THE BOEING C-135 SERIES

By Don Logan

ROCKWELL B-1B: SAC's LAST BOMBER
NORTHROP's T-38 TALON
NORTHROP's YF-17 COBRA
THE 388TH TACTICAL FIGHTER WING AT KORAT RTAFB 1972
REPUBLIC's A-10 THUNDERBOLT II
THE BOEING C-135 SERIES

THE BOEING C-135 SERIES

Stratotanker, Stratolifter and other Variants

Don Logan

Schiffer Military History
Atglen, PA

ACKNOWLEDGEMENTS

I would like to thank the following individuals who have helped me in this project: Don Abrahamson, Gilles Auliard, Peter Becker, Tom Brewer, David F. Brown, Joe Bruch, Jim Goodall, Norris Graser, Mike Grove, Paul Hart, Robert Hopkins III, Renato E. F. Jones, Tom Kaminski, Craig Kaston, Ben Knowles, Ray Leader, Steve Link, Terry Love, Patrick Martin, Don McGary, Roger Messick, Steve Miller, Robert J. Mills Jr., Jack Morris, Jim B. Moseley, Kevin Patrick, Doug Remington, Brian C. Rogers, Mick Roth, Bob Shane, Don Spering/AIR, Douglas Slowiak, Bruce Trombecky, Vance Vasquez, Martin von Wartburg, Randy Walker, Alan Winzerling, and Paul Withers.

THE AUTHOR

After graduating from California State University-Northridge with a BA degree in History, Don Logan joined the USAF in August of 1969. He flew as an F-4E Weapon Systems Officer (WSO), stationed at Korat RTAFB in Thailand, flying 133 combat missions over North Vietnam, South Vietnam, and Laos before being shot down over North Vietnam on July 5 1972. He spent nine months as a POW in Hanoi North Vietnam. As a result of missions flown in Southeast Asia, he received the Distinguished Flying Cross, the Air Medal with twelve oak leaf clusters, and the Purple Heart. After his return to the U.S., he was assigned to Nellis AFB where he flew as a rightseater in the F-111A. He left the Air Force at the end of February 1977.

In March of 1977 Don went to work for North American Aircraft Division of Rockwell International, in Los Angeles, as a Flight Manual writer on the B-1A program. He was later made Editor of the Flight Manuals for B-1A #3 and B-1A #4. Following the cancellation of the B-1A production, he went to work for Northrop Aircraft as a fire control and ECM systems maintenance manual writer on the F-5 program.

In October of 1978 he started his employment at Boeing in Wichita, Kansas as a Flight Manual/Weapon Delivery manual writer on the B-52 OAS/CMI (Offensive Avionics System/ Cruise Missile Integration) program. He is presently the editor for Boeing's B-52 Flight and Weapon Delivery manuals, and Boeing North American B-1B OSO/DSO Flight Manuals and Weapon Delivery Manuals.

Don Logan is also the author of *Rockwell B-1B: SAC's Last Bomber, The 388th Tactical Fighter Wing at Korat Royal Thai Air Force Base 1972, Northrop's T-38 Talon, Northrop's YF-17 Cobra*, and *Republic's A-10 Thunderbolt II* (all titles are available from Schiffer Publishing Ltd.).

Book Design by Robert Biondi.

Library of Congress Catalog Number: 97-80210.

Printed in China.
ISBN: 0-7643-0286-8

We are interested in hearing from authors with book ideas on related topics.

Published by Schiffer Publishing Ltd.
4880 Lower Valley Road
Atglen, PA 19310 USA
Phone: (610) 593-1777
FAX: (610) 593-2002
E-mail: Schifferbk@aol.com.
Please write for a free catalog.
This book may be purchased from the publisher.
Please include $3.95 postage.
Try your bookstore first.

Contents

CHAPTER ONE – PROGRAM HISTORY

CHAPTER TWO – TANKERS

CHAPTER THREE – RECONNAISSANCE AIRCRAFT

CHAPTER FOUR – EC-135 SERIES AIRCRAFT

CHAPTER FIVE – TRANSPORT C-135s

CHAPTER SIX – SPECIAL PURPOSE AIRCRAFT

CHAPTER SEVEN – AIRCRAFT DESCRIPTION

APPENDICES

23567
AIR FORCE

Introduction

Though the C-135 was originally designed over forty years ago as an aerial refueling tanker (749 of 820 were manufactured as KC-135As and Bs), the C-135, with more than 600 C-135s of all types are still in operational service. Boeing's C-135 has been the most successful military jet ever built.

The aircraft's design is technically sound being both aerodynamically and structurally efficient. The C-135 had growth capability in terms of volume with a large compartment, behind the cockpit, running the full width and length of the fuselage. This allowed new mission equipment to be easily incorporated. In addition, an aircraft already in existence can always be modified for less than the cost of designing, developing and manufacturing a new aircraft. With re-engining, the C-135 series received a major increase in performance and fuel economy, and decrease in noise from the engines.

The cold war with the Soviet Union caused a large fleet of tankers to be built to meet the air refueling requirement of the strategic bomber fleet of the 1950s and 1960s. As the number of bombers declined, first due to the growth of the missile forces for strategic deterrence, and second due to the decline of the Soviet Union, additional C-135 aircraft became available for modification to other missions. Due to the decreasing budget available for military procurement, new aircraft were not built for these missions, and because of their availability C-135s were converted to some of the new roles.

The C-135 aircraft is successful because of good basic engineering, and because it can be readily adapted to many different configurations and missions. The C-135 will continue operational for many years because of programs which modernized essential systems and maintained the C-135 fleet's usefulness.

OPPOSITE: Need for inflight refueling of SAC's Bombers like the Boeing's B-52 and B-47 (seen here) led to the development of an all jet powered tanker aircraft. (Boeing)

CHAPTER ONE

Program History

ORIGIN OF THE C-135

The original KC-135 requirements were generated due to post-World War II cold war tension. In Europe, Russia was consolidating its domination of Eastern Europe in the late 1940s. The cold war was in progress with the Berlin blockade in 1948. The Soviet Union first exploded an atomic bomb in 1949. In the Far East the Communists had taken over in China.

In both the East and West the U.S. was confronted with the need to project a strong image to oppose Soviet expansion and Chinese threats. This had to be accomplished with overseas bases no longer secure. One response to this need was to build strategic bomber aircraft — the B-36, B-47, and B-52. These aircraft could be based long distances from an actual trouble spot, and if necessary, be on the scene in a few hours.

The Convair B-36 had global range and a tremendous payload, but it was slow and vulnerable to the postwar generation of jet fighters. The Boeing B-47, first flown in 1947, and the Boeing B-52, first flown in 1952, were designed as high altitude, high speed bombers which could overfly the targets at altitudes and speeds safe from enemy defenses. These highly successful aircraft had one serious limitation, a lack of range. To remedy this lack of global range, the technique of in-flight refueling had to be refined.

Operational in-flight refueling was first accomplished during the flight of a U.S. Army Fokker tri-motor, the "Question Mark," during 1929. During World War II some experimentation was accomplished, but due to the availability of bases in England and on Pacific Islands, in-flight refueling was not required by the strategy employed. It was during the post-World War II years that a serious program of development of in-flight refueling was begun, using the Boeing B-29 as the tanker aircraft.

Two basic methods were tested; the probe and drogue, and the boom and receptacle. Both methods are still in use. In the probe and drogue method, a flexible hose was trailed from the tanker with a conical basket attached. The basket was grappled by a probe on the receiver aircraft. In the boom and receptacle method, a rigid telescoping tube, the refueling boom, was trailed from the tanker. The receiver flew into position. Using control surfaces near the end of the boom, the boom was flown into contact with a receptacle on the receiver aircraft. Because of the control surfaces on the boom, the boom was known as a flying boom. The flying boom was the most suitable method for transferring large quantities of fuel in a short time. Fuel booms developed by the Boeing Company were used on KB-29P and KB-50D/J tankers and later on the most numerous of the flying boom tankers, the Boeing KC-97 (Boeing designation of Model 367) of which 814 were built.

Boeing built the KC-97s as the prime tanker support for the Strategic Air Command's B-47 and B-52 strategic bombers. The propeller powered KC-97, even with the auxiliary jet engines, had a serious drawback in refueling jet powered aircraft. The KC-97s flight envelope did not match that of a jet. The jets with their swept back wings were designed for high speed flight, while the propellers of the straight winged KC-97 were not capable of operation at higher speeds. To accomplish a refueling the KC-97 had to operate at maximum speed while the jet was near minimum speed. The situation was particularly bad when the jet receiver was near maximum weight and flying just a few knots above low speed stall buffet. Even the most skillful pilots had problems maintaining contact at night and in turbulent air. As a result of this situation, the requirement for a jet powered tanker with a compatible flight envelope was born. With a jet tanker, refueling could be accomplished safely at high altitude and high speed minimizing the loss in time and range to the receiver.

Boeing decided to begin development of an improved tanker aircraft based on the KC-97 design. After many preliminary designs, the Model 367-80 resulted in a four-engined swept-wing jet. The Dash 80, a Boeing private venture, rolled out on May 14, 1954, and took to the air on July 15 of the same year.

From the Dash 80 came an Air Force order for the KC-135A Stratotanker. The first KC-135A (Model 717-100A), serial number 55-3118, arrived in 1956. The Model 707-100, developed in a subsequent parallel program, first flew in December 1957. The KC-135A is not a 707! Even the C-135A/Bs are not 707s! The airframes are different. Only the basic shape has a resemblance. The 707 has passenger windows, the C-135 does not. The U.S. Air Force C-137A is a military version of the 707-100. The C-137B evolved from the fan engined 707-100B after the retrofit of fan engines on the C-137As. C-137C resulted from the 707-300B fanjet.

The Boeing model numbers for the C-135 family of aircraft are:

KC-135A	717-100A, 717-146, and 717-148
C-135A	717-157
C-135B	717-158B
C-135F	717-165
KC-135B	717-166
RC-135A	739-700
RC-135B	739-445B

BELOW: Castle AFB, north of Merced California was the first SAC base to receive the new KC-135A. (Joe Bruch Collection)

The U.S. Air Force Strategic Air Command (SAC) and Military Air Transport Service (MATS) ordered the following C-135s from Boeing:

732	KC-135A Stratotankers (SAC)
17	KC-135B Stratotankers (SAC)
10	RC-135B (SAC)
15	C-135A Stratolifters (MATS)
30	C-135B Stratolifters (MATS)
4	RC-135A (MATS)
12	C-135F Stratotankers (French A.F.)
820	Total

From these 820 aircraft in 7 varieties were to come 34 variants, the largest number of variants for a given aircraft type in the U.S. inventory. The C-135s were delivered to the Air Force between April 30, 1957 and January 6, 1966. The first operational mission was flown by a KC-135A of the 93rd Bombardment Wing at Castle AFB, California on June 28, 1957.

After 30 years, of the 820 aircraft built, 75 have been lost due to accidents, 15 are on display in museums, and approximately 100 have been retired, leaving approximately 690 aircraft still in service.

THE PROTOTYPE JET TANKER TRANSPORT

Boeing in the early 1950s was well aware of the potential opportunities in the all-jet transport aircraft, both military and civil. The British Comet jet transport first flew in 1949 and as a result, the British appeared to be well ahead in the competition for the civil jet airliner market. All of the major U.S. aircraft manufacturers were doing design studies of passenger jets and trying to interest potential customers.

The potential military jet tanker and civil airline markets were attractive, and the speed, altitude and payload requirements similar. Boeing began to seriously consider a program to enter this market. This program, a prototype tanker transport aircraft, was destined to demonstrate the benefits of a jet tanker to the military and of a jet transport to the airlines.

Since no government backing was available, a prototype would have to be financed with private funds. After many months of study a proposal was made to the Boeing Board of Directors and in April 1952 approval was given to proceed. The initial investment, sixteen million dollars, was almost the total worth of the company at that time. Had the program failed, it could have meant the collapse of the Boeing Company.

The prototype aircraft, Boeing Model 367-80, was designed to the requirements of both a tanker and a transport. Model 367 was the model number for the Boeing Stratoliner Passenger aircraft and its military brother the C/KC-97. The tanker specifications were given priority since it appeared that the Air Force needs would culminate in a firm requirement for a fleet of new tankers in the near future. This turned out to be true; during the 24 months it took to build the aircraft, the military requirements matured. An Air Force Request For Proposal had been issued to industry and a competition was under way when the Boeing prototype first flew on July 15, 1954. The Dash Eighty was so successful that even thought Boeing had lost the competition, the Boeing tanker design, the KC-135, was immediately put into production.

The prototype aircraft was also successful in generating orders for civil airliners. The 707 program was begun in 1955, about a year after the Dash Eighty's first flight.

The gamble represented by the Boeing prototype Model 367-80 has paid off. This aircraft was the first of a family of over 1600 tanker, transport, and electronic system aircraft. The 707 and its military versions (C-137, E-3. KE-3A, and E-6) was in production for over 30 years. The prototype itself had a twenty year career testing new aeronautical technology and is now in the collection of the National Aeronautics and Space Museum and on display at the Museum of Flight at Boeing Field, Seattle, Washington.

Used 707 airliners have been procured for the USAF and U.S. Navy use, redesignated as C-18s, EC-18s, TC-18s, and E-8s. Other 707s have been converted for use as transports, tankers, and electronics platforms by the militaries of many other countries including Argentina, Australia, Brazil, Canada, Chile, Germany, India, Indonesia, Iran, Israel, Italy, Morocco, NATO, Pakistan, Peru, South Africa, Spain, and Venezuela.

BELOW: KC-135A 59-1512 is seen here as delivered with a short vertical fin and in natural metal finish with red/orange day glow visibility stripes. (Boeing)

THE PRODUCTION PROGRAM

The KC-135A production program extended over ten years with a production rate which varied from six to fifteen aircraft per month. The most notable achievement of the program is that 732 KC-135A model aircraft were built over a period of ten years without a major change in configuration. No new model variants were ordered until the production program was over seven years old.

The KC-135A is a sound basic design. Very few changes were incorporated into the design during the production program, or since. Only about one-third of the Engineering Change Proposals (ECPs) approved for production were retrofitted.

In the early 1960s, the multi-role potential of the 135 design began to be used. The worldwide responsibilities of the United States required airlift capabilities. Since no fuel is carried on the upper cargo deck, the tanker thc was easily converted to an airlift configuration. The C-135A resulted from a change to the tanker configuration which consisted of deletion of the fuel boom and addition of troop accommodations and a more durable cargo floor. The next airlift version was the C-135B. It used the TF33 fan jet engine to decrease takeoff distance and increase range. The TF33 is the same basic engine later used in the airline re-engine program. The C-135A and B models filled the mission requirements for strategic airlift, troop transport, medical air evacuation and executive transport.

The necessity for the United States to maintain surveillance of the growing Soviet activities generated a requirement for a fast, high altitude aircraft of long range and ample payload. The result was the reconnaissance version of the C-135. Both the J57 powered RC-135A and the TF33 powered RC-135B were produced. These RC-135As, initially assigned to MATS, were equipped for photomapping and geodetic surveying, while the RC-135Bs, assigned to SAC, were equipped for electronic surveillance.

Fourteen EC-135C and three EC-135J models with TF33 fan engines were ordered in 1962 for an airborne command and control requirement. Though ordered as KC-135B tanker models these have always been used for the command post mission.

The French Air Force had a requirement for a combined tanker and airlift aircraft to support their forces. This requirement was filled by the C-135F which is a variation of the C-135A with an air refueling boom system.

The total number of C-135 aircraft produced was 820. Of these, 732, or 90 percent, were the KC-135A tanker model.

KC-135A 58-0004 is seen here refueling the fourth B-52G, 57-6471, during B-52G flight test. (Boeing)

GROWTH OF MISSION REQUIREMENTS

The C-135 production program came to an end in 1965. Since then, situations in various areas of the world have generated a need to change the in-flight refueling role of the KC-135 fleet, to broaden it from refueling support of strategic bombers only, to support of a wide variety of missions.

The United States commitment to NATO, together with loss of secure overseas bases, required the building of a strategic airlift capability. These airlift forces require tanker support. For example, a C-5 may require multiple refuelings from several tankers when delivering its maximum cargo to Europe.

The Vietnam conflict used strategic refueling capabilities for the B-52s while at the same time the refueling of tactical aircraft grew to be critical for the prosecution of the Southeast Asia air war. Since the Vietnam war, the use of in flight refueling of fighter aircraft has been a requirement for successful completion of their combat missions.

During the decade of the 1960s there was a growing reliance on missiles for strategic deterrence. The missiles, isolated in underground silos, required secure communication for command and control. The survival of their communication links under nuclear attack became questionable. This problem created the requirement for an airborne command post. An airborne communication relay or command post aircraft is extremely difficult to locate, and thus is highly survivable. An airborne command post requires a large payload, high altitude capability, and the ability to stay aloft for long periods. The C-135 was a natural candidate for this mission and during the early 1960s many were modified to airborne command post configurations. There have been eight EC-135 models serving as airborne command posts. This includes the famous "Looking Glass" SAC airborne command post mission, first begun in 1961. During the Cold War years there was a "Looking Glass" EC-135 aircraft continuously aloft. Some of the EC-135 models were equipped to assume control of and launch strategic ballistic missiles in the event the underground launch control centers were disabled.

Versions of the EC-135 were modified to provide specialized command, control and communication missions for several commands. These aircraft were equipped with communications gear and manned by a battle staff which can be quickly deployed.

Specialized reconnaissance continues to generate the need for a small fleet of aircraft. The C-135 filled the need for a long range aircraft with a large payload. Five RC-135 variants, all modified from C-135 types delivered with TF33 engines, filled this mission requirement.

Additionally C-135 aircraft have been modified into OC-135B Open Skies aircraft. These aircraft are to be used to verify compliance with the Open Skies treaty.

A global communications network to support the manned space program generated another modification to the original fleet, the range instrumented models. These airborne communications platforms provide relay service from remote ocean locations. The C-135 fleet has participated in many test programs because of the large available payload and unobstructed upper deck.

The C-135 variants carrying the "N" prefix have been used as testbeds and for testing support on many system development programs.

CURRENT USAF C-135 UNITS

AMC UNITS

6th Air Refueling Wing, McDill AFB Florida .... (KC-135R)
91st Air Refueling Squadron (transferred from Malmstrom AFB, Montana)

19th Air Refueling Wing, Robins AFB, Georgia. .... (KC-135R)
99th Air Refueling Squadron
712th Air Refueling Squadron

22nd Air Refueling Wing, McConnell AFB, Kansas. .... (KC-135R, KC-135T)
(Operations augmented by the 931st Air Refueling Group Air Force Reserve)
All the air refueling receiver tankers are presently assigned to the 22 ARW.
344th Air Refueling Squadron
349th Air Refueling Squadron
350th Air Refueling Squadron
384th Air Refueling Squadron

89th Airlift Wing, Andrews AFB, Maryland .... (C-135C)
1st Airlift Squadron C-135C

92nd Air Refueling Wing, Fairchild AFB, Washington .... (KC-135R, KC-135T)
92nd Air Refueling Squadron
93rd Air Refueling Squadron
96th Air Refueling Squadron
97th Air Refueling Squadron
98th Air Refueling Squadron

319th Air Refueling Wing, Grand Forks AFB, North Dakota .... (KC-135R AND KC-135T)
905th Air Refueling Squadron
906th Air Refueling Squadron
911th Air Refueling Squadron
912th Air Refueling Squadron

AETC UNITS

97th Air Mobility Wing, Altus AFB, Oklahoma
55th Air Refueling Squadron KC-135R

ACC UNITS

55th Wing, Ofutt AFB, Nebraska OF Tail Code
7th ACCS EC-135C, KC-135E
45th RS RC-135S, TC-135S, OC-135B, WC-135W
38th/343rd RS RC-135U/V/W, TC-135W

366th Wing, Mountain Home AFB, Idaho MO Tail Code
22nd Air Refueling Squadron KC-135R

PACAF UNITS

18th Wing, Kadena AB, Okinawa ZZ Tail Code
909th Air Refueling Squadron KC-135R

15th Air Base Wing, Hickam AFB, Hawaii C-135B, C-135C, EC-135K

USAFE UNITS

100th Air Refueling Wing RAF Mildenhall
351st Air Refueling Squadron KC-135R

AFMC UNITS

AFFTC Edwards AFB, California 412th Test Wing
- 452nd Test Squadron NKC-135B, NKC-135E, C-135E, EC-135E
- 412th Test Squadron C-135C

AFRES UNITS

434th Air Refueling Wing Grissom AFB. Indiana
- 72nd Air Refueling Squadron KC-135R
- 74th Air Refueling Squadron KC-135R

452nd Air Mobility Wing March AFB, California
- 336th Air Refueling Squadron KC-135R

507th Air Refueling Wing Tinker AFB, Oklahoma
- 465th Air Refueling Squadron KC-135R

916th Air Refueling Wing Seymour-Johnson AFB, North Carolina
- 77th Air Refueling Squadron KC-135R

927th Air Refueling Wing Selfridge ANGB, Michigan
- 63rd Air Refueling Squadron KC-135E

940th Air Refueling Wing McClellan AFB, California
- 314th Air Refueling Squadron KC-135E

ANG UNITS

101st Air Refueling Wing 132nd Air Refueling Squadron	BANGOR IAP ME	Maine ANG	KC-135E
107th Air Refueling Wing 136th Air Refueling Squadron	NIAGARA FALLS IAP	New York ANG	KC-135R
108th Air Refueling Wing 141st Air Refueling Squadron 150th Air Refueling Squadron	McGUIRE AFB	New Jersey ANG	KC-135E
117th Air Refueling Wing 106th Air Refueling Squadron	BIRMINGHAM IAP	Alabama ANG	KC-135R
121st Air Refueling Wing 145th Air Refueling Squadron 166th Air Refueling Squadron	RICKENBACKER	Ohio ANG	KC-135R
126th Air Refueling Wing 108th Air Refueling Squadron	O'HARE IAP CHICAGO	Illinois ANG	KC-135E
128th Air Refueling Wing 126th Air Refueling Squadron	GENERAL MITCHELL IAP MILWAUKEE	Wisconsin ANG	KC-135R
134th Air Refueling Wing 151st Air Refueling Squadron	McGHEE-TYSON AIRPORT KNOXVILLE TENN	Tennessee ANG	KC-135E
141st Air Refueling Wing 116th Air Refueling Squadron	FAIRCHILD AFB	Washington ANG	KC-135E
151st Air Refueling Wing 191th Air Refueling Squadron	SALT LAKE CITY	Utah ANG	KC-135E
154th Wing 203rd Air Refueling Squadron	HICKAM AFB	Hawaii ANG	KC-135R

Unit	Location	Component	Aircraft
155th Air Refueling Wing			
173rd Air Refueling Squadron	LINCOLN MAP	Nebraska ANG	KC-135R
157th Air Refueling Wing			
133rd Air Refueling Squadron	PEASE ANGB	New Hampshire ANG	KC-135R
161st Air Refueling Wing			
197th Air Refueling Squadron	SKY-HARBOR IAP	Arizona ANG	KC-135E
163rd Air Refueling Wing			
196th Air Refueling Squadron	MARCH AFB	California ANG	KC-135R
168th Air Refueling Group			
168th Air Refueling Squadron	EIELSON AFB	Alaska ANG	KC-135R
171st Air Refueling Wing			
146th Air Refueling Squadron			
147th Air Refueling Squadron	PITTSBURGH	Pennsylvania ANG	KC-135E
186th Air Refueling Wing	KEY FIELD		
153rd Air Refueling Squadron	MERIDIAN	Mississippi ANG	KC-135R
190th Air Refueling Wing			
117th Air Refueling Squadron	FORBES FIELD	Kansas ANG	KC-135D/E

CHAPTER TWO

Tankers

The first production C-135 tanker, a KC-135A (55-3118), was rolled out from the Boeing plant in Renton, Washington on July 20, 1956. Two months later on August 31, 55-3118 took off on its first flight. The KC-135 flight test program began using the initial production tankers. This first aircraft, named "City of Renton," for the flight test ended its career as an EC-135K assigned to the 552nd ACCW at Tinker AFB, Oklahoma until mid 1996.After a short assignment to the 89th Airlift Wing at Andrews AFB, it was placed on display at McConnell AFB in Wichita, Kansas.

The KC-135A began operational service on April 30, 1957, when Boeing delivered the first three production aircraft to the USAF. The first unit to be equipped with the new tanker was the 93rd Air Refueling Squadron at Castle AFB, California. The 93rd began KC-135A operations in June of 1957, less than a year after the first flight of 55-3118. Deliveries of KC-135As from Boeing eventually hit fifteen aircraft per month. The rate was made possible with the shift of B-52 production from Renton to Boeing's Wichita plant.

The KC-135A was designed to meet the air refueling/ transport needs of the Strategic Air Command (SAC). Lower deck fuselage tanks and wing tanks carry both air refueling and aircraft fuel. The main deck area was available for cargo/ troop transport purposes. Four J57-P-59W or J57-P-43WB turbojet engines equipped with water injection powered the aircraft. A single HF probe antenna is mounted to the top of the vertical fin.

The Stratotanker has a normal crew of four: pilot, copilot, navigator and boom operator, commonly known as the "boomer," who also serves as the loadmaster when required.

The KC-135 has a large fuel capacity, both for transfer and for its own use. The wings each house two primary fuel

Two models of the KC-135 tanker were manufactured. In this photo KC-135A 58-0009 is seen refueling a former KC-135B 63-3585. The KC-135B was in EC-135C configuration in this photo, as evidenced by the wing tip probe antennas. (Joe Bruch Collection)

tanks: the inboard tank has a capacity of 2,275 gallons while the outboard tank has a capacity of 2,062 gallons. Additionally, a 434 gallon reserve tank is mounted outboard of the main tanks in both wings and a 7,306 gallon tank is housed in the wing center section. Within the fuselage, there are nine fuel cells under the cabin floor. The four forward cells have a capacity of 5,800 gallons, while the five rear cells hold a total of 6,378 gallons. There is a 2,174 gallon upper body tank mounted in the rear of the main compartment. Fuselage fuel is normally used for refueling purposes, while wing fuel is used for the tanker's engines. The total fuel load is 31,200 gallons, virtually all of which can be transferred, or the tanker itself can burn all fuel it carries.

The KC-135 flying boom refueling system is controlled by the boom operator. The system is operated from a pod under the rear fuselage. Access to the pod is gained through two openings in the floor in the rear of the main compartment. Once in the pod, the boomer lies on his stomach on a pallet, facing rearward, with the refueling controls and a window in front of him. There are two additional pallets in the pod (right and left of the operator's pallet) for use by boom instructors, students, or observers. The flying boom is stowed upward against the bottom of the rear fuselage when not in use and can be raised or lowered by flying the boom with the ruddevators, as the boom control surfaces are called. The boom can also be lowered with a manual system if the power system should fail. The boom consists of two telescoping sections, capable of extending to a length of 27 feet. It can be moved from 12.5 degrees up to 50 degrees down in the vertical and left or right 30 degrees from the center refueling position.

The inner of the two sections, a fuel pipe, is housed within the boom and is telescopically extended to make contact with the receiving aircraft's refueling receptacle. The end of the pipe has a nozzle and valve attached which opens once the nozzle has locked into the receiver's receptacle. To guide receiver aircraft pilots, KC-135s are equipped with two rows of pilot director lights under the forward fuselage, and colored markings on the telescoping portion of the boom. Early KC-135As had a fluorescent yellow stripe applied to the underside of the fuselage as an aid in the longitudinal alignment of receiver aircraft.

Receiver aircraft monitor the lights on the two blacks under the tankers nose. These lights, called pilot director lights, come on based on boom position and give the receiver pilot up – down and forward – aft position corrections. (Paul Hart)

The boom is marked with florescent red, yellow and green bands. These bands, when aligned with the end of the boom shroud, indicate the extension of the boom. (Don Logan)

KC-135As were equipped with either standard or high speed booms. The standard boom ruddevators had a three piece tab installed on the outboard half of the ruddevators. High speed booms have ruddevators without tabs and the identification HIGH SPEED BOOM initially painted on the black upper and lower surfaces. A majority of the KC-135s in the fleet have since been modified and carry high speed booms. In the 1960s some SAC KC-135As had alphanumeric codes (JJ12, LL12, 4H10 etc.) applied to the ruddevators which identified the unit or aircraft. These markings disappeared by the 1970s. More recently these markings have been replaced with markings indicating the aircraft's owning unit. Many ANG and AFRES units have applied unit unique logos like "Kansas Coyotes." Most AMC units marked the ruddevators with their unit's identity (e.g. 22 ARW).

From its creation, the KC-135A was designed to refuel aircraft using the boom/receptacle combination. By 1960 it became apparent that the KC-135A could also be used to support USAF, US Navy and NATO fighter aircraft equipped with probe and drogue refueling systems. An adapter kit was developed for use with the KC-135. This kit, installed on the ground, converts the flying boom to a drogue/basket unit. With the kit installed, the boom can no longer be used to refuel receptacle type receiver aircraft. The adapter is thirteen feet long and weighs 121 pounds. With the adapter in place, the boom cannot be used for receptacle refueling. KC-135s fitted with drogue units participated in refueling tests of the French Mirage IVA bomber, which led the French Air Force later to purchase twelve KC-135s. The French have since added wing tip drogue refueling pods to their C-135s. The USAF is planning to add similar refueling pods to some of their KC-135Rs.

The production KC-135s had a single cargo door on the left side of the forward fuselage. The door opens outward and upward to allow loading of cargo. Typically, a KC-135 Stratotanker can accommodate eighty passengers or up to 41.5 tons of cargo. Various combinations of personnel and cargo can be accommodated.

The KC-135A is equipped with an inboard aileron on each wing, between the inboard and outboard flaps, and outboard ailerons which can only be operated when the flaps are down. A pair of spoilers is mounted in front of each flap on the wing upper surface. These spoilers enhance roll control when used differentially and can also be used as speed brakes. The aircraft is also equipped with trailing edge Fowler-type flaps and an adjustable horizontal stabilizer.

The KC-135A was powered by four 13,750 lbs thrust Pratt & Whitney J57-P-43WB or J57-P-59 turbojets with water injection for improved takeoff performance. The J57 engines gave the KC-135A a speed of 610 mph, a ceiling of 45,000 feet and a range of 9,942 miles. Despite the use of water injection, the restricted power of the J57s limited fully loaded KC-135s to long (10,000+ feet), hard-surfaced runways.

The crew entry to the aircraft is through an entry hatch and ladder located alongside the nosewheel on the left side of the aircraft. For emergency exit, the KC-135 has an escape hatch on both sides of the fuselage over the wings and an additional escape hatch in the rear fuselage on the right side. The cockpit contains a Pilot, Copilot, and Navigator station, with a seat aft of the entry hatch for the Boom Operator. A stowable jump-seat for an observer can be installed between the pilots, aft of the isle stand. To allow for better visibility of other aircraft traffic while airborne, there are "eyebrow" windows located above the main cockpit windows. Originally, Stratotankers had two rectangular celestial observation windows on the top of the fuselage aft of the cockpit. Following a fatality caused by failure of one of these windows, the windows were replaced with metal plates.

The first 582 KC-135As off the production line were fitted with short vertical fins and non-powered rudders. To improve directional stability, the fin was extended forty inches and the rudder was modified with a power boost system. Aircraft 62-3532 was the first KC-135 manufactured with the modified fin and rudder. All C-135 versions currently flying have the extended fin and powered rudder modifications. The modification increased the overall height to the top of the fin to 41 feet 8 inches.

The KC-135As, RC-135As, C-135As, and C-135Fs (763 of the 820 135 versions built) were each powered by four J57 turbojets like this one. (Don Logan)

Crew entry to all 135 versions was through this hatch and ladder on the left side of the nose gear. The top of the ladder enters the cockpit just behind the pilots seat. (Boeing)

The original design had one serious restriction to airframe life — the aluminum alloy selected for the lower wing skin. To save weight, high strength 7178-T6 aluminum was used. This material was satisfactory for the original design objective of 10,000 hours of life, but has low durability and damage tolerance and proved unsatisfactory in the crack resistance required for the extended service life of the aircraft. As a result of this design problem, the Air Force modified all 135s between 1976 and 1990 under TCTO 1C-135-989 (Boeing ECP-405) which replaced the lower wing skin with a skin made from much tougher 2024 aluminum with stiffeners of 7075 aluminum. This modification program increased the expected lifespan of the KC-135 fleet to some 27,000 flight hours. The wing reskin took place at approximately 8,500 flying hours. The schedule was to modify three to six aircraft per month at a projected cost of $400 million for the full fleet of 640 KC and RC-135s.

At one point, it was planned to retrofit all KC-135s with winglets (tested on NKC-135A 55-3129) as a fuel-saving measure, but this modification was not incorporated.

The KC-135Qs were KC-135As modified to carry the special fuel required to refuel the SR-71 Blackbird. They had a steerable flood light installed in the tail. This light could be pointed by the boomer at the refueling receptacle on the back of the SR-71 to make night refueling of the black jet easier. As a result of the success of the Q model flood light, two non-steerable down facing floodlights for night refueling of dark camouflaged aircraft was added to the top of the vertical fin of all KC-135s. These lights are aimed at the point the refueling boom nozzle would plug into the receptacle of a properly positioned receiver. The new light is commonly called the "streetlight" by tanker crews.

In order to increase the C-135's capability for refueling of U.S. Navy and NATO aircraft equipped with refueling probes, Boeing is presently under contract to modify U.S. Stratotankers with wing tip mounted hose and drogue pods similar to those installed on the French Air Force C-135FRs. In the first phase of this modification, called the Multipoint Refueling System (MPRS), Boeing's Wichita facility modified one KC-125R. The first modified aircraft rolled out on March 20, 1997. Up to 150 additional MPRS conversions will be accomplished by the USAAF at Tinker AFB using kits supplied by Boeing. This modification has been especially useful for the French, whose receiver aircraft are probe equipped.

Nine KC-135s have had refueling receiver receptacles installed. Eight are KC-135Rs and one is a KC-135E. These

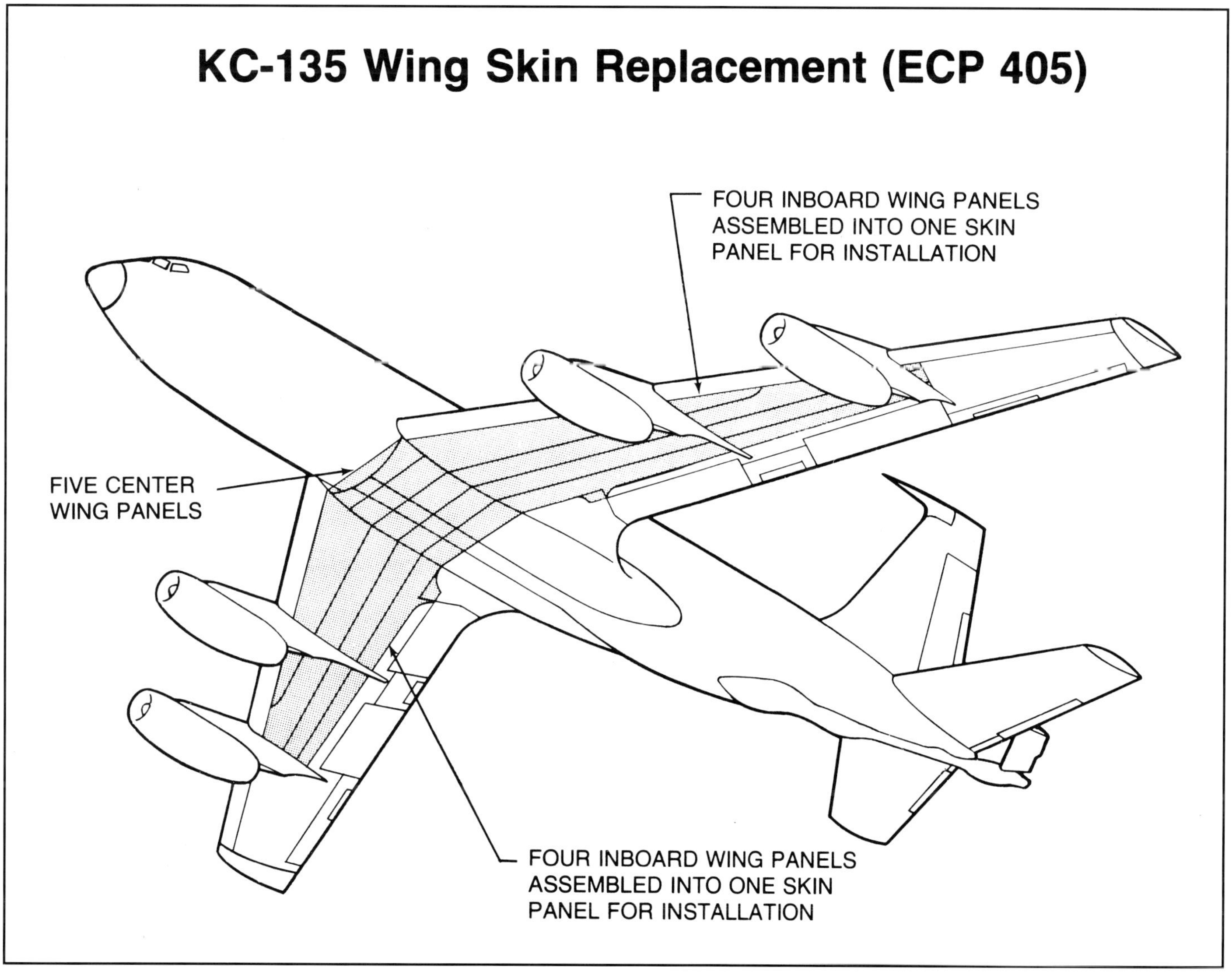

KC-135R, 62-3499, was photographed on June 20, 1997 and assigned to the 22 ARW at McConnell AFB, was the first USAF KC-135 fitted with the wing tip refueling pods. (Don Logan)

ARR capable KC-135s are referred to as ART (air refuelable tankers) or RT (refuelable tankers).

Though details are not firm, a program is now underway to add the UARRSI (Universal Air Refueling Receiver Slipway Installation) to some KC-135Rs.

Presently the KC-135 refueling fleet consists of over 500 aircraft. All A to R and Q to T conversions are complete. Sixteen KC-135E models have been converted to R models. A mix of four different KC-135 models are now in use and are manned by active duty, Air Force Reserve, and Air National Guard aircrews.

Description of the different models follows:

KC-135 DERIVATIVE TANKER MODELS

KC-135D: Four tankers modified from the RC-135A, re-engined with TF33-PW-102 turbofan engines with thrust reversers (formerly commercial JT-3D)

KC-135E: KC-135A aircraft re-engined with TF33-PW-102 turbofan engines with thrust reversers (formerly commercial JT-3D)

KC-135R: Re-engined/Modernized KC-135A/ KC-135E with F108-CF-100 engines (CFM56 commercial designation)

KC-135T: Re-engined/Modernized KC-135Q with F108-CF-100 engines (CFM56 commercial designation), and can isolate its body fuel tanks and offload specialized fuels

Maximum cargo weight of the KC-135 is approximately 55,000 pounds, however maximum loads are usually limited to approximately 35,000 pounds due to cargo volume and floor loading limitations. They can carry a maximum crew/ passenger load of 58. Both cargo and passenger loads affect the maximum fuel load of approximately 200,000 pounds (K/ T-model).

KC-135A 58-0124 was the first tanker to be fitted with an air refueling receiver receptacle. The aircraft was nicknamed "Christine" referring to Christine Jorgenson (the recipient first publicized male-to-female sex change). (Joe Bruch Collection)

All KC-135s produced were delivered as KC-135As (except for seventeen KC-135B command post tankers, which were designated as EC-135Cs upon delivery). KC-135 tanker assets are assigned to Air Mobility Command (AMC), Air Combat Command (ACC), Air Education and Training Command (AETC), Pacific Air Force (PACAF), United States Air Forces in Europe (USAFE), the Air National Guard, and the Air Force Reserve. The Oklahoma City Air Logistics Center at Tinker AFB provides system management for the KC-135/C-135 family and the J-57 TF33 and F108 engines. Crew training of KC-135 aircrews is carried out at Altus AFB, Oklahoma by the 97th Air Mobility Wing (AETC).

During 1975, the Air National Guard began to receive Stratotankers, which allowed the ANG's aging KC-97s to be retired. Eventually, twenty two ANG squadrons were equipped with the Stratotanker. The Air Force Reserve also received KC-135s, equipping seven squadrons.

60-0362, a KC-135R, photographed at McConnell AFB on August 9, 1995 received its air refueling receiver receptacle when it was modified to RC-135D configuration. (Don Logan)

KC-135A 59-1505 was photographed on September 21, 1962 at Nellis AFB is SAC markings. (W. M. Jefferies via Dave Menard)

This KC-135A, 56-3654 wears both types of SAC "milky way" stripes, the original stripe on the nose and the mid fuselage stripe which replaced it. (Dave Menard)

RE-ENGINE PROGRAMS

During the late 1970s and early 1980s re-engining of the C-135 series fleet was being studied as a means to increase the aircraft's service life and reduce maintenance cost, and at the same time, increase performance, fuel economy and reduce noise. The C/KC-135 airframe, being structurally sound, needed only a reskin of the lower wing already being accomplished to last well into the 21st century. The J57 engines however, were becoming obsolete, with more powerful engines not requiring water injection available.

A major study conducted by Boeing in 1976 and 1977 came up with different modernization configurations which included re-engining. The configurations were grouped into three categories:

1) Engine change only
2) Engine change plus install a new wing using the 720-320 commercial wing design
3) Engine Change with an all new wing.

Three engine types were included in the configurations; the Pratt and Whitney JT8-209, the Pratt and Whitney TF33-P-7, and the General Electric/SNECMA CFM56.

The Pratt and Whitney JTB-209 was a derivative of the commercial JT8D-9 engine then used on 727, 737, and DC-9 airliners. The -209 version was modified with an advanced technology fan, low pressure compressor and low pressure turbine. The JT8D-209 was rated at 19,000-pound takeoff thrust on a standard day at sea level. It was a twin spool turbofan engine with a mechanically coupled fan and low pressure compressor, which at takeoff power setting had a 1.63 bypass ratio and an overall compressor ratio of 19. Because the engine was being updated with new fan stages, the engine was simply referred to in this study as the "RF", standing for Re-Fanned, engine.

The TF33-P-7 was a improved version of the TF33 used on the TF33 powered C-135s. This improved engine was in the USAF inventory, being used on the C-141 aircraft. In addition it was in commercial service as the JT3D on 707 and DC-8 airliners. The re-engine version of the TF33-P-7 engine takeoff thrust was rated at 21,000 pounds at sea level on a standard day. Like the JT8B-209, it was a twin spool turbofan engine with a mechanically coupled fan and low pressure compressor. At takeoff power setting it had a 1.26 bypass ratio and an overall compressor ratio of 15.6. The TF33-P-7 engine was simply referred to as the P-7 in this study.

The CFM56 engine is a joint General Electric/SNECMA engine based on core engine components from the F101-GE-F100 engine designed for the B-1A. Three exhaust configurations (mixed, confluent, and separate) were available giving the engine takeoff thrust at sea level on a standard day between 22,000 and 24,000 pounds. The Fan is mechanically coupled to the low pressure compressor and low pressure turbine providing takeoff bypass ratio of 6.05 and an overall compressor ratio of 22.4. Because of the 22,000 pounds of thrust, the CFM56 engine was simply referred to as the Ten-Ton or TT engine in this study.

From these configuration categories and engine options, seven different aircraft configurations with the following temporary designations were developed:

Designation	Wing Type	Engines
KC-135P7	KC-135A	(4) TF33-P-7
KC-135ME (Mixed Engines)	KC-135A	(2) CFM56 Inboard (2) J57 Outboard
KC-135TT	KC-135A	(4) CFM56
KC-135RF	KC-135A	(4) JT8D-209
KC-135X	707-320	(4) CFM56
KC-135H	707-320	(4) TF33-P-7
KC-135Y	NEW DESIGN	(4) CFM56

Two different programs were eventually adopted to re-engine the C-135s; airline re-engine, using used components from retired airliners including the JT3D engines, and the RE program which used new off-the-shelf CFM56 commercial engines. Even though the rollout of the first KC-135R occurred almost six months after rollout of the first KC-135E, the RE (CFM56) re-engine program began before the JT3D re-engine program.

KC-135 Modernization Study Configurations

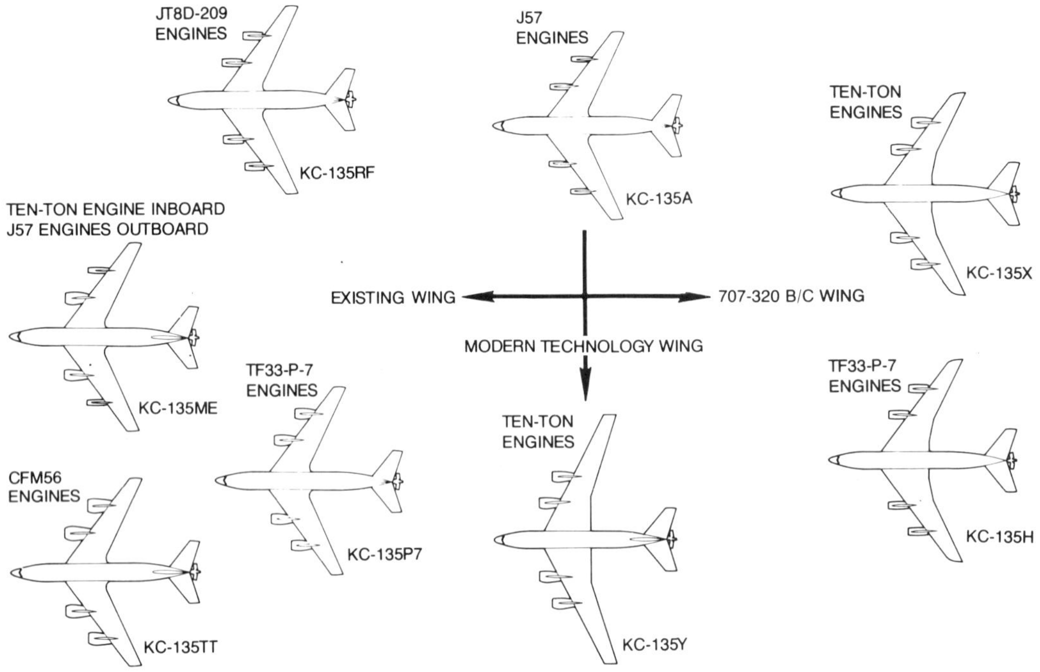

KC-135 Reengine Candidates

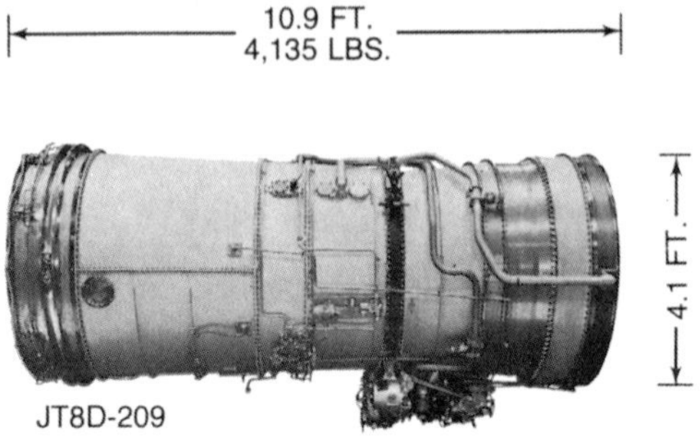

JT8D-209

TF33-P-7

P&WA JT8-209 – COMMERCIAL VENTURE FOR MODEL IMPROVEMENTS AND NEW A/C REFAN ON JT8D SERIES ENGINES USED ON CURRENT 727, 737, DC-9, ETC.

P&WA TF33-P-7 – USED ON C-141 AND E-3A IMPROVED VERSION OF JT3D/TF33 SERIES USED ON 707, DC-8, B-52H AND C/VC-135B

CFM56 – "TEN-TON" GE/SNECMA JOINT COMMERCIAL VENTURE FOR NEW AND MODIFIED CORE BASED ON F101 ENGINE

CFM56

Airline Re-engine Program (KC-135E)

A Request For Proposal (RFP) was issued on August 10, 1981, and Boeing Military Airplanes, Wichita, Kansas was awarded the contract on September 18, 1981. The airline re-engine program used surplus commercial 707 and 720 aircraft purchased by the USAF as donors to provide JT3D (Military designation TF33PW-102) engines and components for the re-engining. The TF33-P-5 or -9 used on the KC-135B and C-135B is another military version of the JT3D.

Both KC and C versions of J57 powered aircraft were to be re-engined under this program. Four major components would be changed; engines, engine struts, aisle stand throttle quadrant, and the surface area of the horizontal stabilizers. The airline re-engined tankers (KC-135E and KC-135D) were assigned to Air National Guard and Air Force Reserve units.

The JT3D turbofan engines and struts were removed and refurbished before being installed on the C-135s. In order to take advantage of the thrust reverser system from the airliners, the throttle quadrant had to be removed, replacing it with the throttle quadrant from the airliners. The increased size (sq. ft. area) of the horizontal stabilizers was required to dampen the increased pitch oscillation tendency caused by the increase in the frontal area of the engines. The first 81 "E" conversions used horizontal tails from the donor aircraft. The following 82 through 187 "E" conversions used kits which modified the existing C-135 horizontal stabilizers. A similar modification was accomplished on the KC-135R re-engine modification. The increased size horizontal stabilizer had been installed during production on the TF33 turbofan powered KC-135B, C-135B, and RC-135B models. To handle the additional capability, the anti-skid system and wheel brakes were upgraded.

187 KC-135A and C-135A aircraft were re-engined with the JT3D (USAF designation TF33-PW-102), producing the following models:

JT3D Re-engine Program
Aircraft Modifications

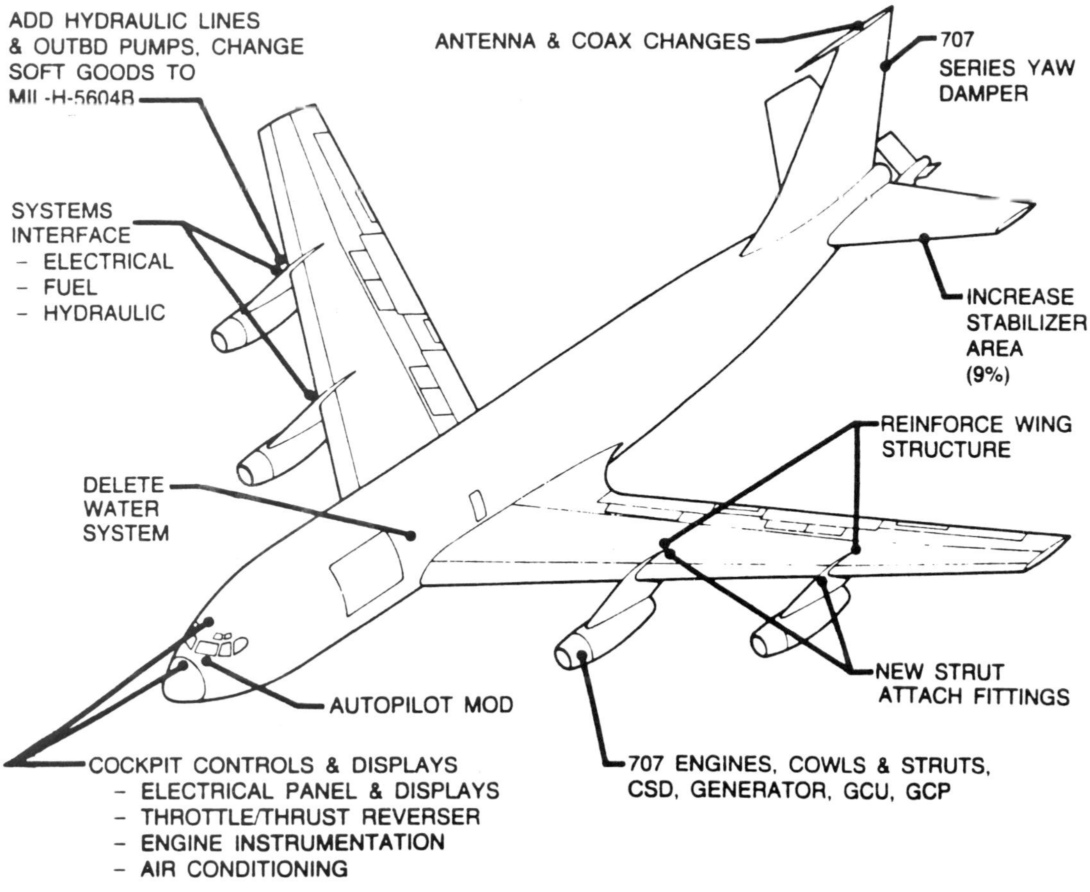

From aircraft manufactured as KC-135As:

KC-135E	(161)
NKC-135E	(2)
EC-135H	(5)
EC-135K	(2)
EC-135P	(3)
EC-135Y	(1)
RC-135T	(1)

From aircraft manufactured as RC-135A/KC-135Ds:

KC-135D	(4)

From aircraft manufactured as C-135As:

C-135E	(3)
EC-135E	(4)
EC-135N	(1)

This TF33-PW-102, the number 3 engine (right inboard) on a KC-135E is typical of the JT3D engines removed from Boeing 707 and 720 airliners for use on -135 models. (Don Logan)

KC-135E 59-1514, the first "E" model, photographed at Boeing Military Airplanes facility at Wichita, Kansas, taxing out for its first flight after reengining in January, 1982. This aircraft was one of the four R (reconnaissance) models. It is now based with the 55th Wing at Offutt AFB, Nebraska and is used as a STRATCOMM command support airplane. (Boeing)

These Boeing 707s, photographed at AMARC in January, 1992, are some of the donor aircraft used in the "Airline Re-engine" program. (Randy Walker)

Some of the donor engine struts had humps, or "dog houses" as they were called on the leading edge of the pylon where the pylon meets the top of the engine inlet. These humps, while installed on the airliners, housed the turbo compressors used to supply pressurized air to the airliner's passenger compartment. The -135's pressurization system uses engine bleed air ducted from the engine compressor section, rather than separate turbo compressors. As a result the turbo compressors were not required and the inlet at the front of the pylon humps were blocked. The number of pylons on the re-engined -135s with the hump was based on the configuration of the donor aircraft, and is not standard on all E models.

The first "E" model, 59-1514, a KC-135E, was delivered on January 29, 1982, just over four months after contract award. A full flight test program for the "E" modification was accomplished using 59-1514. This aircraft had been one of the original KC-135R (Reconnaissance) models and was fitted with an inflight refueling receptacle. This receptacle allowed testing of the new KC-135E as both a tanker and a receiver. The testing of the receiver capability was required before re-engining the non-tanker versions, also having a receiver capability. The air refueling receiver capability also allowed for longer test mission durations.

59-1514, the first KC-135E was photographed on January 29, 1982, at the delivery ceremony. (Boeing)

JT3D/TF33-P-102 RE-ENGINED 135 MODELS AND THEIR COMMERCIAL DONORS

* These KC-135Es were modified to KC-135R configuration beginning in January 1996.

MOD UNIT NO.	C/KC-135 MDS	AIRCRAFT SERIAL NO.	COMMERCIAL MODEL	DONOR AIRCRAFT SERIAL NO.
1	KC-135E	59-1514	707-123B	19337
2	RC-135T	55-3121	707-123B	18885
3	EC-135K	55-3118	707-123B	18882
4	EC-135H	61-0274	707-123B	19344
5	EC-135E	61-0330	707-123B	19326
6	NKC-135E	55-3135	707-123B	19342
7	EC-135H	61-0285	707-123B	19325
8	EC-135E	60-0374	707-123B	19332
9	C-135E	60-0376	707-123B	19329
10	EC-135K	59-1518	707-123B	19328
11	C-135E	60-0375	707-123B	19187
12	EC-135H	61-0286	707-123B	19330
13	EC-135P	58-0022	707-123B	19341
14	C-135E	60-0372	707-123B	19340
15	EC-135H	61-0291	707-123B	19334
16	EC-135H	61-0282	707-123B	19331
17	EC-135P	58-0019	707-123B	19343
18	EC-135P	55-3129	707-123B	19327
19	KC-135E	57-1496	707-131B	18394
20	KC-135E	57-1510	707-131B	18396
21	KC-135E	58-0080	707-131B	18392
22	KC-135E	57-1452	707-131B	18389
23	KC-135E	57-1485	707-131B	18391
24	KC-135E	57-1433	707-131B	18403
25	KC-135E	58-0107	707-131B	18385
26	KC-135E	57-1455	707-131B	19220
27	KC-135E	56-3638	707-131B	19219
28	KC-135E	57-1478	707-131B	19223
29	KC-135E	55-3143	707-131B	19436
30	KC-135E	56-3607	707-131B	20057
31	KC-135E	58-0006	707-131B	18988
32	KC-135E	56-3609	707-131B	19216
33	KC-135E	58-0043	707-131B	20056
34	KC-135E	57-1495	707-131B	18402
35	KC-135E	57-1473	707-131B	18397
36	KC-135E	57-1425	707-131B	18387
37	KC-135E	57-2604	707-131B	18759
38	KC-135E	57-1484	707-131B	19221
39	KC-135E	59-1519	707-131B	18400
40	KC-135E	57-1475	707-131B	18989
41	KC-135E	58-0012	707-131B	19222
42	KC-135E	56-3643	707-131B	18386
43	KC-135E	59-1489	707-131B	18401
44	KC-135E	58-0111	707-131B	19218
45	KC-135E	57-1503	707-131B	18761
46	KC-135E	59-1479	707-131B	19217
47	KC-135E	59-1484	707-131B	18986
48	KC-135E	56-3612	707-131B	18761
49	KC-135E	57-2606	707-131B	18393
50	KC-135E	58-0003	707-131B	18404
51	KC-135E	57-1431	707-131B	19215
52	KC-135E	58-0115	707-131B	18388
53	KC-135E	57-1458	707-131B	18390
54	KC-135E	58-0024	707-131B	18762
55	KC-135E	57-1509	707-131B	18758
56	KC-135E	58-0087	707-131B	19568
57	KC-135E	57-1480	707-131B	19569
58	KC-135E	59-1456	707-123B	18884
59	KC-135E	59-1497	707-123B	19188
60	KC-135E	59-1487	707-123B	19324
61	KC-135E	59-1506	707-123B	18883
62	KC-135E	56-3626	720-047B	19438
63	KC-135E	58-0032	720-047B	19413
64	KC-135E	58-0078	720-047B	19028
65	KC-135E	58-0068	720-047B	19207
66	KC-135E	57-2595	720-047B	19414
67	KC-135E	58-0040	707-123B	17646
68	KC-135E	56-0067	707-123B	19333
69	KC-135E	59-1485	707-123B	19336
70	KC-135E	57-2589	720-047B	19523
71	KC-135E	57-2608	707-123B	19338
72	KC-135E	59-1457	707-123B	17636
73	KC-135E	57-2594	707-123B	17640
74	KC-135E	58-0057	720-023B	18022
75	KC-135E	57-2607	707-138B	17700
76	EC-135E	61-0329	720-051B	18382

59-1514, the first KC-135E takes off on its maiden flight. (Boeing)

77	KC-135E	56-3648	720-051B	18383
78	KC-135E	55-3141	720-058B	18425
79	KC-135E	56-3641	707-123B	17652
80	KC-135E	56-3606	720-030B	18059
81*	KC-135E	58-0008	707-123B	17651
82	KC-135E	57-1429	720-051B	18381
83	KC-135E	57-1464	707-331B	18980
84	KC-135E	56-3654	707-331B	18982
85	KC-135E	57-1505	707-331B	18405
86	KC-135E	57-1448	707-331B	18984
87	KC-135E	56-3631	707-131B	18764
88	KC-135E	56-3631	707-331B	18916
89	KC-135E	58-0017	707-331B	20061
90*	KC-135E	57-1428	707-331B	18408
91	KC-135E	57-1463	707-331B	18406
92	KC-135E	56-3640	707-331B	18913
93	KC-135E	56-3604	707-331B	18981
94*	KC-135E	59-1499	707-331B	18918
95	KC-135E	57-1465	707-331B	18983
96	KC-135E	57-1481	707-331B	20058
97	KC-135E	57-1450	707-331B	18979
98	KC-135E	57-1460	707-321B	19697
99	KC-135E	55-3146	707-321B	20019
100	KC-135E	56-3630	707-321B	20020
101	KC-135E	57-1507	707-321B	19698
102*	KC-135E	59-1450	707-321B	19699
103	KC-135E	56-3622	707-331B	18409
104	KC-135E	57-1426	707-331B	20059
105*	KC-135E	59-1505	707-331B	19224
106	KC-135E	57-1482	707-331B	19227
107	KC-135E	56-3593	707-321B	20024
108	KC-135E	57-1445	707-321B	18840
109	KC-135E	57-1494	707-331B	19226
110*	KC-135E	59-1448	707-331B	18407
111	KC-135E	56-3611	707-331B	18914
112	KC-135E	57-1443	707-331B	18915
113	KC-135E	56-3658	707-331B	19225
114	KC-135E	59-1494	707-323C	19383
115*	KC-135E	59-1509	707-323C	19237
116	KC-135E	57-1491	707-331B	20064
117	EC-135E	61-0326	707-331B	20067
118	KC-135E	57-1501	707-331C	18756
119	KC-135E	57-1434	707-321B	19275
120	KC-135E	57-1438	720-023B	18037
121	KC-135E	58-0096	720-059B	18831
122*	KC-135E	57-1468	707-331C	19567
123	KC-135E	57-1421	720-040B	18380
124	KC-135E	58-0020	707-123B	19185
125	KC-135E	59-1445	707-123B	19186
126	KC-135E	59-1452	707-123B	19323
127	KC-135E	57-2600	707-123B	19339
128	EC-135N	61-0327	720-023B	18033
129	KC-135E	58-0082	707-321B	20026
130*	KC-135E	58-0085	720-030B	18251
131	KC-135E	57-1504	707-321B	20027
132	KC-135E	58-0064	707-331B	20066
133	EC-135Y	55-3125	720-023B	18016
134	KC-135E	58-0041	707-331B	20065
135	KC-135E	58-0108	720-024B	18419
136*	KC-135E	58-0052	707-323C	20089
137	KC-135E	59-1451	720-024B	18418
138	KC-135E	58-0090	707-338C	18954
139*	KC-135E	57-1479	707-351C	19034
140	KC-135E	59-1477	707-321B	18836
141	KC-135E	57-1511	707-321B	18834
142*	KC-135E	57-2598	720-023B	18014
143	KC-135E	59-1447	707-321B	18842
144	KC-135E	55-3145	707-321B	19693
145	KC-135E	56-3623	707-139B	17903
146	KC-135E	58-0013	707-338C	18953
147	KC-135E	58-0058	707-323G	18691
148*	KC-135E	57-2603	707-323C	16690
149	KC-135E	58 0053	707-321B	18833
150	KC-135E	57-1422	707-321B	18336
151*	KC-135E	57-1512	707-331B	20062
152	KC-135E	57-1471	707-324C	19351
153*	KC-135E	57-1436	720-051B	18422
154	KC-135E	58-0014	707-138B	18068
155	KC-135E	59-1503	720-051B	18792
156*	KC-135E	59-1516	707-328B	18686
157	KC-135E	58-0005	707-123B	17645
158	KC-135E	58-0037	707-368B	19810
159	KC-135E	57-1492	720-051B	18421
160	KC-135E	57-1493	707-336B	20456
161	KC-135E	57-1441	707-123B	17639
162	KC-135E	61-0271	707-321C	20018
163	KC-135E	61-0280	720-060B	18455
164*	KC-135E	61-0303	720-024B	18417
165	KC-135E	61-0270	720-047B	18063
166	KC-135D	63-8060	707-331B	18985
167	KC-135D	63-8058	707-358B	19502
168	KC-135D	63-0061	707-358B	20097
169	KC-135D	63-8059	707-337B	19247
170	KC-135E	56-3645	707-337B	18873
171	KC-135E	61-0268	707-358B	19004
172	KC-135E	58-0044	707-321B	18339
173	KC-135E	57-1447	707-337B	18708
174	KC-135E	58-0116	720-051B	18688
175	KC-135E	61-0281	707-321B	18832
176	NKC-135E	55-3132	707-123B	17631
177	KC-135E	57-1451	707-323C	19383
178	KC-135E	60-0316	707-384B	20036
179	KC-135E	59-1496	707-323B	20179
180	KC-135E	57-1423	707-351C	19163
181	KC-135E	60-0327	707-123B	17635
182	KC-135E	57-1497	720-047B	18829
183	KC-135E	62-3566	707-344B	19133
184	KC-135E	57-2601	707-321B	19266
185	KC-135E	62-3527	707-321B	18837
186*	KC-135E	57-1459	707-330B	19315
187	KC-135E	57-2602	707-384B	20035

Tanker Re-engine Program (KC-135R and T)

Early in 1980 the U.S. Air Force, continuing with their upgrade program of the 135 fleet, began planning for a program to re-engine SAC's 135 tanker fleet with new engines, rather than using used airline engines as was done in the "E" program.

The goal of this re-engine program was to increase the performance of the 135 tanker. By increasing the performance there would be a increase in fuel off-load capability, and at the same time, the re-engined tankers could be dispersed to more sites with shorter runways than could the J57/TF33 powered tankers. This would allow greater survivability in case of a surprise nuclear attack. The new engines would be safer and more reliable, with decreased maintenance, and be more fuel efficient.

The design configuration was narrowed to three versions, updates of the three re-engine recommendations from earlier Boeing studies; the KC-135P7 using the TF33-P-101, the KC-135RF using the JT8D-209B, and the KC-135TT using the CFM56-1B1. The CFM56 configuration was selected. Boeing's initial design for the CFM56 configuration used the nacelles which had been designed for use on the 707. These nacelles had cascade thrust reversers, reversing the fan thrust, but not the exhaust thrust. The Air Force felt thrust reversers were unnecessary, and if removed the weight savings would allow a greater fuel offload. As a result the nacelles were redesigned without thrust reversers.

As part of the rebuilding program, the J57 engines were removed and replaced by four 22,000 lb thrust CFM International CFM56-2B-1 turbofans (military designation F108-CF-100). This type of engine is also used on the E-6 Mercury (TACAMO) and export models of the E-3 Sentry. In addition to its far greater thrust (8,250 lbs per engine more than the J-57), the F108/CFM56 burns less fuel, is cleaner and quieter than its turbojet predecessor. The F108 weighs 8,300 pounds, some 2,800 pounds more than the original J57. To handle the additional weight and thrust the wing spars were strengthened and the horizontal stabilizers were enlarged to improve longitudinal stability. In addition to replacing the engines and pylons, the horizontal stabilizer received the same modification as on the later "E" re-engined aircraft.

The increased power and reduced fuel consumption of the F108 radically improves the KC-135Rs performance. As with the KC-135E, the takeoff run is reduced, without the need for water injection and takeoffs can be made under adverse conditions without reducing the fuel load. The KC-135R has an improved fuel offload capability and under some mission scenarios two KC-135Rs could transfer as much fuel as three KC-135As. In addition to the new engines, the KC-135R has a number of other improvements. There are two Turbomach T-T-62-40LCLL-2-2 auxiliary power units in the rear of the cargo compartment to provide high-pressure air to start the engines or to operate the air conditioning system on the ground.

KC-135 CFM56 Re-engine Program Aircraft Modifications

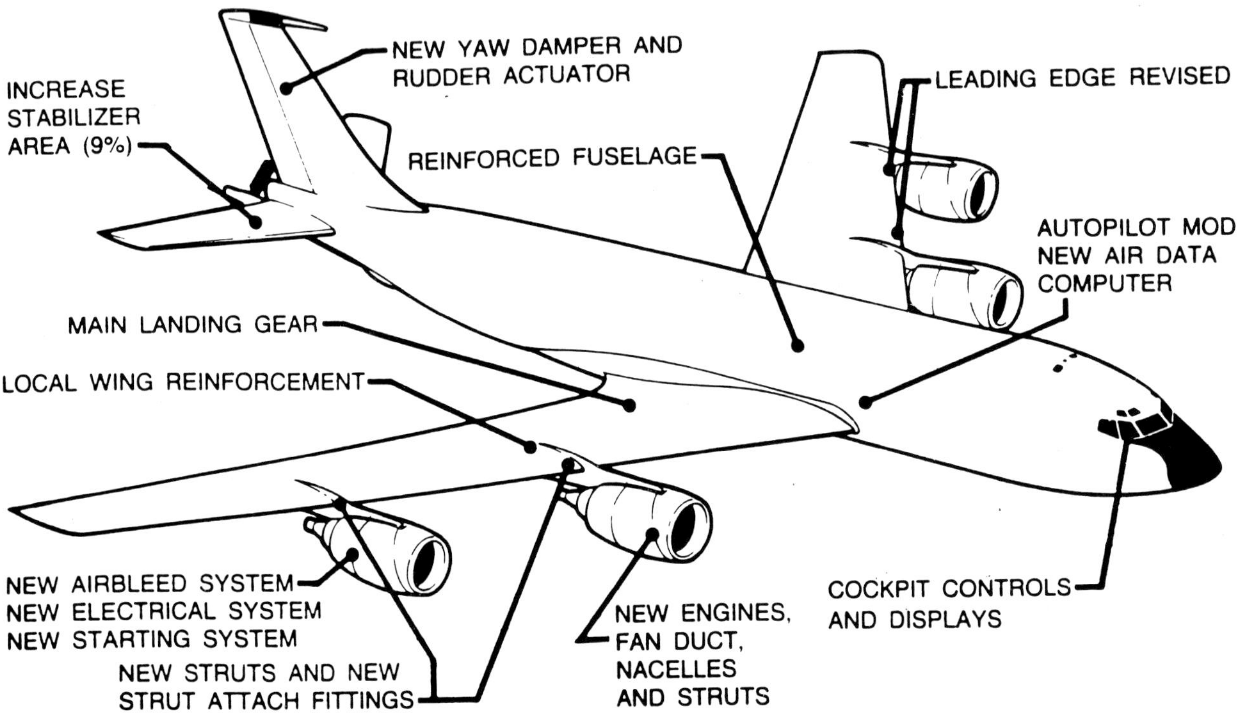

This F108-CF-100 engine (military version of the CFM International CFM56-2B-1), photographed at Boeing's Wichita plant, is one of the engines used on 61-0293, the first KC-135R model tanker. (Boeing)

The KC-135R has 2 F108-CF-100 engines mounted on short pylons on each wing. (Don Logan)

The increased weight capability of the KC-135R made it necessary to install strengthened landing gear and MK III five-rotor anti-skid brakes which replaced the four-rotor brakes of the KC-135A A high-speed pitch trim system was added for stabilization during refueling of large aircraft. A flight control augmentation system was installed. This system provides automatic rudder control inputs to assist the pilots with yaw control in case of an outboard engine failure at high power settings. A series yaw damper was installed to provide automatic rudder input in response to adverse yaw conditions. In the cockpit, there are instrumentation changes, some related to the new engines, while others are for the Engine Failure Assist System (EFAS) and other new systems.

The new re-engined tanker was designated as the KC-135R. The military designation given the CFM56 engine was F108-CF-100. The designation KC-135R had been previously used, but since there were no longer any of the four original reconnaissance KC-R's still in service using that designation, the designation was re-used.

The first KC-135R, 61-0293, was rolled out of the Boeing Wichita modification facility on June 22, 1982. A full flight test program was accomplished at Edwards AFB using 61-0293, previously an EC-135A. As with the KC-135E flight test aircraft, this aircraft had a previous modification which added an inflight refueling receptacle. This refueling receiver capability allowed flight testing of the new KC-135R as both a tanker and a receiver.

The 384th Air Refueling Wing at McConnell AFB in Wichita, Kansas was the first unit to receive KC-135Rs. The first R model, 61-0293 was delivered to the 384th ARW on June 20, 1984 two years later, after completing flight test.

Under this program 336 KC-135As have been modified to the KC- 135R configuration. Twenty KC-135Es were re-engined and are now KC-135Rs.

The 54 KC-135Qs, also equipped with J57 engines, received the F108 engine modification. The resulting aircraft are designated KC-135Ts.

F108 re-engining is still continuing with Boeing-Wichita re-engining KC-135Es and RC-135s for the USAF. KC-135As are also being converted to KC-135Rs for foreign military sales.

KC-135A 61-0293, the first tanker to be re-engined with CFM56 (F108) engines is seen here on arrival at Boeing's Wichita military modification center. 61-0293 had received an air refueling receiver receptacle when it was in service as an EC-135A. (Boeing)

61-0293 is seen here during checkout on the Boeing Wichita ramp after installation of F108 engines. (Boeing)

During flight test 61-0293 had a special test pitot boom fitted to the nose. (Boeing)

As part of flight test the refueling receiver characteristics of the KC-135R were tested. (Boeing)

MISSION MODIFIED KC-135As

KC-135A COMBAT LIGHTNING/RADIO RELAY

In order to provide airborne communications relay capability for tactical aircraft conducting combat operations in Southeast Asia during the Vietnam War, seven KC-135As were converted for the radio relay role. These aircraft were modified with 19 small antennas on the upper fuselage and 9 on the lower fuselage, carrying an AN/ARC-89 communications relay set internally.

The Combat Lightning mission can be traced back to June 1966. Headquarters USAF informed Headquarters SAC that month of an urgent requirement for airborne relay platforms to support the USAF command and control system in Southeast Asia. Headquarters USAF first suggested using two EC-135L aircraft of the SAC Post Attack Command Control System (PACCS) fleet, but Headquarters SAC eventually decided to use two basic KC-135 tankers with AN/ARC-89 equipment installed. The first two, one from Travis AFB, California, and one from Blytheville AFB, Arkansas, were modified by the end of summer, tested in early September and arrived at Kadena on September 14. After a short delay to get clearance to enter Thailand, they arrived at U-Tapao on September 20 and 22 and flew their first mission on October 5, 1966. These aircraft provided only interim coverage, however, as it was realized from the outset that full, 24-hour coverage would be needed in 1967 and would require five aircraft.

Combat Lightning was designed to extend the range of ground communications stations. Tied in to an operational control system at Monkey Mountain, South Vietnam, it first functioned mainly to pass warning information to aircraft operating over North Vietnam, a mission it performed while orbiting over the Gulf of Tonkin. Although air refueling was not the normal or main function of these tankers, they could and often did provide this service in emergencies. Three additional KC-135As joined the Combat Lightning fleet in the first part of October. In addition to carrying regular radio relay equipment, these aircraft were outfitted with secure voice communications equipment. The modification of the original Combat Lightning aircraft was completed by the end of 1967. During the period of their operations in Southeast Asia, the Combat Lightning aircraft moved several times. At first they operated from U-Tapao, but they moved to Ching Chuan Kang Air Base, when it opened on February 2, 1968. When SAC KC-135s left Ching Chuan Kang late in 1970, the Combat Lightning aircraft resumed operations from U-Tapao. On February 23, 1971 the aircraft moved again, this time to Kadena, to make room for other aircraft during Operation Lam Son 719. They returned to U-Tapao AB, Thailand on June 8, 1971. One of the earlier actions taken in connection with the 1972 buildup was to move the radio relay tankers to Kadena again, the move taking place between April 9 and 11, 1972. They returned to U-Tapao on February 2 and 3, 1973.

After the relay aircraft were withdrawn from SEA during 1973, two aircraft were reconfigured back to standard KC-135A configurations. The remaining five had some of the radio relay equipment removed and operated as standard tankers. They retained their antennas, internal provisions for the installation of relay gear and their J57 power plants and were known as KC-135A Relay. Because the former Combat Lightning aircraft had a heavier basic weight due to the retained racks and antennas, they would not carry as much fuel as standard KC-135As. As a result, they were not usable for SIOP (Single Integrated Operations Plan) alert mission. Consequently, when ANG units began converting to the KC-135A, the ex-Combat Lightning aircraft were logical choices to serve as aircrew trainers for the newly forming Guard tanker squadrons. Later all were completely demodified from the Combat Lightning and converted to E or R tankers. 61-0268, 61-0270,

The Combat Lightning KC-135A, 61-0280 is seen here in its silver paint. (Joe Bruch Collection)

61-0271, 61-0280, and 61-0303 were converted to KC-135Es, and 61-0321, and 63-8881 were converted to KC-135Rs.

KC-135A aircraft that served as Combat Lightning/Radio Relay aircraft (7):

61-0268 61-0303
61-0270 61-0321
61-0271 63-8881
61-0280

The Combat Lightning KC-135A, 61-0280, now a KC-135E, is seen here in gloss gray paint. (Joe Bruch Collection)

KC-135A 61-0280 seen on landing. (Don Logan Collection)

Combat Lightning 63-8881 was photographed at Plattsburg AFB on June 19, 1971. (Tom Brewer Collection)

KC-135A COMMAND SUPPORT AIRCRAFT

U.S. AIR FORCE CHIEF OF STAFF
(SPECKLED TROUT)KC-135A and C-135B

KC-135A 55-3126 was converted to a VIP transport for the USAF Chief of Staff and operated out of Andrews AFB, Maryland. 55-3126 was retired to MASDC (Military Aircraft Storage and Disposition Center) now Aircraft Maintenance and Regeneration Center (AMARC) on July 31, 1975 given the storage number CA004. The aircraft was cut up at AMARC and used for systems mock-up and testing by Boeing at Wichita, Kansas.

61-2669, originally a C-135B, replaced 55-3126 as Speckled Trout after having been in storage at MASDC as CA003. 61-2669 is presently based at Edwards AFB and used as a VIP transport for the USAF Chief of Staff, and as a testbed for C/KC-135 avionics programs. (See C-135B)

Speckled Trout Serial Numbers:

55-3126 Ex – KC-135A
61-2669 Ex – C-135B/WC-135B

The present "Speckled Trout", seen flying banked over Edwards AFB runway. (USAF)

BELOW: 55-3126, a KC-135A was the first "Speckled Trout" aircraft. It went to AMARC at Davis-Monthan AFB, AZ on July 31, 1975 for storage, and was stored as #CA004. The engines were sealed, and numerous items were removed for spares for the new Speckled Trout, 61-2669. Other parts were salvaged and used to support the 135 fleet. Its last flight occurred on July 31, 1975. It had a total of 9,975 flight hours when retired. (Joe Bruch Collection)

61-2669, built as a C-135B, was the second and last "Speckled Trout." It is now assigned to the 412th Test Squadron at Edwards AFB, California. (Boeing)

STRIKE COMMAND

In 1967 KC-135A 61-0316 was converted into an airborne command and control aircraft for United States Strike Command (USSTRICOM), McDill AFB, Florida. The aircraft had improved communications and navigation capability. Its mission was to support deployments of tactical fighters and other aircraft. The aircraft had HF probe antennas mounted over the wingtips, Additional static dischargers were located on the wingtips, vertical fin tip, elevator tip, and on the boom ruddevators.

Different antennas were installed along the fuselage.

This aircraft later served with the 2nd Bomb Wing at Barksdale AFB, as "CASEY 08," the 8th Air Force Command support aircraft.

On March 19, 1985, the aircraft was destroyed by fire while on the ground at Cairo, Egypt. The fire started in the area of the APU.

61-0316 wore this paint scheme when photographed on June 5, 1969, while assigned to the U.S. Strike Command (USSTRICOM) at McDill AFB, Florida. (Jack Morris via Tom Brewer)

61-0316 later served as the support aircraft for the 8th Air Force commander, and was stationed at Barksdale AFB. It burned on the ramp at Cairo International Airport, Egypt on March 19, 1985. The left outboard wing section was used at Wurtsmith AFB, Michigan to repair a KC-135A (58-0014) which had suffered a wing overpressure mishap. Total flight hours when destroyed were 10,235. (Tom Brewer Collection)

UNITED STATES AIR FORCES – EUROPE

KC-135A 63-8020 was used by USAFE (United States Air Forces – Europe) as a command support aircraft.

BELOW: KC-135A, 63-8020, photographed at Elmendorf AFB on May 29, 1968 while serving as the European Commander's airplane. It has a VIP configured interior. It was later converted back to a standard KC-135A then to a KC-135R. (Tom Brewer Collection)

STRATEGIC AIR COMMAND

Three KC-135As were used as Command support aircraft for SAC. 57-2589, assigned to the 55th SRW at Offutt AFB, supported CINCSAC and SAC Headquarters. It flew with the callsign "CASEY 01."

57-2589 was re-engined as a KC-135E and is still assigned to the 55th at Offutt AFB, supporting U.S. Strategic Command.

61-0316, the ex-STRIKE COMMAND aircraft, served with the 2nd Bomb Wing at Barksdale AFB as "CASEY 08", the 8th Air Force Command support aircraft.

61-0300 served with the 22nd Air Refueling Wing at March AFB as "CASEY 15", the 15th Air Force Command support aircraft.

KC-135A 57-2589, photographed on May 27, 1973, was used as the SAC Commander's Airplane, with call sign "Casey-01"(pronounced KC-01). (Tom Brewer Collection)

KC-135A 57-2589, seen here at Offutt AFB in July, 1982 was converted to a KC-135E. (Tom Brewer Collection)

KC-135A 61-0300, a one time a Combat Lightning airplane, Served as a transport for the Commander of the 15th Air Force, and was known as "Casey 15" (KC-15). (Douglas Slowiak/Vortex Photographics)

While serving as Casey 15 for the 15th Air Force, 61-0300 was assigned to the 22nd Bombardment Wing at March AFB, California. 61-0300 was converted to a KC-135R. (Don McGarry)

KC-135 TANKERS

KC-135A

The most numerous of the C-135 series was the KC-135A. Of the 820 C-135 aircraft manufactured, 732 were built as KC-135As.

KC-135A Serial Numbers (Original Production)

Serial Numbers	Count
55-3118 thru 55-3146	(29)
56-3591 thru 56-3658	(68)
57-1418 thru 57-1514	(97)
57-2589 thru 57-2609	(21)
58-0001 thru 58-0130	(130)
59-1443 thru 59-1523	(81)
60-0313 thru 60-0368	(56)
61-0261 thru 61-0325	(65)
62-3497 thru 62-3580	(84)
63-7976 thru 63-8045	(70)
63-8871 thru 63-8888	(18)
64-14828 thru 64-14840	(13)
Total	**(732)**

KC-135B

Seventeen aircraft were ordered as KC-135Bs, powered with TF33-P-9. The first fourteen were modified and redesignated as EC-135C airborne command posts and the last three were modified as EC-135J before delivery to the USAF. EC-135C, 63-8050 was converted back to tanker configuration, designated a NKC-135B and is now assigned to the 412th Test Wing, 452nd Test Squadron at Edwards AFB.

The following aircraft were originally ordered as KC-135Bs:

KC-135B Serial Numbers (17):

62-3581	63-8050
62-3582	63-8051
62-3583	63-8052
62-3584	63-8053
62-3585	63-8054
63-8046	63-8055
63-8047	63-8056
63-8048	63-8057
63-8049	

62-3581, seen here in EC-135C configuration, was the first of 17 KC-135Bs produced by Boeing. (Boeing)

KC-135D

The four RC-135As operated by MATS/MAC were converted to tanker configuration by the late 1970s and transferred to SAC, redesignated as KC-135Ds.

All four were assigned to the 55th SRW at Offutt AFB where they served as command support aircraft.

The KC-135Ds were next assigned to the 305th Air Refueling Wing at Grissom AFB as tankers. In 1990 all four received JT3D (TF33-PW-102) engines as part of the KC-135E re-engine program, but kept their KC-135D designation.

The aircraft were then reassigned to the 168th Air Refueling Group, Alaska ANG at Eielson AFB. With the Alaska ANG now receiving KC-135Rs, the aircraft were transferred to the 161st ARG, Arizona ANG, and later to the 190th ARG, Kansas ANG.

KC-135D Serial Numbers (4):

63-8058
63-8059
63-8060
63-8061

BELOW: 63-8058, a KC-135D, when photographed on June 6, 1981, still was equipped with J57 engines while assigned to the 305th Air Refueling Wing (ARW), Grissom AFB, Indiana. (Don McGarry)

KC-135D 63-8058, In the markings of the 190th ARW when photographed August, 1996, has been re-engined with TF-33 engines as part of the airline re-engine program. (Jerry Geer)

KC-135D 63-8059, one of four KC-135Ds originally produces as RC-135As, is seen here on July 22, 1995, in the markings of the 161st Air Refueling wing, Arizona Air National Guard. (Carey Mavor)

KC-135D 63-8060, along with the other three KC-135Ds, were assigned to 168th Air Refueling Group Alaska Air National Guard until replaced by KC-135Rs during 1995. (David F. Brown)

63-8061, the fourth KC-135D, photographed in February, 1996, in 163rd Air Refueling Wing, California Air National Guard markings, with an acceptance date of January 6, 1966, was the last C-135 version to be delivered to the US Air Force. It was delivered as an RC-135A, specially equipped for reconnaissance work. (Jerry Geer)

KC-135E

The KC-135E is a KC-135A modified with uprated engines salvaged from used 707/720 airliners. These aircraft were all part of a modernization program involving 161 Air National Guard and Air Force Reserve Stratotankers. The rebuild program involved replacing the original J57 engines with 18,000 lb thrust JT3D turbofans removed from 707/720s, the installation of the larger horizontal stabilizers from the donor airliners, and various cockpit avionics improvements. The TF33-PW-102 turbofan engines (military equivalent of the commercial JT-3D) provided a considerable increase in thrust (approximately 5,000 lbs per engine) and reliability over the earlier J57 engines. Additionally, engine noise, smoke emissions and fuel consumption were reduced. The increased thrust of the JT3D allowed removal of the water injection system, and provided a wider safety margin during runway operations. The inclusion of thrust reversers made it possible for the KC-135E to use shorter runways.

The airline engines had a cartridge start capability added as part of the conversion to TF33-PW-102s. The conversion program used already existing parts, providing the Air National Guard (ANG) and Air Force Reserve (AFRES) with a quick and cost-effective way of dealing with the emissions, noise, and performance problems encountered with standard KC-135A operations. The ANG and AFRES operate all of the KC-135Es, except for two aircraft assigned to Offutt AFB

One of these aircraft (59-1514) had been a KC-135R/RC-135R (RC-135R was an unofficial designation) that was reverted to KC-135A status before becoming a KC-135E. This aircraft has a refueling receiver installed and is the only KC-135E with this feature. It is used as a flight crew trainer by the 55th Wing at Offutt AFB.

The second, 57-2589, was used for many years at Offutt AFB as a support aircraft for the Commander-in-Chief, Strategic Air Command (CINCSAC). It has remained at Offutt and is now flown by the 55th Wing as a command support aircraft for STRATCOM.

The first ANG unit to be equipped with the KC-135E was the 197th ARS, 161 ARG, Arizona Air National Guard.

Two KC-135Es have been lost since conversion. 57-1481 exploded and burned on the ramp at Eielson AFB, Alaska on September 20, 1989. 59-1494 exploded and burned on the ramp at Pease AFB, New Hampshire on January 11, 1990.

A number of KC-135Es are planned to be further modified receiving the F108 engines and being redesignated as KC-135Rs. Due to engine noise restrictions, all KC-135Es are planned to be re-engined or retired by the early 2000s.

KC-135E 59-1473, from 151st Air Refueling Wing, Utah ANG, lands at Davis-Monthan AFB on January 10, 1997. (Don Logan)

The following KC-135As have been modified with TF33-PW-102 engines converting them to KC-135Es (Notes: * This aircraft has air refueling receiver capability; E/R – These aircraft have been modified to KC-135R configuration):

55-3141	57-1423	57-1475	57-2600	58-0058	59-1484
55-3143	57-1425	57-1478	57-2601	58-0064	59-1485
55-3145	57-1426	57-1479E/R	57-2602	58-0067	59-1487
55-3146	57-1428E/R	57-1480	57-2603E/R	58-0068	59-1489
56-3593	57-1429	57-1481	57-2604	58-0078	59-1493
56-3604	57-1431	57-1482	57-2606	58-0080	59-1494
56-3606	57-1433	57-1484	57-2607	58-0082	59-1496
56-3607	57-1434	57-1485	57-2608	58-0085E/R	59-1497
56-3609	57-1436E/R	57-1491	58-0003	58-0087	59-1499E/R
56-3611	57-1438	57-1492	58-0005	58-0090	59-1503
56-3612	57-1441	57-1494	58-0006	58-0096	59-1505E/R
56-3622	57-1443	57-1495	58-0008E/R	58-0107	59-1506
56-3623	57-1445	57-1496	58-0012	58-0108	59-1509E/R
56-3626	57-1447	57-1497	58-0013	58-0111	59-1514 *
56-3630	57-1448	57-1501	58-0014	58-0115	59-1516E/R
56-3631	57-1450	57-1503	58-0017	58-0116	59-1519
56-3638	57-1451E/R	57-1504	58-0020	59-1445	60-0316
56-3640	57-1452	57-1505	58-0024	59-1447	60-0327
56-3641	57-1455	57-1507	58-0032	59-1448E/R	61-0268
56-3643	57-1458	57-1509	58-0037	59-1450E/R	61-0270
56-3645	57-1459E/R	57-1510	58-0040	59-1451	61-0271
56-3648	57-1460	57-1511	58-0041	59-1452	61-0280E/R
56-3650	57-1463	57-1512E/R	58-0043	59-1456	61-0281
56-3654	57-1464	57-2589	58-0044	59-1457	61-0303
56-3658	57-1465	57-2594	58-0052E/R	59-1473	62-3527
57-1421	57-1468	57-2595	58-0053	59-1477	62-3566E/R
57-1422	57-1471	57-2598E/R	58-0057	59-1479	

KC-135Q

Externally identical to the KC-135A, the KC-135Q aircraft were KC-135As modified with special valves to isolate tanks used for carrying JP-7 fuel. These aircraft were the dedicated tankers used for the SR-71 Blackbird strategic reconnaissance aircraft. While the KC-135Qs were modified to transfer the Blackbird's exotic JP-7 fuel, they also retained the capability to pass conventional JP-4. Additionally, the aircraft are fitted with a secure communications link in the form of a boom interphone which allowed communications through the boom when it was latched in the SR-71's receptacle. Additional navaids were added to aid in rendezvous with the SR-71. A total of fifty-six KC-135As were converted to the KC-135Q configuration.

The Qs were initially delivered to the 456th SAW at Beale AFB, California; the 43rd Bomb Wing at Little Rock AFB, Arkansas; and the 306th Bomb Wing at McCoy AFB, Florida. The 43rd and 306th aircraft later moved to Plattsburgh AFB, Beale AFB, and Kadena AB.

During the Vietnam conflict KC-135Qs were used to support Blackbird (SR-71/A-12) flights out of Kadena AB, Okinawa. Between September 27 and October 30, 1967, ten KC- 135Qs arrived at Kadena and began to fly bomber refueling missions. In their first few months their purpose was to broaden the base of KC-135 operations, and as each "Q" model arrived, Kadena would release a KC-135A, a regular tanker, to the 4258th Strategic Wing at U-Tapao.

The 376th SW on Okinawa operated a number of KC-135Qs. The 380th BW at Plattsburgh AFB, New York operated a number of KC-135Qs alongside the unit's standard KC-135As.

Some KC-135Qs were always assigned to Beale AFB, the home of the SR-71 during the Blackbird's operational life.

Two KC-135Qs were destroyed. 58-0039 crashed while flying an approach at Torrejon AB, Spain on June 3, 1971. 60-0338 burned on the ground at Plattsburgh AFB, New York on February 8, 1980.

KC-135Q Serial Numbers (56):

58-0039	58-0071	58-0125	59-1512
58-0042	58-0072	58-0129	59-1513
58-0045	58-0074	59-1460	59-1520
58-0046	58-0077	59-1462	59-1523
58-0047	58-0084	59-1464	60-0335
58-0049	58-0086	59-1467	60-0336
58-0050	58-0088	59-1468	60-0337
58-0054	58-0089	59-1470	60-0338
58-0055	58-0094	59-1471	60-0339
58-0060	58-0095	59-1474	60-0342
58-0061	58-0099	59-1480	60-0343
58-0062	58-0103	59-1490	60-0344
58-0065	58-0112	59-1504	60-0345
58-0069	58-0117	59-1510	60-0346

KC-135Q 58-0112 was one of 56 KC-135As converted to KC-135Q configuration and used to refuel the SR-71 fleet. All the KC-135Qs were latter converted to KC-135Ts. (USAF)

KC-135R

KC-135Rs are KC-135A airframes which had previously completed the lower wing reskin modification and were put through an extensive rebuilding program carried out at the Boeing facility in Wichita, Kansas. The RE program included the installation of advanced turbofan engines to overcome the KC-135As biggest problem, that of being underpowered. During the initial phases of the project, the Air Force referred the aircraft to be rebuilt as KC-135REs, possibly to avoid confusion with the KC-135R reconnaissance aircraft (which no longer existed). Several engines were considered including the TF33-P-7 and JT10D, as well as the CFM56 (built by a consortium of General Electric of the U.S., and Snecma of France). The Air Force also considered the possibility of retrofiting 707-320B wings to the KC-135A airframe. The CFM56 turbofan was ultimately chosen as the engine, but the wing modification was rejected.

Since all operational KC-135A tankers have been re-engined, some KC-135Es are currently being modified into KC-135Rs. Additional KC-135As are being removed from storage at AMARC and being re-engined for Foreign Military Sales (FMS).

The first unit to receive the KC-135R was the 384th ARW at McConnell AFB, Kansas (across the runway from Boeing's Wichita facility that accomplished the modifications). The 384th Wing accepted its first aircraft during July of 1984. One KC-135R named Cherokee Rose (62-3554), flying from Altus AFB, set sixteen time-to-climb records on November 19, 1988.

One KC-135R has been lost. 57-1470 exploded and burned on the ramp at General Mitchell International Airport, Milwaukee, Wisconsin.

KC-135R AIRCRAFT BY SERIAL NUMBER

E/R – These aircraft were modified from KC-135As to KC-135Es, and then to KC-135Rs
AR – These aircraft have air refueling receiver capability
FR – KC-135As re-engined for France
TK – KC-135As re-engined for Turkey
SP – KC-135As re-engined for Singapore

57-1418
57-1419
57-1427
57-1428 E/R
57-1430
57-1432
57-1435
57-1436 E/R
57-1437
57-1439
57-1440
57-1451 E/R
57-1453
57-1454
57-1456
57-1459 E/R
57-1461
57-1462
57-1468 E/R
57-1469
57-1470
57-1472
57-1473
57-1474
57-1479 E/R
57-1483
57-1486
57-1487
57-1488
57-1493
57-1499
57-1502
57-1506
57-1508
57-1512 E/R
57-1514
57-2593
57-2597
57-2598 E/R
57-2599
57-2603 E/R
57-2609 TK
57-2605
58-0001
58-0004
58-0008 E/R
58-0009
58-0010
58-0011 AR
58-0015
58-0016
58-0018 AR
58-0021
58-0023
58-0027
58-0030
58-0034
58-0035
58-0036
58-0038
58-0051
58-0052 E/R
58-0056
58-0059
58-0063
58-0066
58-0073
58-0075
58-0076
58-0079
58-0083
58-0085 E/R
58-0092
58-0093
58-0098
58-0100
58-0102
58-0104
58-0106
58-0109
58-0110 TK
58-0113
58-0114
58-0118
58-0119
58-0120
58-0121
58-0122
58-0123
58-0124 AR
58-0126 AR
58-0128
58-0130
59-1444
59-1446
59-1448 E/R
59-1450 E/R
59-1453
59-1454 SP
59-1455
59-1458
59-1459
59-1461
59-1463
59-1466
59-1469
59-1472
59-1475
59-1476
59-1478
59-1482
59-1483
59-1486
59-1488
59-1492
59-1495
59-1498
59-1499 E/R
59-1500
59-1501
59-1502
59-1505 E/R
59-1507
59-1508
59-1509 E/R
59-1511
59-1515
59-1516 E/R
59-1517
59-1521
59-1522
60-0313
60-0314
60-0315
60-0318
60-0319
60-0320
60-0321
60-0322
60-0323
60-0324
60-0325 TK
60-0326 TK
60-0328
60-0329
60-0331
60-0332
60-0333
60-0334
60-0341
60-0347
60-0348
60-0349
60-0350
60-0351
60-0353
60-0355
60-0356 AR
60-0357 AR
60-0358
60-0359
60-0360
60-0362 AR
60-0363
60-0364
60-0365
60-0366
60-0367
61-0264
61-0266
61-0267
61-0272
61-0275
61-0276
61-0277
61-0280 E/R
61-0284
61-0288
61-0290
61-0292
61-0293 AR
61-0294
61-0295
61-0298
61-0299
61-0300
61-0302
61-0303 E/R
61-0304
61-0305
61-0306
61-0307
61-0308
61-0309
61-0310
61-0311
61 0312
61-0313
61-0314
61-0315
61-0317
61-0318
61-0320
61-0321
61-0323
61-0324
62-0325 SP
62-3497 FR
62-3498
62-3499
62-3500
62-3502
62-3503
62-3504
62-3505
62-3506
62-3507
62-3508
62-3509
62-3510
62-3511
62-3512
62-3513
62-3514
62-3515
62-3516
62-3517
62-3518
62-3519
62-3520
62-3521
62-3523
62-3524
62-3525 FR
62-3526
62-3528
62-3529
62-3530
62-3531
62-3533

KC-135R 59-1516, in 163rd Air Refueling Wing, California Air National Guard markings, was one of the first group of KC-135Es to be modified to KC-135Rs. (Roger Messick)

62-3534	62-3553	62-3573	63-7988	63-8012	63-8029	63-8872	64-14829
62-3537	62-3554	62-3574 FR	63-7991	63-8013	63-8030	63-8873	64-14830
62-3538	62-3556	62-3575	63-7992	63-8014	63-8031	63-8874	64-14831
62-3539 TK	62-3557	62-3576	63-7993	63-8015	63-8032	63-8875	64-14832
62-3540	62-3558	62-3577	63-7995	63-8016 SP	63-8033	63-8876	64-14833
62-3541	62-3559	62-3578	63-7996	63-8017	63-8034	63-8877	64-14834
62-3542	62-3561	62-3580	63-7997	63-8018	63-8035	63-8878	64-14835
62-3543	62-3562	63-7976	63-7999	63-8019	63-8036	63-8879	64-14836
62-3544	62-3563 TK	63-7977	63-8000	63-8020	63-8037	63-8880	64-14837
62-3545	62-3564	63-7978	63-8002	63-8021	63-8038	63-8881	64-14838
62-3546	62-3565	63-7979	63-8003	63-8022	63-8039	63-8883	64-14839
62-3547	62-3566 E/R	63-7980	63-8004	63-8023	63-8040	63-8884	64-14840
62-3548	62-3567 TK	63-7981	63-8006	63-8024	63-8041	63-8885	
62-3549	62-3568	63-7982	63-8007	63-8025	63-8043	63-8886	
62-3550	62-3569	63-7984	63-8008	63-8026	63-8044	63-8887	
62-3551	62-3571	63-7985	63-8009 SP	63-8027	63-8045	63-8888	
62-3552	62-3572	63-7987	63-8011	63-8028	63-8871	64-14828	

KC-135T

KC-135Ts are KC-135Q airframes with the F108 re-engining modification. The KC-135T is externally identical to the KC-135R, with the serial number being the only means of identifying the aircraft as a KC-135T. All 54 remaining KC-135Qs have been modified to the KC-135T configuration.

The KC-135Ts are presently assigned to the 22nd ARW at McConnell AFB, Kansas, the 92nd ARW at Fairchild AFB, Washington, and the 319th ARW at Grand Forks AFB, North Dakota, all active USAF units.

KC-135T Serial Numbers (54):

58-0042	58-0072	58-0129	59-1512
58-0045	58-0074	59-1460	59-1513
58-0046	58-0077	59-1462	59-1520
58-0047	58-0084	59-1464	59-1523
58-0049	58-0086	59-1467	60-0335
58-0050	58-0088	59-1468	60-0336
58-0054	58-0089	59-1470	60-0337
58-0055	58-0094	59-1471	60-0339
58-0060	58-0095	59-1474	60-0342
58-0061	58-0099	59-1480	60-0343
58-0062	58-0103	59-1490	60-0344
58-0065	58-0112	59-1504	60-0345
58-0069	58-0117	59-1510	60-0346
58-0071	58-0125		

BELOW: 58-0088, a KC-135T, photographed on August 9, 1995, is assigned to the 349th Air Refueling Squadron, 22nd Air Refueling Wing, McConnell AFB, Kansas. (Don Logan)

58-0086, a KC-135T, photographed on September 24, 1996, is assigned to the 96th Air Refueling Squadron, 92nd Air Refueling Wing, Fairchild Air Force Base, Washington. (Brian C. Rogers)

TANKER OPERATIONS IN SOUTHEAST ASIA 1964-1973

The Air War in Southeast Asia could not have been fought without the presence of a substantial tanker force. The air offensive against North Vietnam and the B-52 ARC Light strikes could not have been carried out without the tanker support provided by SAC's KC 135As. The tankers were primarily operated from Andersen Air Base on Guam, U-Tapao Air Base in Thailand, and Kadena Air Base in Japan.

Southeast Asia totals were 1.4 billion gallons supplied to 813,878 receivers over the nine years of air operations.

SAC Units, Southeast Asia War 1964-1975

Eighth Air Force

Moved without personnel or equipment, from Westover AFB Massachusetts to Andersen AFB, Guam on April 1, 1970. Following the end of the conflict, moved without personnel or equipment to Barksdale AFB, Louisiana on January 1, 1975.

3rd Air Division

Activated at Andersen AFB, Guam on June 18, 1954. Inactivated on March 31, 1970 when it was replaced by 8th Air Force. Activated at Andersen AFB, Guam on January 1, 1975, replacing the 8th Air Force.

17th Air Division (Provisional)

Activated on June 1, 1972 at U-Tapao Airfield Thailand, attached to 8th AF (SAC). Inactivated January 1, 1975.

57th Air Division (Provisional)

Activated on June 1, 1972 at Andersen AFB, Guam, attached to 8th AF (SAC). Inactivated November 15, 1973.

43rd Strategic Wing

Activated on April 1, 1970 at Andersen AFB, Guam, assigned to 8th AF (SAC) and later attached to 57 Air Division (P). Replaced the 3960 Strategic Wing.

72nd Strategic Wing (Provisional)

Activated on June 1, 1972 at Andersen AFB, Guam, attached to 57 Air Division (P). Inactivated November 15, 1973.

307th Strategic Wing (Provisional)

Activated on April 1, 1970 at U-Tapao Airfield Thailand, assigned to 8th AF (SAC) and attached to 17 Air Division (P). Replaced the 4258th Strategic Wing. Inactivated September 30, 1975.

310th Strategic Wing (Provisional)

Activated on June 1, 1972 at U-Tapao Airfield Thailand, attached to 17 Air Division (P). Inactivated July 1, 1974.

376th Strategic Wing

Activated on April 1, 1970 at Kadena Air Base, Okinawa. Replaced the 4252nd Strategic Wing.

3960th Strategic Wing

Activated on April 1, 1955 at Andersen AFB, Guam, assigned to 3rd Air Division. Underwent changes of designation to Air Base Wing and Combat Support Group. Inactivated on March 31, 1970 and replaced by the 43rd Strategic Wing.

4252nd Strategic Wing

Activated on January 12, 1965 at Kadena Air Base, Okinawa. Inactivated on April 1, 1970. Replaced by the 376th Strategic Wing.

4258th Strategic Wing

Activated on June 2, 1966 at U-Tapao Airfield Thailand. Redesignated the 307th Strategic Wing on April 1, 1970.

4101 Air Refueling Squadron (Provisional)

Activated at Takhli Air Base, Thailand June 6, 1972, attached to 17th Air Division (Provisional). Inactivated February 15, 1973.

4102 Air Refueling Squadron (Provisional)

Activated at Clark Air Base, Republic of Philippines June 6, 1972, attached to 376th Strategic Wing, relocated to Ching Chuan Kang Air Base Taiwan, inactivated November 8, 1972. Activated at Clark Air Base on December 18, 1972, inactivated January 22, 1973.

4103 Air Refueling Squadron (Provisional)

Activated at Don Muang Airport, Thailand July 1, 1972, attached to 17th Air Division (Provisional). Inactivated October 10, 1972.

4104 Air Refueling Squadron (Provisional)

Activated at Korat Air Base, Thailand June 6, 1972, attached to 17th Air Division (Provisional). Inactivated November 8, 1972.

4220 Air Refueling Squadron

Activated at Ching Chuan Kang Air Base, Taiwan February 2, 19682, assigned to 4252nd Strategic Wing. Inactivated January 31, 1971.

An F-102 with a temporary air refueling probe receives fuel from the drogue basket attached to the boom of KC-135A 56-3631. The temporary probe allowed deployment ferry flights from the U.S. to Vietnam during the Vietnam war. (Joe Bruch Collection)

SOUTHEAST ASIA TANKER OPERATIONS 1964 – 1973

1964

SORTIES	
B-52 Support	-
Combat Lightning	-
Other SAC*	-
Total SAC	-
Tactical Air	237
TOTAL	237

REFUELINGS	
B-52 Support	-
Combat Lightning	-
Other SAC*	-
Total SAC	-
Tactical Air	948
TOTAL	**948**

Total Fuel Offload (Millions of pounds)	11.9

* Includes support of reconnaissance operations, deployments, redeployments, training, logistics, test hops, and related activities.

1965

SORTIES	
B-52 Support	1,804
Combat Lightning	-
Other SAC*	313
Total SAC	2,117
Tactical Air	7,165
TOTAL	**11,399**

REFUELINGS	
B-52 Support	1,600
Combat Lightning	-
Other SAC*	450
Total SAC	2,450
Tactical Air	29,200
TOTAL	**31,250**

Total Fuel Offload (Millions of pounds)	315.0

* Includes support of reconnaissance operations, deployments, redeployments, training, logistics, test hops, and related activities.

1966

SORTIES	
B-52 Support	6,164
Combat Lightning	102
Other SAC*	999
Total SAC	7,265
Tactical Air	10,938
TOTAL	**18,203**

REFUELINGS	
B-52 Support	5,590
Combat Lightning	0
Other SAC*	289
Total SAC	5,879
Tactical Air	73,067
TOTAL	**78,946**

Total Fuel Offload (Millions of pounds)	851.7

* Includes support of reconnaissance operations, deployments, redeployments, training, logistics, test hops, and related activities.

1967

SORTIES	
B-52 Support	7,279
Combat Lightning	808
Other SAC*	1,093
Total SAC	9,180
Tactical Air	13,711
TOTAL	**22,891**

REFUELINGS	
B-52 Support	7,032
Combat Lightning	69
Other SAC*	368
Total SAC	7,469
Tactical Air	95,946
TOTAL	**103,415**

Total Fuel Offload (Millions of pounds)	1,037.2

* Includes support of reconnaissance operations, deployments, redeployments, training, logistics, test hops, and related activities.

1968

SORTIES	
B-52 Support	10,510
Combat Lightning	828
Other SAC*	1,995
Total SAC	13,333
Tactical Air	18,667
TOTAL	**32,000**

REFUELINGS	
B-52 Support	13,086

Combat Lightning	5
Other SAC*	1,360
Total SAC	14,461
Tactical Air	114,744
TOTAL	**129,205**

Total Fuel Offload 1,642.9
(Millions of pounds)

* Includes support of reconnaissance operations, deployments, redeployments, training, logistics, test hops, and related activities.

1969

SORTIES

B-52 Support	5,241
Combat Lightning	746
Other SAC*	2,691
Total SAC	8,678
Tactical Air	19,188
TOTAL	**27,866**

REFUELINGS

B-52 Support	6,464
Combat Lightning	0
Other SAC*	1,568
Total SAC	8,032
Tactical Air	130,132
TOTAL	**138,164**

Total Fuel Offload 1,433.1
(Millions of pounds)

* Includes support of reconnaissance operations, deployments, redeployments, training, logistics, test hops, and related activities.

1970

SORTIES

B-52 Support	1,750**
Combat Lightning	746
Other SAC*	3,422
Total SAC	5,918
Tactical Air	13,532
TOTAL	**19,450**

REFUELINGS

B-52 Support	2,802**
Combat Lightning	0
Other SAC*	1,579
Total SAC	4,381
Tactical Air	82,050
TOTAL	**86,431**

Total Fuel Offload 888.2
(Millions of pounds)

* Includes support of reconnaissance operations, deployments, redeployments, training, logistics, test hops, and related activities.
** From September 19, 1970 through February 14, 1972, B-52 bombing sorties were launched only from U-Tapao Airfield Thailand and did not require KC-135 tanker support.

1971

SORTIES

B-52 Support	0**
Combat Lightning	703
Other SAC*	3,137
Total SAC	3,840
Tactical Air	10,587
TOTAL	**14,427**

REFUELINGS

B-52 Support	0**
Combat Lightning	1
Other SAC*	1,547
Total SAC	1,548
Tactical Air	61,044
TOTAL	**62,592**

Total Fuel Offload 618.5
(Millions of pounds)

* Includes support of reconnaissance operations, deployments, redeployments, training, logistics, test hops, and related activities.
** From September 19, 1970 through February 14, 1972, B-52 bombing sorties were launched only from U-Tapao Airfield Thailand and did not require KC-135 tanker support.

1972

SORTIES

B-52 Support	6,294**
Combat Lightning	1,389
Other SAC*	5,513
Total SAC	13,196
Tactical Air	21,532
TOTAL	**34,728**

REFUELINGS

B-52 Support	6,553**
Combat Lightning	12
Other SAC*	1,794
Total SAC	8,359
Tactical Air	106,913
TOTAL	115,272

Total Fuel Offload 1,438.5
(Millions of pounds)

* Includes support of reconnaissance operations, deployments, redeployments, training, logistics, test hops, and related activities.

** From September 19, 1970 through February 14, 1972, B-52 bombing sorties were launched only from U-Tapao Airfield Thailand and did not require KC-135 tanker support.

1973

SORTIES	
B-52 Support	1,840
Combat Lightning	480
Other SAC*	4,617
Total SAC	6,937
Tactical Air	8,666
TOTAL	15,603

REFUELINGS	
B-52 Support	2,238
Combat Lightning	4
Other SAC*	2,487
Total SAC	4,729
Tactical Air	62,926
TOTAL	**67,655**

Total Fuel Offload 726.7
(Millions of pounds)

* Includes support of reconnaissance operations, deployments, redeployments, training, logistics, test hops, and related activities.

Total Southeast Asia Tanker Operations

June 9, 1964 Through August 15, 1973

SORTIES	
B-52 Support	40,882
Combat Lightning	5,802
Other SAC*	23,780
Total SAC	70,464
Tactical Air	124,223
TOTAL	194,687

REFUELINGS	
B-52 Support	45,375
Combat Lightning	91
Other SAC*	11,442
Total SAC	56,908
Tactical Air	756,970
TOTAL	813,878

Total Fuel Offload 8,963,700,000 pounds
Approximately 1.4 Billion gallons

* Includes support of reconnaissance operations, deployments, redeployments, training, logistics, test hops, and related activities.

Without the refueling support of KC-135As, the air war against North Vietnam could not have been carried out. F-105s like these with KC-135A 62-3572, and F-4s flying from their bases in Thailand required two air refuelings to complete their missions over North Vietnam. (Joe Bruch Collection)

TANKER FORCES IN DESERT SHIELD/STORM

As with the Air War in Southeast Asia two decades before, Desert Storm could not have been fought had it not been for the presence of a substantial tanker force. The air offensive which preceded the ground war would have lasted even longer and might well have been significantly more costly in terms of losses.

During the early stages of the air war the allies sought to gain air supremacy by knocking out key Iraqi air bases and command and control centers. The availability of airborne tankers permitted the coalition strike forces to carry a greater payload of ordnance and inflict a greater damage on the targets.

As the U.S. Military was the biggest contribution to the coalition, it follows that the United States assembled the largest tanker task force in the Gulf. Statistics released by the Pentagon after the war reveal that 256 KC-135 Stratotankers and 46 KC-10A Extenders were deployed to the region during Operations Desert Shield and Desert Storm. The previous high for a deployed tanker task force was 172 KC-135 tankers deployed in mid-1972 to support Linebacker missions in Southeast Asia. 15,434 sorties were flown in support of Desert Shield/Storm missions and a total of 110 million gallons of fuel was supplied to 46,000 receivers in less than a year of operations. Southeast Asia totals were 1.4 billion gallons supplied to 813,878 receivers over the nine years of air operations.

As single manager of the Air Force tanker fleet, Strategic Air Command was heavily committed. The scale of the operation required mobilization of Air National Guard and Air Force Reserve tanker units. The mobilization process began as early as August 22, 1990 and eventually encompassed all second-line units.

To facilitate operational control of SAC bomber and tanker assets in the Gulf the 17th Air Division (Provisional) was organized in Saudi Arabia. This in, turn directed the activities of a number of temporary units including the 1702nd Air Refueling Wing (Provisional) at Seeb, Oman, and the 1703rd ARW (Prov) at King Khalid International Airport, Saudi Arabia. Other airfields hosting tankers included Jeddah and Dhahran in Saudi Arabia; Cairo West in Egypt; and Al Dhafra and Dubai in the United Arab Emirates. Tankers also operated from bases in Europe in support of SAC B-52Gs engaged on long-range bombing missions from Fairford, England, and Moron, Spain.

France deployed a small number of its C-135FRs at King Khalid.

DESERT SHIELD/STORM C-135 Units

807th Air Refueling Wing (Provisional)	(KC-135R)	(Mont-de-Marsan AB, France)
1702nd Air Refueling Wing (Provisional)	(KC-135R)	(Muscat-Seeb, Oman)
1703rd Air Refueling Wing (Provisional)	(KC-135A/R)	(Riyadh/King Khalid International Airport)
1706th Air Refueling Wing (Provisional)	(KC-135E)	(Cairo West Airport, Egypt)
1707th Air Refueling Wing (Provisional)	(KC-135R)	(Masirah)
1709th Air Refueling Wing (Provisional)	(KC-135A/E/Q)	(Jeddah/King Abdul Aziz International Airport)
1711th Air Refueling Wing (Provisional)	(KC-135A/Q)	(Riyadh Military City Airport)
1712th Air Refueling Wing (Provisional)	(KC-135E/R)	(Abu Dhabi International Airport)
1713th Air Refueling Wing (Provisional)	(KC-135E)	(Dubai International Airport)

CURRENT USAF KC-135 UNITS
June 1992 to June 1997

Air Mobility Command KC-135 Units

Altus AFB, Oklahoma	
304 Air Refueling Wing	June 1, 1992, thru October 1, 1992
11 Air Refueling Squadron	
306 Air Refueling Squadron	
97 Air Mobility Wing	October 1, 1992, thru July 1, 1993
11 Air Refueling Squadron	
457 Operations Group – 19 Air Refueling Wing	July 1, 1993, thru October 1, 1994
11 Air Refueling Squadron	Inactivated October 1, 1994
97 Air Mobility Wing Transferred to Air Education and Training Command (AETC)	
55 Air Refueling Squadron	Activated October 28, 1994, to Present
Barksdale AFB, Louisiana	
458 Operations Group – 22nd Air Refueling Wing	June 1, 1992, thru July 1, 1993
380th Air Refueling Wing	July 1, 1993, thru April 1, 1994
71 Air Refueling Squadron	
Beale AFB, California	
43 Operations Group – 43 Air Refueling Wing	October 1, 1993, thru July 1, 1994
350 Air Refueling Squadron	
Carswell AFB, Texas	
19 Operations Group – 19 Air Refueling Wing	June 1, 1992, thru January 1, 1993
7 Air Refueling Squadron	
Castle AFB, California	
398 Operations Group – 340 Air Refueling Wing	June 1, 1992, thru October 1, 1992
97 Air Mobility Wing	October 1, 1992, thru June 1, 1993
93 Air Refueling Squadron	
Dyess AFB	
43 Operations Group – 43 Air Refueling Wing	June 1, 1992, thru July 1, 1994
917 Air Refueling Squadron	
Ellsworth AFB	
43 Operations Group – 43 Air Refueling Wing	June 1, 1992, thru July 1, 1994
28 Air Refueling Squadron	
Fairchild AFB	
453 Operations Group – 43 Air Refueling Wing	June 1, 1992, thru July 1, 1994
43 Air Refueling Squadron	
92 Air Refueling Squadron	
96 Air Refueling Squadron	April 1, 1994, (activated) thru July 1, 1994
97 Air Refueling Squadron	April 1, 1994, (moved from Malmstrom) thru July 1, 1994
98 Air Refueling Squadron	April 1, 1994, (activated) thru July 1, 1994
92 Air Refueling Wing	July 1, 1994, to Present
43 Air Refueling Squadron	July 1, 1994, thru March 31, 1995
92 Air Refueling Squadron	March 31, 1995, to Present
93 Air Refueling Squadron	July 1, 1994, to Present
96 Air Refueling Squadron	July 1, 1994, to Present
97 Air Refueling Squadron	July 1, 1994, to Present
98 Air Refueling Squadron	July 1, 1994, to Present

Grand Forks AFB, North Dakota	
305 Operations Group, 305 Air Mobility Wing	June 1, 1992, thru July 1, 1993
905 Air Refueling Squadron	
43 Operations Group, 43 Air Refueling Wing	July 1, 1993, thru October 1, 1993
905 Air Refueling Squadron	
319 Air Refueling Wing	October 1, 1993, to Present
905 Air Refueling Squadron	October 1, 1993, to Present
906 Air Refueling Squadron	January 30, 1994, to Present
911 Air Refueling Squadron	April 29, 1994, to Present
912 Air Refueling Squadron	April 1, 1994, to Present
Griffiss AFB, New York	
380 Operations Group – 380 Air Refueling Wing	
41 Air Refueling Squadron	June 1, 1992, thru February 15, 1993 (Inactivated)
509 Air Refueling Squadron	June 1, 1992, thru October 1, 1994 (Inactivated)
Grissom AFB, Indiana	
305 Air Mobility Wing	
70 Air Refueling Squadron	June 1, 1992, thru April 1, 1993 (Inactivated)
305 Air Refueling Squadron	June 1, 1992, thru August 20, 1993 (Inactivated)
K.I. Sawyer AFB, Michigan	
305 Operations Group, 305 Air Mobility Wing	June 1, 1992, thru October 8, 1993
46 Air Refueling Squadron	
Loring AFB, Maine	
380 Operations Group – 380 Air Refueling Wing	
42 Air Refueling Squadron	June 1, 1992, thru April 30, 1994 (Inactivated)
MacDill AFB, Florida	
6th Air Refueling Wing	
91st Air Refueling Squadron	October 1, 1996 to Present
Malmstrom AFB, Montana	
43 Operations Group	
91 Air Refueling Squadron	June 1, 1992, thru July 1, 1994
97 Air Refueling Squadron	October 1, 1992, thru April 1, 1994
43 Air Refueling Group/Wing	
91 Air Refueling Squadron	July 1, 1994, to October 1, 1996
McConnell AFB, Kansas	
19 Operations Group – 19 Air Refueling Wing	June 1, 1992, thru January 1, 1994
384 Air Refueling Squadron	
22 Air Refueling Wing	
344 Air Refueling Squadron	April 29, 1994, to present
349 Air Refueling Squadron	January 1, 1994, to present
350 Air Refueling Squadron	July 1, 1994, to present
384 Air Refueling Squadron	January 1, 1994, to present
Minot AFB, North Dakota	
43 Operations Group	
906 Air Refueling Squadron	June 1, 1992, thru January 30, 1994

Plattsburgh AFB, New York	
380 Air Refueling Wing	June 1, 1992, thru October 1, 1994
310 Air Refueling Squadron	(Inactivated October 1, 1994)
380 Air Refueling Squadron	(Inactivated October 1, 1994)
Robins AFB, Georgia	
19 Air Refueling Wing	
99 Air Refueling Squadron	June 1, 1992, to present
912 Air Refueling Squadron	June 1, 1992, to 1 April 1994
712 Air Refueling Squadron	April 1, 1994, to present
Wurtsmith AFB, Michigan	
305 Air Mobility Wing	
920 Air Refueling Squadron	June 1, 1992, thru September 30, 1992 (Inactivated)

Air Combat Command KC-135 Unit

Mountain Home AFB, Idaho	
366 Wing	
22 Air Refueling Squadron	Activated October 1, 1992, to Present

Air Education And Training Command KC-135 Units

Altus AFB, Oklahoma
97 Air Mobility Wing Transferred to Air Education and Training Command (AETC)

55 Air Refueling Squadron	Activated October 28, 1994, to Present

Air Force Reserve KC-135 Units

Grissom AFB. Indiana	
434 Air Refueling Wing	
72 Air Refueling Squadron	1987, to present
74 Air Refueling Squadron	August 1, 1992, (Activated) to present
March AFB, California	
452 Air Mobility Wing	
336 Air Refueling Squadron	January, 1976, to present
McClellan AFB, California	
940 Air Refueling Group/Wing	
314 Air Refueling Squadron	1976, to present
Selfridge ANGB, Michigan	
927 Air Refueling Group/Wing	
63 Air Refueling Squadron	August, 1992, to present
Seymour-Johnson AFB, North Carolina	
916th Air Refueling Wing	
77th Air Refueling Squadron	October, 1995 to present
Tinker AFB, Oklahoma	
507 Air Refueling Group/Wing	
465 Air Refueling Squadron	April 1, 1994, to present

Air National Guard KC-135 Units

Alabama Air National Guard, Birmingham International Airport
117 Air Refueling Wing
106 Air Refueling Squadron — October 1, 1994, to present

Alaska Air National Guard, Eielson AFB
168 Air Refueling Group
168 Air Refueling Squadron — October, 1986, to present

Arizona Air National Guard, Sky-Harbor International Airport, Phoenix
161 Air Refueling Wing
197 Air Refueling Squadron — October, 1977, to present

Arkansas Air National Guard, Little Rock AFB
189 Air Refueling Group
154 Air Refueling Squadron — January 1, 1976, to October 1, 1986

California Air National Guard, March AFB
163 Air Refueling Wing
196 Air Refueling Squadron — October 1, 1993, to present

Hawaii Air National Guard, Hickam AFB
154 Wing
203 Air Refueling Squadron — January 16, 1993 to present

Illinois Air National Guard, O'Hare International Airport, Chicago
126 Air Refueling Wing
108 Air Refueling Squadron — December, 1976, to present

Kansas Air National Guard, Forbes Field
190 Air Refueling Wing
117 Air Refueling Squadron — July 8, 1978, to present

Maine Air National Guard, Bangor International Airport
101 Air Refueling Wing
132 Air Refueling Squadron — April 1, 1976, to present

Mississippi Air National Guard, Key Field. Meridian
186 Air Refueling Wing
153 Air Refueling Squadron — April 1, 1992, to present

Nebraska Air National Guard, Lincoln Municipal Airport
155 Air Refueling Wing
173 Air Refueling Squadron — January 1, 1994, to present

New Hampshire Air National Guard, Pease Air National Guard Base
157 Air Refueling Wing
133 Air Refueling Squadron — June, 1975, to present

New Jersey Air National Guard, McGuire AFB
108 Air Refueling Wing
141 Air Refueling Squadron — September, 1991, to present
150 Air Refueling Squadron — April 1, 1977, to present

New York Air National Guard, Niagara Falls International Airport
107 Air Refueling Wing
136 Air Refueling Squadron — July 1, 1994, to present

Ohio Air National Guard, Rickenbacker Air National Guard Base
121 Air Refueling Wing
145 Air Refueling Squadron — January 1, 1993, to present
166 Air Refueling Squadron — April 1, 1975, to present

Pennsylvania Air National Guard, Pittsburgh International Airport
171 Air Refueling Wing
146 Air Refueling Squadron — October 1, 1993, to present
147 Air Refueling Squadron — July 1, 1977, to present

Tennessee Air National Guard, McGhee-Tyson Airport, Knoxville
134 Air Refueling Wing
151 Air Refueling Squadron — July 1, 1976, to present

Utah Air National Guard, Salt Lake City International Airport
151 Air Refueling Wing
191 Air Refueling Squadron — April 1, 1978, to present

Washington Air National Guard, Fairchild AFB
141 Air Refueling Wing
116 Air Refueling Squadron — July 1, 1976, to present

Wisconsin Air National Guard, General Mitchell International Airport, Milwaukee
128 Air Refueling Wing
126 Air Refueling Squadron — December 1, 1977, to present

This unusual paint scheme on KC-135A 62-3500 is one half gloss gray and one half painted silver. (Dave Menard)

STRATEGIC AIR COMMAND KC-135 UNITS – JUNE 1957 TO JUNE 1992

ALTUS AFB, OKLAHOMA			
	11 SAW/BW/ARW		
	11 AREFS	KC-A	June 25, 1965 – March 25, 1969
	96 AREFS	KC-A	March 8, 1958 – June 15, 1965
	918 AREFS	KC-A	October 1, 1960 – December 15, 1960
	921 AREFS	KC-A	October 1, 1960 – December 15, 1960
	340 ARG/ARW		
	11 ARS,	KC-A, KC-R	July 1, 1977 – June 1, 1992
	306 AREFS	KC-A, KC-R	October 1, 1984 – June 1, 1992
AMARILLO AFB, TEXAS			
	461 BW		
	909 AREFS	KC-A	April 1, 1963 – June 23, 1966
ANDERSEN AFB, GUAM			
	43 SW	Tankers assigned on temporary basis	
BARKSDALE AFB, LOUISIANA			
	4238 SW		1958 – April 1, 1963
	2 BW/WG		April 1, 19163 – present
	71 AREFS	KC-A, KC-Q	April 15, 1968 – June 1, 1992
	913 AREFS	KC-A	June 1, 1958 – November 1, 1981
BEALE AFB, CALIFORNIA			
	4126 SW		April 1, 1959 – February 1, 1963
	456SAW/BW		February 1, 1963 – September 30, 1975
	17 BW		
	9 AREFS	KC-Q	September 30, 1975 – September 30, 1976
	903 AREFS	KC-Q	September 30, 1975 – September 30, 1976
	100 AREFW		September 30, 1976 – March 15, 1983
	9 AREFS	KC-Q	September 30, 1976 – January 28, 1982
	349 AREFS	KC-Q	September 30, 1976 – March 15, 1985
	350 AREFS	KC-Q	January 28, 1982 – March 15, 1983
	9 SRW/WG		
	349 AREFS	KC-Q	March 15, 1993 – June 1, 1992
	350 AREFS	KC-Q	March 15, 1983 – 1 June 1, 1992
BERGSTROM AFB, TEXAS			
	4130 SW		1958 – September 1, 1963
	340 BW		September 1, 1963 – October 2, 1966
	910 AREFS	KC-A	October 15, 1958 – October 2, 1966
BIGGS AFB, TEXAS			
	95 BW		
	917 AREFS	KC-A	May 1, 1959 – January 15, 1965
CARSWELL AFB, TEXAS			
	7 BW/WG		
	7 AREFS	KC-A	April 1, 1958 – June 1, 1992
	919 AREFS	KC-A	April 15, 1960 – July 1, 1960

CASTLE AFB, CALIFORNIA
93 BW
93 AREFS KC-A, KC-R March 1, 1957 – June 1, 1992
924 AREFS KC-A July 1, 1959 – 1 April 1, 1992

CLINTON-SHERMAN AFB, OKLAHOMA
4123 SW December 1, 1968 – February 1. 1963
70 BW February 1, 1963 – December 31, 1969
902 AREFS KC-A December 1, 1958 – December 31, 1969

COLUMBUS AFB, MISSISSIPPI
4228 SW 1958 – February 1, 1963
454 BW February 1, 1963 – July 2, 1969
901 AREFS KC-A August 1, 1958 – July 2, 1969

DOW AFB, MAINE
397 BW
71 AREFS KC-A March 1, 1964 – April 15, 1968

DYESS AFB, TEXAS
96 SAW/BW/WG
917 AREFS KC-A January 15, 1965 – June 1, 1992

EAKER AFB/BLYTHEVILLE AFB, ARKANSAS
97 BW/WG
97 AREFS KC-A October 23, 1964 – April 1, 1992
914 AREFS KC-A October 1, 1961 – October 23, 1964

ELLSWORTH AFB , SOUTH DAKOTA
28 BW/WG
28 AREFS KC-A, KC-R October 1, 1960 – June 1,1992
928 AREFS KC-A February 1, 1959 – October 1, 1960

FAIRCHILD AFB, WASHINGTON
92 SAW/BW/WG
43 AREFS KC-A, KC-R April 2, 1966 – June 1, 1992
92 AREFS KC-A, KC-R September 13, 1957 – June 1, 1992

GLASGOW AFB, MONTANA
91 BW
907 AREFS KC-A July 1, 1963 – June 25, 1968

GRAND FORKS AFB, NORTH DAKOTA
4133 SW 1960 – February 1, 1963
319 BW February 1, 1963 – June 1, 1992
905 AREFS KC-A, KC-R February 1, 1963 – June 1, 1992

GRIFFISS AFB, NEW YORK
4039 SW 1961 – February 1, 1963
416 BW February 1, 1963 – September 30, 1995
41 AREFS KC-A, KC-R February 1, 1963 – June 1, 1992
509 AFRES KC-R July 1, 1990 – June 1, 1992

GRISSOM AFB/BUNKER HILL AFB, INDIANA			
	305 ARW		
	68 AREFS	KC-A	July 1, 1959 – March 25, 1965
	70 AREFS	KC-A, KC-R	January 1, 1970 – June 1, 1992
	305 AREFS	KC-A, KC-R	March 25, 1965 – June 1, 1992
HOMESTEAD AFB, FLORIDA			
	19 BW		
	407 AREFS	KC-A	April 1, 1962 – July 25, 1968
KADENA AB, OKINAWA			
	376 SW		
	909 AREFS	KC-A, KA-Q,	July 1, 1971 – September 1, 1991
KINCHELOE AFB, MICHIGAN			
	449 BW		
	908 AREFS	KC-A	July 1, 1963 – September 30, 1977
K. I. SAWYER AFB, MICHIGAN			
	4042 SW		1961 – February 1, 1963
	410 BW		February 1, 1963 – September 30, 1995
	46 AREFS	KC-A	April 1, 1961 – June 1, 1992
	307 AREFS	KC-A	October 1, 1985 – August 1, 1990
LARSON AFB, WASHINGTON			
	4170 SW		1960 – February 1, 1963
	462 SAW		February 1, 1963 – April 2, 1966
	43 AREFS	KC-A	November 15, 1960 – April 2, 1966
LORING AFB, MAINE			
	42 BW/WG		
	42 AREFS	KC-A, KC-R	July 1, 1957 – June 1, 1992
	407 AREFS	KC-A	July 2, 1968 – October 1, 1990
LITTLE ROCK AFB, ARKANSAS			
	384 BW		
	70 AREFS	KC-A, KC-Q	July 1, 1963 – January 1, 1970
MALMSTROM AFB, MONTANA			
	301 AREFW		
	91 AREFS	KC-R	January 5, 1989 – June 1, 1992
MATHER AFB, CALIFORNIA			
	4134 SW		1959 – February 1, 1963
	320 BW		February 1, 1963 – October 1, 1986
	904 AREFS	KC-A	March 1, 1959 – October 1, 1986
MARCH AFB, CALIFORNIA			
	22 BW/ARW		
	22 AREFS	KC-A	1 Jul 63 – 1 Dec 89
	909 AREFS	KC-A	25 Jun 66 – 1 Jul 71
McCHORD AFB, WASHINGTON			
	92 BW		
	22 AREFS	KC-A	June 15, 1960 – July 1, 1962

McCONNELL AFB, KANSAS			
384 ARW/BW/WG			
	91 AREFS	KC-A, KC-R	December 1, 1972 – July 1, 1987
	384 AREFS	KC-A. KC-R	September 30, 1973 – June 1, 1992
McCOY AFB, FLORIDA			
306 BW			
	306 AREFS	KC-A, KC-Q	July 1, 1962 – September 30, 1973
	919 AREFS	KC-A	March 25, 1967 – June 30, 1971
RAF MILDENHALL, ENGLAND			
306 SW		Tankers only temporarily assigned	
MINOT AFB, NORTH DAKOTA			
4136 SW			1959 – February 1, 1963
450 BW			February 1, 1963 – July 25, 1968
	906 AREFS	KC-A	June 1, 1959 – July 25, 1968
5 BW/WG			
	906 AREFS	KC-A	July 25, 1968 – June 1, 1992
OFFUTT AFB, NEBRASKA			
4321 SW			
385 SAW			January 1, 1963 – December 15, 1964
55 SRW			August 16, 1966 – June 1, 1992
	34 AREFS	KC-A	October 1, 1958 – June 25, 1966
PEASE AFB, NEW HAMPSHIRE			
509 BW			
	34 AREFS	KC-A	June 25, 1966 – March 31, 1976
	509 AREFS	KC-A	October 2, 1966 – June 30, 1990
	900 AREFS	KC-A	April 22, 1966 – June 25, 1966
PLATTSBURGH AFB, NEW YORK			
380 BW/AREFW			
	310 AREFS	KC-A, KC-Q	January 25, 1967 – June 1, 1992
	380 AREFS	KC-A, KC-Q	July 1, 1964 – June 1, 1992
RAMEY AB, PUERTO RICO			
72 BW			
	915 AREFS	KC-A	September 1, 1958 – June 30, 1971
RICKENBACKER AFB/LOCKBOURNE AFB, OHIO			
376 BW			
	91 AREFS	KC-A	January 1, 1963 – June 15, 1964
301 AREFW			
	32 AREFS	KC-A	March 15, 1965 – September 30, 1979
	91 AREFS	KC-A	June 15, 1964 – July 1, 1971
	301 AREFS	KC-A	September 30, 1973 – December 31, 1975
	321 AREFS	KC-A	April 1, 1963 – March 15, 1965

Base / Unit	Aircraft	Dates
ROBINS AFB, GEORGIA		
4137 SW		1961 – February 1, 1963
465 BW		February 1, 1963 – July 25, 1968
19 BW/AREFW		July 25, 1968 – June 1, 1992
99 AREFS	KC-A, KC-R	October 1, 1983 – 1 June 1, 1992
912 AREFS	KC-A, KC-R	December 1, 1961 – 1 June 1, 1992
SEYMOUR-JOHNSON AFB, NORTH CAROLINA		
4241 SW		December 15, 1958 – April 15, 1963
68 BW		April 15, 1963 – October 1, 1982
68 AREFG/W		October 1, 1982 – 1985
SCHILLING AFB, KANSAS		
310 SAW		
310 AREFS	KC-A	December 1, 1963 – June 25, 1965
911 AREFS	KC-A	December 15, 1958 – 1965
SHEPPARD AFB, TEXAS		
4245 SW		1962 – February 1, 1963
494 BW		February 1, 1963 – April 2, 1966
900 AREFS	KC-A	October 1, 1962 – April 2, 1966
TRAVIS AFB, CALIFORNIA		
5 BW		
916 AREFS	KC-A	September 1, 1959 – July 25, 1968
47 AD		
916 AREFS	KC-A	July 25, 1968 – July 1, 1977
307 AREFG		
916 AREFS	KC-A	July 1, 1977 – October 31, 1983
TURNER AFB, GEORGIA		
4138 SW		1960 – February 1, 1963
484 BW		February 1, 1963 – March 25, 1969
919 AREFS	KC-A	1 Jul 60 – 25 Mar 67
WALKER AFB, NEW MEXICO		
6 BW/SAW		
6 AREFS	KC-A	November 1, 1957 – January 25, 1967
310 AREFS	KC-A	June 25, 1965 – January 25, 1967
WESTOVER AFB, MASSACHUSETTS		
4050 AREFW		August 7, 1957 – January 1, 1966
99 BW		January 1, 1966 – September 30, 1973
99 AREFS	KC-A	August 7, 1957 – September 30, 1973
WRIGHT-PATTERSON AFB, OHIO		
4043 SW		1959 – February 1, 1963
17 BW		February 1,1963 – July 25, 1968
922 AREFS	KC-A	December 1, 1959 – September 30, 1975
WURTSMITH AFB, MICHIGAN		
4026 SW		1960 – January 9, 1961
379 BW		January 9, 1961, – June 1, 1992
920 AREFS	KC-A	June 15, 1960 – June 1, 1992

TANKER MARKINGS

Originally SAC KC-135s carried the Milky Way band on the nose. SAC later moved the band aft to the mid fuselage. The SAC crest appeared on the left Milky Way. Bomb Wing or Air Refueling Wing insignia were normally applied to the right Milky Way band. Units specific colored bands were normally applied to the top-most portion of the vertical fin of their C-135s.

Commencing in the summer of 1975, the Air Force began transferring 129 KC-135As to Air Force Reserve and Air National Guard units. These airplanes were later painted overall gloss gray FS 16473 and carried the same markings as regular SAC KC-135s. Additionally, the Reserve/Guard units have applied their own distinctive tail markings.

The 8th Air Force, SAC's numbered Air Force based at Barksdale AFB Louisiana, started painting the tops of the tails of their tankers with distinctive patterns and colors to identify the units. The markings were as follows:

19th Air Division – Diamond pattern
7th Bomb Wing – Carswell AFB, Texas Black and Yellow
340th Air Refueling Wing – Altus AFB, Oklahoma Blue and Silver
384th Air Refueling Wing – McConnell AFB, Kansas Light Blue and Dark Blue

40th Air Division – Vertical stripes
379th Bomb Wing – Wurtsmith AFB Michigan Red and Yellow
410th Bomb Wing – K.I. Sawyer AFB, Michigan Red and White
416th Bomb Wing – Griffiss AFB, New York Blue and Yellow

42nd Air Division – Checkerboard
2nd Bomb Wing – Barksdale AFB, Louisiana Green and Yellow
19th Air Refueling Wing – Robins AFB, Georgia Navy Blue and Yellow
68th Air Refueling Wing – Seymour Johnson AFB, North Carolina Red and Blue
97th Bomb Wing – Blytheville AFB, Arkansas Red and White
305th Air Refueling Wing – Grissom AFB, Indiana Blue and White

45th Air Division – Diagonal stripes.
42nd Bomb Wing – Loring AFB, Maine Blue and Yellow
380th Bomb Wing – Plattsburgh AFB, New York Green and White
509th Bomb Wing – Pease AFB, New Hampshire Red and Royal Blue

In the early 1980s Unit tail markings started to appear and nose art was officially permitted on SAC aircraft.

In the mid 1980s flat dark gray (FS 36081) was painted on the aircraft sides and upper surfaces. This paint scheme was referred to as the "Shamu" scheme. Emergency markings were painted flat red. The bottom of the fuselage and under surfaces remained gloss gray (FS 16473). Nose art was added by some units.

With the reorganization of the USAF and the creation of Air Mobility Command and Air Combat Command the C-135 markings were once again changed. Tanker aircraft were painted overall flat light gray (FS 36173) and had flat black markings. The using command abbreviation was painted above the five digit tail number; ACC for Air Combat Command, AETC for Air Education and Training Command, AFRES for Air Force Reserve, AMC for Air Mobility Command, ANG for Air National Guard, and SAC for Strategic Air Command. On ACC C-135s the serial number was displayed in the tactical format with AF and a two digit number stacked followed by three digits, along with the unit tail code.

Nose art was no longer allowed on AMC aircraft. Some Air National Guard and AFRES tanker units did continue the tradition of nose art, but with subjects more "politically correct."

U.S. AIR FORCE TANKER BASES

ALTUS AIR FORCE BASE, OKLAHOMA

Altus Air Force Base, located in Altus, Oklahoma, has been the home for KC-135s since 1958. The 11th Bomb Wing/ Strategic Aerospace Wing/Air Refueling Wing was assigned, equipped with KC-135As, to Altus AFB from March 1958 until March 1969. While the wing was at Altus, four Air Refueling Squadrons assigned to the 11th Air Refueling Wing. The 11th Air Refueling Squadron was assigned to the 11th Wing at Altus AFB from June 25, 1965, until March 25, 1969. The 96th Air Refueling Squadron was assigned to the 11th at Altus AFB from March 8, 1958, until June 15, 1965. The 918th and the 921st Air Refueling Squadrons were assigned for a short period, from October 1, 1960, to December 15, 1960.

The 340th Air Refueling Group (later Wing), assigned to SAC, was active at Altus from July 1, 1977, until October 1, 1992. The 11th and 306th Air Refueling Squadrons were assigned to the 340 Air Refueling Wing.

The 11th Air Refueling Squadron was activated at Altus on July 1, 1977, and remained until inactivated on October 1, 1994. The 306th Air Refueling Squadron was assigned to Altus from October 1, 1984. At the same time the 340th Air Refueling Group became the 340th Air Refueling Wing. From October 1, 1992, after transitioning to Air Mobility Command (AMC) when SAC inactivated, the two squadrons were assigned to the 97th Air Mobility Wing. From July 1, 1993, until inactivated, the squadrons were assigned to the 457th Operations Group, a geographically separated unit of the 19th Air Refueling Wing at Robins AFB, Georgia. The 11th Air Refueling Squadron was inactivated on October 1, 1994, and the 306th was inactivated on August 1, 1994.

The 55th Air Refueling Squadron was activated on October 28, 1994 and was assigned to the 97th Air Mobility Wing, a unit of Air Education and Training Command (AETC). Upon activation, the 55th assumed KC-135 aircrew training from the 93rd Air Refueling Squadron at Castle Air Force Base, California.

On July 1, 1993, the 97th AMW and its squadrons transferred to Air Education and Training Command (AETC).

This view of KC-135A 58-0021 of the 340th ARW, Altus AFB, Oklahoma was photographed on August 13, 1987. (Brian C. Rogers)

KC-135R 61-0317 from the 340th ARW is photographed here refueling a four ship of F-16Cs from the 50th TFW, based at the now closed Hahn AB, Germany. The aircraft is marked with the 19th Air Division diamond tail cap in the blue and silver colors of the 340th ARW. (Boeing)

62-3564, a KC-135R of the 97th Air Mobility Wing (AMW), displays the Air Education and Training Command (AETC) shield. (Don Logan)

The KC-135Rs of Altus AFB now carry, along with AETC, the flaming spear tail cap of the 97th AMW. (Don Logan)

KC-135R 62-3531 of the 340th ARW photographed during December, 1989 while supplying air refueling support to F-4s from Edwards AFB. (Don Logan Collection)

KC-135R 62-3551 was photographed in June, 1996 marked as the flagship for the 55th Air Refueling Squadron. (Jerry Geer)

BARKSDALE AIR FORCE BASE, LOUISIANA

Barksdale Air Force Base is located in Bossier City, Louisiana and is the home of the 2nd Bomb Wing. Barksdale had been home to KC-135s since June, 1958. The 2nd Bombardment Wing, was assigned to SAC until June 1, 1992. The 71st and 913th Air Refueling Squadrons were assigned to the 2nd Bomb Wing at Barksdale AFB.

The 71st moved to Barksdale from Dow AFB on April 15, 1968, and remained until inactivated on April 1, 1994. From April 15, 1968, until June 1, 1992, the 71st was equipped with KC-135As. From June 1, 1992, until October 1, 1993, while still assigned to the 2nd Wing, and a unit of Air Combat Command, the 71st flew KC-135A and KC-135Q model tankers with LA tail codes. On October 1, 1993, the 71st was transferred from the 2nd Wing to the 458 Operations Group, a geographically separate unit of the 380th Air Refueling Wing, assigned to AMC. The 71st squadron was inactivated on April 1, 1994. KC-135s are no longer assigned to Barksdale AFB.

The 913th Air Refueling Squadron was assigned to Barksdale from June 1, 1958, until inactivated on November 1, 1981, and flew KC-135As. The 913th was initially assigned to the 4238th Strategic Wing from 1958 through 1963.

KC-135A 63-8037 photographed in the markings of the 2nd Bomb Wing on January 20, 1987. (Brian C. Rogers)

KC-135A 57-1467 wears the modified 2nd Bomb Wing Barksdale markings when photographed on April 13, 1989. (Craig Kaston)

Dark camouflaged KC-135s like 63-8000 carried flat black markings for the 2nd Bomb Wing and Barksdale AFB when photographed at Forbes Field, Kansas in August, 1992. (Jerry Geer)

KC-135Q 59-1512 photographed on the PDM (Programmed Depot Maintenance)line at Tinker AFB, Oklahoma, on November 16, 1992, wears the LA tail code and markings of the 2nd Wing at Barksdale. (Randy Walker)

RIGHT: The tail of KC-135A 63-8005 displays the ACC style markings and the LA tail code of the 2nd Wing. (Brian C. Rogers)

BELOW: KC-135Qs, including 59-1504 pictured here were assigned to the 2nd Wing at Barksdale during 1992 and 1993. (Brian C. Rogers)

KC-135Q 58-0060, photographed on June 9, 1993, in the new AMC light gray paint scheme is in the markings of the 71st Air Refueling Squadron, 2 Wing. (Tom Kaminski)

BEALE AIR FORCE BASE, CALIFORNIA

Beale Air Force Base is located 13 miles east of Marysville in northern California. KC-135s were assigned at Beale AFB from April, 1959, through July 1, 1994. Beale AFB was also the home of the SR-71 for most of its operational life.

Tankers were first assigned to the 903rd Air Refueling Squadron, 4126th Strategic Wing (SW) in April 1959. The 4126th SW was replaced by the 456th Strategic Aerospace Wing (SAW) on February 1, 1963. The 903rd KC-135A were converted to KC-135Qs during the mid 1960s. On January 1, 1970 the 9th Air Refueling Squadron was activated with KC-135Qs.

The 456th SAW was redesignated the 456th Bombardment Wing Heavy on July 1, 1972, and was replaced by the 17 Bomb Wing on September 30, 1975.

The 17th Bomb Wing was assigned to Beale AFB from September 30, 1975, until replaced by the 100th Air Refueling Wing on September 30, 1976. While at Beale AFB two Air Refueling Squadrons, the 9th and the 903rd, were assigned to the 17th Bomb Wing. Both squadrons operated KC-135Qs.

On September 30, 1976, with departure of the B-52s from Beale, the 17th Bomb wing was inactivated, replaced by the 100th Air Refueling Wing (ARW). The 100th ARW initially consisted of the 9th and 349th Air Refueling Squadrons (the 349th replaced the 903rd on September 30, 1976). In 1982 the 350th replaced the 9th. In 1983, the 100th ARW was inactivated and its squadrons absorbed into the 9th Strategic Reconnaissance Wing (SRW).

The 9th SRW, now the 9th Reconnaissance Wing, has operated at Beale since September of 1976. When SAC was inactivated on June 1, 1992, the wing transferred to ACC. Two Air Refueling Squadrons (the 349th and 350th) were assigned to the 9th SRW. The 349th operated KC-135Qs from September 30, 1976, until inactivated on June 1, 1992. The 349th was again activated, on January 1, 1994, as part of the 22nd Air Refueling Wing at McConnell AFB, Kansas. KC-135s are no longer assigned to Beale AFB.

On June 1, 1992, the 350th transitioned to ACC and wore BB tail codes until transferring to AMC. On October 1, 1993, the 350th was reassigned to the 43rd Operations Group, part of the 43rd Air Refueling Wing at Malmstrom AFB, Montana. The 350th was reassigned to the 22nd Air Refueling Wing at McConnell AFB on July 1, 1994.

This photo taken during 1968 shows the aircraft types assigned to Beale AFB at the time. The KC-135Q (58-0054) and B-52G (59-2567) belong to the 456th Bomb Wing, while the SR-71A (64-17970) and the T-38 (61-3282) belong to the 9th Strategic Reconnaissance Wing. (Joe Bruch Collection)

KC-135Q 58-0099 of the 456th Bomb Wing seen at Mildenhall on June 14, 1976. (Tom Brewer Collection)

This KC-135Q, 58-0054 photographed at Offutt on July 12, 1975 wears the markings of the 9th Air Refueling Squadron, 9th Strategic Reconnaissance Wing (SRW) based at Beale AFB. (Don McGarry)

KC-135Q 59-1504 photographed on June 30, 1984, in the painted silver scheme, wears the yellow tail stripe with black iron crosses of the 9th SRW. (Brian C. Rogers)

KC-135Q 58-0088, also photographed on June 30, 1984 is painted in the gloss gray paint scheme. (Brian C. Rogers)

KC-135Q 58-0088, photographed in May, 1992, wears the two color camouflaged paint scheme and the flat black unit markings. (David F. Brown)

KC-135Q 58-0084, photographed in September, 1993, wears the ACC style markings and the BB tail code of the 9th SRW. (David F. Brown)

KC-135Q 58-0072, photographed on May 13, 1993, in the new AMC light gray paint scheme is in the markings of the 350th Air Refueling Squadron, 9th SRW. (Norris Graser)

KC-135Q 60-0342, photographed in July, 1994, carrying the blue tail stripe of the 43rd Air Refueling Wing based at Malmstrom AFB, was assigned to 43rd Operations Group. (Mike Grove)

KC-135Q, 58-0071, 9th SRW.

KC-135Q, 58-0086, 9th SRW. (Ben Knowles Collection)

KC-135Q, 58-0088, 9th SRW. (Ben Knowles Collection)

KC-135Q, 58-0074, 9th SRW. (Ben Knowles Collection)

KC-135Q, 58-0055, 9th SRW. (Ben Knowles Collection)

KC-135Q, 59-1523, 9th SRW. (Jerry Geer)

KC-135Q, 58-0054, 9th SRW. (Ben Knowles Collection)

KC-135Q, 58-0086, 9th SRW. (Craig Kaston)

CARSWELL AIR FORCE BASE, TEXAS

Carswell Air Force Base was located in Fort Worth, Texas, and was the home of the 7th Bomb Wing. KC-135s were assigned at the base from April 1, 1958, until January 1, 1993. On October 1, 1993, in preparation for the realignment of Carswell AFB base, the 7th Bomb Wing was reassigned to Dyess Air Force Base.

Two Air Refueling Squadrons, the 7th and the 919th, were assigned to the 7th Bomb Wing. The 7th Air Refueling Squadron operated KC-135As, as part of the 7th Bomb Wing from April 1, 1958, until SAC's demise on June, 1992. From June 1, 1992, until its inactivation on January 1, 1993, the 7th Air Refueling Squadron was assigned to the 19th Operations Group part of the 19th Air Refueling Wing at Robins AFB, Georgia. The 919th was assigned to the 7th Bomb Wing for a short time, from April 15, 1960, until July 1, 1960.

KC-135A 56-3656, photographed at Carswell AFB in March 1986 with the 19th Air Division diamond tail cap in the black and yellow colors of the 7th Bomb Wing. (Brian C. Rogers)

KC-135A 57-1470, photographed at Carswell AFB on July 25, 1988 wears the 7th Bomb wing tail cap of the steer head and "FORT WORTH TEXAS." (Don Logan)

CASTLE AIR FORCE BASE, CALIFORNIA

Castle Air Force Base, located near Merced California, and was the home of the 93rd Bomb Wing from March, 1957 until the base closed. The 93rd Bomb Wing was the first SAC unit to operate the KC-135. The Castle AFB supplied KC-135 aircrew training until training was transferred to Altus AFB due to the planned closing of the base.

Two Air Refueling Squadrons, the 93rd and the 924th, were assigned to the 93rd Bomb Wing. The 93rd Air Refueling Squadron was the first squadron to operate KC-135As, beginning operations in June 1957. On June 1, 1992, following the inactivation of SAC, the 93rd Bomb wing transferred to ACC. On the same date, the 93rd Air Refueling Squadron was transferred to the 398th Operations Group (OG) a part of the 340th Air Refueling Wing at Altus AFB. The 398th OG was assigned to AMC from June 1, 1992, until July 1, 1993. On July 1, 1993, the 398th OG was transferred to Air Education and Training Command (AETC). On March 31, 1995, the 348 Operations Group and the 93rd Air Refueling Squadron were inactivated as a result of the planned closing of Castle AFB. The 924th Air Refueling Squadron was assigned to the 93rd Bomb Wing from July 1, 1959, until the squadron was inactivated on April 1, 1992.

On May 6, 1987, 57-1499 was forced to land at Edwards AFB, when the nose gear could not be extended. The aircraft was repaired and has since been modified to KC-135R configuration. (USAF)

BELOW: KC-135A 62-3502 photo graphed at Castle AFB on July 5, 1990. The black Castle tail stripe contains the light gray castle tower used on aircraft of the 93rd Bomb Wing. (Brian C. Rogers)

KC-135A 57-14523 photo graphed at Castle AFB on July 5, 1990. On the camouflaged aircraft the light gray castle tower is applied without the black stripe. (Brian C. Rogers)

KC-135A Aircraft 58-0073, 93rd Bomb Wing. (Brian C. Rogers)

KC-135A, 59-1496, 93rd Bomb Wing. (Brian C. Rogers)

KC-135A, 62-3502, 93rd Bomb Wing. (Brian C. Rogers)

KC-135A, 63-8045, 93rd Bomb Wing. (Brian C. Rogers)

KC-135A, 60-0353, 93rd Bomb Wing. (Brian C. Rogers)

KC-135A, 61-0272, 93rd Bomb Wing. (Brian C. Rogers)

KC-135A, 62-3573, 93rd Bomb Wing. (Brian C. Rogers)

KC-135A, 63-8024, 93rd Bomb Wing. (Brian C. Rogers)

KC-135A 62-3501, this photograph taken at Castle on May 27, 1993, shows the 97th Air Mobility Wing (AMW) markings carried by aircraft of the 398th Operations Group (OG). Castle KC-135A's assigned to the 97th AMW at Altus AFB displayed their unit tail stripe in mid-tail, while the KC-135Rs 97th AMW stripe was in its standard position at the top of the tail. (Don Logan)

KC-135R 60-0331, the 93rd Air Refueling Squadron (AREFS) flagship, carries Air Education and Training Command (AETC) markings on the tail and the AETC shield on the nose. (Ben Knowles)

KC-135R 62-3502 represented the 97th AMW, 398th OG, and 93rd ARS at the Airlift Rodeo during July, 1994. The crew, with the aircraft marked as the 398th Operations Group flagship, took first place in the tanker competition. (Don Abrahamson)

This closeup of 62-3502's nose shows the celebration markings added to the aircraft following the win. (Don Abrahamson)

The flagship tail markings for 62-3502 do not include the aircraft serial number. (Renato E. F. Jones)

KC-135R 62-3551, in AMC light gray is seen here marked as the 93rd Air Refueling Squadron (ARS) flagship. (Carl Porter via Ben Knowles)

DYESS AIR FORCE BASE, TEXAS

Dyess Air Force Base, located west of Abilene, Texas was the home of the 96th Bomb Wing. The 96th Bomb Wing operated KC-135As from January, 1965, until the KC-135s were reassigned to the 43rd Operations Group on October 1, 1993. The 96th Bomb Wing transferred to ACC as the 96th Wing when SAC was inactivated. The 96th Wing remained as the flying unit at Dyess AFB until replaced by the 7th Wing following the closing of Carswell AFB

The 917th Air Refueling Squadron was assigned to the 96th from January 15, 1965, to October 1, 1993. After the 96th Wing transferred to ACC, the 917th received KC-135Qs which, along with the KC-135As at Dyess, carried DY tail codes. After October 1, 1993, the 917th Air Refueling Squadron was assigned as a geographically separated unit of the 43rd Operations Group, 43rd Air Refueling Wing at Malmstrom AFB. The 917th was inactivated on July 1, 1994. KC-135s are no longer assigned to Dyess AFB.

KC-135A 56-3616 of the 917th Air Refueling Squadron. 96th Bomb Wing, photographed on November 3, 1987, sits at the north end of the Dyess AFB runway awaiting its turn to takeoff. (Don Logan)

KC-135A 63-8886 caught on July 25, 1988, over the Dyess AFB runway just prior to touchdown. (Don Logan)

KC-135A 56-3652, 96th Bomb Wing. (Don Logan)

KC-135A 56-3639, 96th Bomb Wing. (Don Logan)

KC-135A 56-3616, 96th Bomb Wing. (Don Logan)

KC-135A 58-0073, 96th Bomb Wing. (Don Logan)

KC-135A 55-3136, 96th Bomb Wing. (Don Logan)

KC-135A 63-8019, 96th Bomb Wing. (Don Logan)

KC-135A 58-0102, 96th Bomb Wing. (Don Logan)

KC-135A 63-8874, 96th Bomb Wing. (Don Logan)

KC-135A 60-0318, 96th Bomb Wing. (Don Logan)

ABOVE: KC-135A 60-0326, photographed on January 23, 1993, wears the DY tail code of the 96th Wing with the steer skull tail stripe. (Alan Winzerling)

RIGHT: With the inactivation of SAC, the old SAC bomb wings became part of ACC and used tail codes and ACC style markings as seen here on 62-3539 photographed on August 31, 1992. The tankers of the 917th Air Refueling Squadron wore a red and dark blue tail stripe with a steer skull. (Brian C. Rogers)

KC-135A 63-8888 is seen here at Dyess AFB on January 23, 1993, in AMC gray with 96th Wing markings. (Alan Winzerling)

KC-135Q 58-0112, after the 917th ARS transferred to AMC was photographed at Dyess AFB on December 30, 1993, while assigned to the 43rd Operations Group at Dyess was attached to the 43rd ARW at Malmstrom. (Don Logan)

EAKER/BLYTHEVILLE AIR FORCE BASE, ARKANSAS

Blytheville Air Force Base, renamed Eaker Air Force Base in 1988, was located in Blytheville, Arkansas and was the home of the 97th Bomb Wing. KC-135s were assigned at the base from October, 1961, until inactivation of the 97th Bomb Wing on April 1, 1992, in preparation for the closing of the base. The wing was reassigned to AMC and activated at Altus AFB, Oklahoma, on October 1, 1992, as the 97th Air Mobility Wing.

The 97th Bomb Wing had two Air Refueling Squadrons, the 97th and the 914th, assigned. The 97th operated KC-135As from October 23, 1964, until its inactivation, coinciding with the inactivation of the wing on April 1, 1992. The 914th was assigned to the 97th Bomb Wing on October 1, 1961, until its inactivation on October 23, 1964.

RIGHT: The flaming spear on the top of the tail of 63-8012, a KC-135A of 97th Bomb Wing comes from the spear in the unit emblem. A modification of this tail cap is now used on aircraft of the 97th Air Mobility Wing at Altus AFB. (Jim Mosley Collection)

KC-135A 61-0276 from the 97th Bomb Wing wore this razorback on its nose for the annual SAC Bombing and Navigation Competition held in November, 1974. (Tom Brewer Collection)

KC-135A 61-0304 in 97th Bomb Wing markings was on display for this August, 1970 Open House. (Terry Love)

ELLSWORTH AIR FORCE BASE, SOUTH DAKOTA

Ellsworth Air Force Base, located at Box Elder, South Dakota, 12 miles east of Rapid City is the home of the 28th Bomb Wing. KC-135s were operated at Ellsworth from February 1959, until May 15, 1994. In 1986, KC-135R replaced the KC-135As. The 28th Bomb Wing transferred to ACC when SAC was inactivated. The 28th Bomb Wing remained as the flying unit at Ellsworth AFB presently flying B-1Bs.

The 928th Air Refueling Squadron was assigned to the 28th Bomb Wing from February 1, 1959, until October 1, 1960. The 28th Air Refueling Squadron replaced the 928th on October 1, 1960, and was assigned to the 28th Bomb Wing until June 1, 1992. After the 28th Bomb Wing transferred to ACC on June 1, 1992, the 28th Air Refueling Squadron was reassigned as a geographically separated unit of the 43rd Operations Group, 43rd Air Refueling Wing at Malmstrom AFB. The 28th Air Refueling Squadron inactivated on May 15, 1994. KC-135s are no longer assigned to Ellsworth AFB.

KC-135R 60-0321 in 28th Bomb Wing markings crosses the runway threshold for landing at Ellsworth AFB on July 17, 1987. (Don Logan)

KC-135A 55-3143 was photographed in March, 1978 on the 161 Air Refueling Group ramp at Sky Harbor International Airport, Phoenix, Arizona. (Douglas Slowiak/Vortex Photographics)

KC-135R 57-1462 photographed on takeoff at Ellsworth AFB on June 17, 1991. In late 1988 the 28th Bomb wing changed their tail stripe from the yellow and blue scalloped tail stripe for an outline of Mount Rushmore. (Don Logan)

KC-135A 59-1455 photographed over South Dakota. (USAF)

KC-135R 60-0321 photographed taxing past the fire station at Ellsworth AFB on July 17, 1987.

ABOVE: KC-135R 63-8032 "ORCA" photographed on April 19, 1989, shows the 28th Bomb Wing markings on the dark gray camouflage scheme. (Brian C. Rogers)

RIGHT: KC-135R 59-1455 photographed flying past Mount Rushmore. With the Mount Rushmore National Monument less than 100 miles from Ellsworth AFB. (USAF)

BELOW: KC-135R 63-8040 in AMC gray wears the light blue stripe of the 43rd Operations Group, 43rd ARW based at Malmstrom AFB. (Don Logan)

FAIRCHILD AIR FORCE BASE, WASHINGTON

Fairchild Air Force Base, located 12 miles west Spokane, Washington, has been the home for KC-135s since September, 1957. The 43rd and 92nd Air Refueling Squadrons were assigned to the 92nd Bomb Wing during Fairchild's SAC years. The 43rd was assigned to the 92nd Bomb Wing from April 2, 1966 until the wing transferred to ACC on June 1, 1992. The 92nd Air Refueling Squadron was assigned to the 92nd Bomb Wing from July 1, 1959 until June 1, 1992.

With the inactivation of SAC, the 43rd and 93nd were assigned to the 453rd Operations Group(OG) a geographically separated unit of the 43rd Air Refueling Wing, AMC, headquartered at Malmstrom AFB. The 96th and 98th Air Refueling Squadrons (ARS) were activated, and the 97th reassigned from the 43rd Operations Group at Malmstrom. All three squadrons became units of the 453rd Operations Group on April 1, 1994. This brought the total number of Air Refueling Squadrons assigned to the 453rd OG to five.

On July 1, 1994 the 92nd Bomb Wing was redesignated as the 92nd Air Refueling Wing and reassigned from ACC to AMC. The 92nd ARW gained the 93rd Air Refueling Squadron from Castle replacing the 43rd Air Refueling Squadron on March 31, 1995. The 92nd ARW, one of AMC's tanker hubs, is equipped with KC-135R and KC-135T models and presently has five Air Refueling Squadrons assigned; the 92nd, the 93rd, the 96th, the 97th, and the 98th. The 92nd, 93rd, and 97th ARS operate KC-135Rs, and the 96th and 98th operate KC-135Ts.

KC-135A 59-1498, photographed on September 15, 1987 is wearing changed 92nd Bomb Wing Seahawk tail stripe. (Doug Remington)

KC-135A 59-1444, photographed on May 18, 1986 shows the 92nd Bomb Wing blue tail stripe containing "FAIRCHILD" in script with a crown below the stripe. (Tom Brewer Collection)

KC-135R 60-0328 in camouflage paint was photographed on November 18, 1993 with the light blue tail stripe of the 453rd Operations Group, 43rd Air Refueling Wing. (Alan Winzerling)

ABOVE: KC-135R 57-1430 in AMC gray paint was photographed on November 18, 1993 with the light blue tail stripe of the 453rd Operations Group, 43rd Air Refueling Wing. (Alan Winzerling)

RIGHT: The tail of KC-135R 59-1469, photographed on June 12, 1995 wears the blue seahawk of the 43rd Air Refueling Squadron, 92nd Air Refueling Wing. (Brian C. Rogers)

The tail of KC-135R 60-0328 photographed in April, 1995 wears the black seahawk of the 92nd Air Refueling Squadron, 92nd Air Refueling Wing. (Don Logan)

The tail of this KC-135R 59-1468 photographed on January 21, 1995 wears the green seahawk of the 96th Air Refueling Squadron, 92nd Air Refueling Wing. (Brian C. Rogers)

KC-135T 59-0125, photographed on September 24, 1996 wears the yellow seahawk of the 97th Air Refueling Squadron, 92nd Air Refueling Wing. (Brian C. Rogers)

KC-135T 58-0084 photographed on September 24, 1995 wears the red seahawk of the 98th Air Refueling Squadron , 92nd Air Refueling Wing. (Brian C. Rogers)

GRAND FORKS AIR FORCE BASE, NORTH DAKOTA

Grand Forks Air Force Base, located 18 miles west of Grand Forks, North Dakota, has been the home for KC-135s since February 1960. The 905th Air Refueling Squadron was assigned to the 319th Bomb Wing during Grand Forks SAC years. The 905th was assigned to the 4133 Strategic Wing from February, 1960 thru 1963, and to the 319th Bomb Wing from February 1, 1963 until the wing transferred to ACC on 1 June, 1992.

With the inactivation of SAC, the 905th Air Refueling Squadron was assigned to the 305th Operations Group a part of the 305th wing AMC, on June 1, 1992. On July 1, 1993, the 905th was reassigned to the 43rd Operations Group part of the 43rd ARW at Malmstrom AFB.

On October 1, 1993 the 319th Bomb Wing was redesignated as the 319th Air Refueling Wing (ARW) and reassigned from ACC to AMC. The 905th Air Refueling Squadron was reassigned to the 319th also on October 1, 1993. The 319th ARW gained the 906th Air Refueling Squadron from Minot AFB on January 30, 1994. The 911th Air Refueling Squadron, which had been a KC-10 squadron at Seymour Johnson AFB, was assigned to the 319th ARW on April 29, 1994, and the 912th Air Refueling Squadron from the 19th ARW at Robins AFB, Georgia, was assigned to the 319th ARW on April 1, 1994. These additional squadrons picked up their aircraft from closing bases such as Griffiss and Plattsburgh. The 319th ARW, as one of AMC tanker hubs, is equipped with KC-135R and KC-135T models and presently has four Air Refueling Squadrons assigned; the 905th, the 906th, the 911th, and the 912nd.

A fourship of F-106As of the 94th Fighter Interceptor Squadron (FIS) returning from a deployment to Korea in 1969, await their turn on the boom of a KC-135A from the 319th Bomb Wing. (USAF)

KC-135A 63-7997 of the 905th Air Refueling Squadron, 319th Bomb Wing photographed on September 30, 1976. (Don McGary)

KC-135A 59-1500 in gloss gray when photographed on February 4, 1986, is wearing the "Sunflake" and blue and orange tail stripe of the 319th Bomb Wing. (Brian C. Rogers)

KC-135R 62-3565, photographed on the taxiway at Grand Forks AFB on August 12, 1989, shows the 319th Bomb Wing Sunflake", which is half sunburst and half snowflake. (Don Logan)

KC-135R 59-1475, in the "Shamu" camouflage scheme was photographed in January 1990. (Don Logan Collection)

KC-135R 63-8886 905th Air Refueling Squadron (Blue tail stripe), 319th Air Refueling Wing was photographed on August 7, 1996. The 319th Bomb Wing was changed to the 319th Air Refueling Wing on October 1, 1993, following the transfer of the wing's B-1B Lancers. (Brian C. Rogers)

KC-135R 63-8885, photographed on April 28, 1995 at Grand Forks AFB, wears the white tail stripe of the 912th Air Refueling Squadron, 319th Air Refueling Wing. (Brian C. Rogers)

KC-135T 58-0042, photographed on January 31, 1995, wears the yellow tail stripe of the 906th Air Refueling Squadron, 319th Air Refueling Wing. (Brian C. Rogers)

KC-135R 62-3519, photographed on August 7, 1996, wears the red tail stripe of the 911th Air Refueling Squadron, 319th Air Refueling Wing. (Brian C. Rogers)

GRIFFISS AIR FORCE BASE, NEW YORK

Griffiss Air Force Base is located in Rome, New York, and was the home of the 416th Bomb Wing. KC-135s were first assigned to the base in 1959 as part of the 4039th Strategic Wing. The 416th Bomb Wing replaced the 4039th SW on February 1, 1963. With the inactivation of SAC on June 1, 1992, the KC-135s were reassigned to 380th Operations Group, AMC. The 416th Bomb Wing retained their B-52s and transferred to ACC. With the closing of the base the 416th Bomb Wing was inactivated on September 30, 1995.

The 41st Air Refueling Squadron was assigned to the 416th Bomb Wing, operating as part of the wing from February 1, 1963 until SAC's demise on June, 1992. From June 1, 1992 until its inactivation on February 15, 1993, the 41st Air Refueling Squadron was assigned to the 380th Operations Group part of the 380th Air Refueling Wing at Plattsburgh AFB, New York.

The 509th was reassigned from the 509th Bomb Wing to the 416th Bomb Wing on July 1, 1990, as a result of the closing of Pease AFB. The 509th remained part of the 416th Bomb Wing until June 1, 1992. As with the 41st Air Refueling Squadron, the 509th Air Refueling Squadron was assigned to the 380th Operations Group beginning on June 1, 1992. The 509th was inactivated on October 1, 1994 in preparation for re-alignment of Griffiss AFB as a result of the BRAC commission decision.

KC-135A 62-3521 of the 41st Air Refueling Squadron, 416th Bomb Wing at Griffiss AFB, New York, was photographed on October 18, 1971. (Nelson Hare)

KC-135R 64-14829, photographed in April, 1992, shows the addition of the silhouette of the State of New York to the 416th Bomb Wing's markings. (Don Logan Collection)

KC-135A 62-3526, photographed on April 22, 1988, is now wearing the Statue Of Liberty tail stripe of the 416th Bomb Wing. (Douglas Sloviak Vortex Photographics)

KC-135A 61-0294 of the 41st Air Refueling Squadron, wears the tail stripe in the blue and white colors of the 416th Bomb Wing applied in the vertical stripe pattern of the 40th Air Division, 8th Air Force. (Brian C. Rogers)

ABOVE: KC-135R 61-0321, painted in the "Shamu" paint scheme was photographed at Griffiss AFB in April, 1992. (Don Logan Collection)

RIGHT: KC-135R 60-0323 wears the flying horse of the 509th Air Refueling Squadron which was reassigned to Griffiss AFB following the closure of Pease AFB in Vermont. (Tom Kaminiski)

BELOW: KC-135R 60-0323, photographed at Griffiss AFB in April 1994. (Paul Hart)

GRISSOM AIR FORCE BASE, INDIANA

Grissom Air Force Base is located 15 miles north of Kokomo, Indiana, and was the home of the 305th Air Refueling Wing. The base, originally named Bunker Hill AFB, was renamed Grissom AFB in May, 1968 in honor on Astronaut Lt. Col. Gus Grissom. Grissom was killed on January 27, 1967 in an Apollo space capsule fire at Cape Kennedy. KC-135s were first assigned to the 305th Bomb Wing on July 1, 1959. The wing was redesignated the 305th Air Refueling Wing on January 1, 1970. With the inactivation of SAC on June 1, 1992, the wing was reassigned to AMC. Due to the re-alignment of the base, the 305th Air Refueling Wing was redesignated the 305th Air Mobility Wing and moved to McGuire AFB, New Jersey on October 1, 1994.

The 68th Air Refueling Squadron was assigned to the 305th Bombardment Wing, operating as part of the wing from July 1, 1959, until replaced by the 305th Air Refueling Squadron on March 25, 1965.

The 70th Air Refueling Squadron moved from Little Rock AFB and was assigned to the 305th wing on January 1, 1970. The 70th remained part of the wing until the squadron was inactivated on April 1, 1993.

The 305th Air Refueling Squadron replaced the 68th Air Refueling Squadron on March 25, 1965, and remained part of the 305th Air Refueling Wing until the squadron was inactivated on August 20, 1993.

This closeup of the nose of KC-135A 63-8027, of the 305th Air Refueling Wing at Grissom AFB, shows the "Hoosier Hotshots" added for the SAC Bombing and Navigation Competition held in November, 1974. (Don Logan Collection)

BELOW: As seen here on 63-8027, in addition to the nose art the competitors from the 2nd Air Force wore the 2nd Air Force crest on the tail. (Don Logan Collection)

KC-135A 63-8026, photographed on July 22, 1979, wears the black and white checkerboard of the 305th Air Refueling Wing. (Don Logan Collection)

KC-135D 63-8059, photographed at Ellsworth AFB in August of 1989, wears the black and white checkerboard tail stripe and checkered flag emblem of the 305th ARW. (Don Logan)

This closeup of the nose of KC-135R 60-0362, shows the "Circus City Peru Indiana" nose art. (Jerry Geer)

The "Shamu" paint scheme's unit markings are applied in flat black and gray. This closeup of the tail of KC-135R 62-3515, photographed on June 19, 1991 shows the 305th Air Refueling Wing "Pacesetters" emblem. (Brian C. Rogers)

HOMESTEAD AIR FORCE BASE, FLORIDA

Homestead Air Force Base, located 5 miles north of Homestead, Florida, was the home of the 19th Bombardment Wing. KC-135s were assigned to the 407th Air Refueling Squadron from April 1, 1962, until July 2, 1968.

BELOW: KC-135A 56-3623 of the 19th Bomb Wing, Homestead Air Force Base, Florida, was photographed at McCoy AFB, just outside Orlando, Florida. (Tom Brewer Collection)

KADENA AIR BASE, OKINAWA, JAPAN

Kadena Air Base is located on the island of Okinawa (part of Japan) 15 miles north of the city of Naha. Kadena was the home of the 376th Strategic Wing (SW). KC-135s were first permanently assigned to the wing on July 1, 1971. Prior to that date, many tankers had been assigned, on a temporary basis, to the 4252nd Strategic Wing in support of Southeast Asia air operations. In preparation for the inactivation of SAC, the 376th Strategic Wing was inactivated, and on October 30, 1991, the KC-135s were reassigned to PACAF's 18th Wing already in place at Kadena AB.

The 909th Air Refueling Squadron was assigned to the 376th SW and operated KC-135As and KC-135Qs. The 909th converted to the KC-135Rs during 1991. The 909th was reassigned to the 18th Wing, Pacific Air Forces (PACAF), on October 1, 1991. The 909th ARS aircraft carry the 18th Wing's ZZ tail code.

ABOVE: As one of the non-AMC units, belonging to PACAF, the KC-135Rs of the 909th Air Refueling Squadron wear the ZZ tail code of the 18th Wing. (Jerry Geer)

BELOW: KC-135A 63-8012 of the 376th Strategic Wing was photographed at the SAC Bombing and Navigation Competition held at Barksdale AFB in November, 1974. (Ray Leader)

RIGHT: A closeup of the nose of 63-8012 shows the insignia of the 376th Strategic Wing and a Torii gate straddling a map of Okinawa. (Ray Leader)

BELOW: KC-135A 63-8044 of the 376th Strategic Wing photographed on May 10, 1985 with the new wing tail stripe. (Brian C. Rogers)

KC-135R 61-0323 wears the ZZ tail code and ACC style serial number when photographed in April, 1992. (Alan Winzerling)

KC-135R 63-8883 of the 18th Wing, photographed in April, 1992 wears the emblem of the 5th Air Force on the nose. (Alan Winzerling)

KC-135R 62-3520 of the 18th Wing wears the Young Tiger emblem. Young Tiger was the name given to the rotating deployment of SAC KC-135A to Southeast Asia during the war in Vietnam. (Alec Fushi)

KC-135R 61-0306 of the 18th Wing carried nose art called "Tsunami" when photographed in August 1992. (Jerry Geer)

RIGHT: KC-135R 61-0323 carried nose art titled "Island Born" when photographed at Tinker AFB on August 5, 1994. (Don Logan)

K. I. SAWYER AIR FORCE BASE, MICHIGAN

K.I. Sawyer Air Force Base was located 21 miles south of Marquette, Michigan, and was the home of the 410th Bomb Wing. KC-135As were first assigned to 4052nd Strategic Wing on April 1, 1961. The 4052nd SW was redesignated the 416th Bombardment Wing Heavy on February 1, 1963. With the inactivation of SAC on June 1, 1992, the KC-135s were reassigned to 305th Operations Group, AMC. The 410th Bomb Wing retained their B-52s and transferred to ACC. With the closing of the base, the 410th Bomb Wing was inactivated on September 30, 1995.

The 46th Air Refueling Squadron was assigned to the 4052nd SW and later the 410th Bomb Wing from April 1, 1961 until SAC's demise on June 1, 1992. From June 1, 1992 until its inactivation on October 8, 1993, the 46th Air Refueling Squadron was assigned to the 305th Operations Group part of the 305th Air Refueling Wing at Grissom AFB, Indiana.

The 307th Air Refueling Squadron was assigned to the 410th Bomb Wing on October 1, 1985 and remained part of the 410th Bomb Wing until the squadron was inactivated on August 1, 1990.

A closeup of the nose of KC-135A 60-0313 shows the nose art worn by the representative of the 410th Bomb Wing at the SAC Bombing and Navigation Competition held at Barksdale AFB in November, 1974. (Don Logan Collection)

KC-135A 59-1572 of the 46th Air Refueling Squadron, 410th Bomb Wing was photographed on October 10, 1982. (Don McGary)

KC-135A 63-8038 of the 46th Air Refueling Squadron, photographed on July 18, 1986, wears the tail stripe in the red and white colors of the 410th Bomb Wing applied in the vertical stripe pattern of the 40th Air Division, 8th Air Force. (Brian C. Rogers)

KC-135A 60-0366, photographed on June 4, 1987 at Carswell AFB wear the rainbow tail stripe of the 410th Bomb Wing. (Brian C. Rogers)

RIGHT: This closeup of the nose of KC-135A 58-0110 in storage at AMARC as CA-089 shows the 46th Air Refueling Squadron emblem. This aircraft was removed from storage, converted to a KC-135R, and was the first of the KC-135Rs for the Turkish Air Force. (Douglas Sloviak Vortex Photographics)

LORING AIR FORCE BASE, MAINE

Loring Air Force Base was located 4 miles west of Limestone, Maine, and was the home of the 42nd Bomb Wing. KC-135As were first assigned to the base on July 1, 1957. With the inactivation of SAC on June 1, 1992, the KC-135s were reassigned to 380th Operations Group, AMC. The 42nd Bomb Wing retained their B-52s and transferred to ACC. The 42nd Bomb Wing was inactivated on September 30, 1994, in preparation for the closing of the base.

The 42nd Air Refueling Squadron was assigned to the 42nd Bomb Wing, operating as part of the wing from July 1, 1957, until SAC's demise on June 1, 1992. From June 1, 1992, until its inactivation on April 30, 1994, the 42th Air Refueling Squadron was assigned to the 380th Operations Group part of the 380th Air Refueling Wing at Plattsburgh, New York.

The 407th Air Refueling Squadron was assigned to the 42nd Bomb Wing on July 2, 1968, and remained part of the 42nd Bomb Wing until the squadron was inactivated on October 1, 1990.

The tail of KC-135R 60-0316, photographed on December 31, 1990, shows the Loring AFB 42nd Bomb Wing markings of a moose head over the outline of the state of Maine. (Brian C. Rogers)

KC-135A 58-0030 of the 42nd Air Refueling Squadron, photographed on August 19, 1986, wears the tail stripe in the blue and yellow colors of the 42nd Bomb Wing applied in the diagonal stripe pattern of the 45th Air Division, 8th Air Force. (Brian C. Rogers)

KC-135A 56-3624, photographed at Carswell AFB on September 14, 1988, wears the moose head of the 42nd Bomb Wing and Loring in green on the tail. (Brian C. Rogers)

KC-135A 56-3619 of the 42nd bomb Wing was photographed at RAF Mildenhall on March 18, 1988 with tail markings of the moose head and Loring in red. (Keith Svendsen)

KC-135R 61-0323 photographed at Ellsworth AFB on December 31, 1990, painted in the "Shamu" scheme has 42nd Bomb Wing markings in green. (Brian C. Rogers)

MacDILL AIR FORCE BASE, FLORIDA

MacDill AFB is located adjacent to the southwest city limits of Tampa, Florida. The base, in the post-World War II years, performed crew training for SAC's B-50 aircraft. It was the home of B-47s and KC-97s starting in 1951. TAC took over the base in 1962 hosting the 12th, 15th and 1st Tactical Fighter Wings before becoming a KC-135R base.

The 6th Air Refueling Wing traces its lineage to the 6th Strategic Reconnaissance Wing (SRW), which flew RC-135S and RC-135X aircraft from Eilson AFB. The 6th SRW changed to the 6th Wing in October 1991, and was inactivated in 1992, transferring its RC-135s to the 55th Wing at Offutt AFB.

The 6th Wing was activated as the 6th Air Base Wing (ABW) at MacDill AFB to replace the 56th FW when it moved to Luke AFB in April 1994. The 6th ABW became the 6th Air Refueling Wing with the 91st Air Refueling Squadron transferring from the 43rd Air Refueling Group at Malmstrom AFB, Montana in October, 1996. Like the other active duty Air Force squadrons, the 91st ARS flies KC-135Rs.

During April 1997, the EC-135N (61-0327) and EC-135Y (55-3125), which had been assigned to the 19th ARW at Robins, were reassigned to the 6th ARW at MacDill.

BELOW: KC-135R, 60-0355, assigned to the 6th Air Refueling Wing at MacDill AFB, Florida was photographed here at Nellis AFB on June 12, 1997. (Brian C. Rogers)

MALMSTROM AIR FORCE BASE, MONTANA

Malmstrom Air Force Base is located at Great Falls, Montana and is the home of the 43rd Air Refueling Group. KC-135Rs , the first KC-135 type at Malmstrom, were assigned to the base on January 5, 1989 as part of the 91st Air Refueling Squadron, 301st Air Refueling Wing. With the inactivation of SAC on June 1, 1992, the 301st Air Refueling Wing was replaced by the 43rd Air Refueling Wing. The 43rd ARW had previously been assigned to Andersen AFB, Guam as the 43rd Bomb Wing. The 43rd Air Refueling Wing was redesignated the 43rd Air Refueling Group (ARG) on July 1, 1994. The 91st Air Refueling Squadron remained at Malmstrom AFB assigned to the 301st ARW, the 43rd ARW, and presently the 43rd ARG.

The 97th Air Refueling Squadron, previously assigned to the 97th Bomb Wing at Eaker AFB, inactivated on April 1, 1992, due to the closing of Eaker AFB, was reactivated at Malmstrom AFB on October 1, 1992. The 97th ARS moved to Fairchild AFB on April 1, 1994. The 43rd ARG was inactivated and the 91st ARS moved to MacDill, AFB, Florida as part of the 6th Air Refueling Wing on October 1, 1996.

ABOVE: The light blue tail stripe and MALMSTROM on the tail of 61-0306 seen here on July 16, 1993, were the standard markings of the 43rd Air Refueling Wing. After the transfer of a majority of the KC-135 tankers to AMC, Air Refueling Squadrons at many of the ACC bomber bases such as Dyess, Ellsworth, Fairchild and Minot, were assigned to Operations Groups reporting to the 43rd ARW, the tankers of these operations groups carried light blue tail stripes containing their base name instead of Malmstrom. (Don Logan)

BELOW: KC-135R 61-0309, seen here in November of 1988, at Malmstrom AFB wears the tail stripe of the 301st Air Refueling Wing. (James Benson)

KC-135R 61-0306, photographed at Forbes Field, Kansas on July 16, 1993, painted in "Shamu" scheme. (Don Logan)

KC-135R 59-1475 wears the yellow tail stripe of the 91st Air Refueling Squadron, 43rd Air Refueling Group. (Alan Winzerling)

MARCH AIR FORCE BASE, CALIFORNIA

March Air Force Base is located 9 miles southeast of Riverside, California, was the home of the 22nd Bomb Wing. KC-135As were first assigned to the 22nd Air Refueling Squadron on July 1, 1963, as part of the 22nd Bomb Wing. After the retirement of the wing's B-52s, the 22nd Bomb Wing was redesignated as the 22nd Air Refueling Wing. On December 1, 1989, with the inactivation of the 22nd Air Refueling Squadron, the KC-135s left March, and the 22nd ARW continued as a KC-10 Wing. With the inactivation of SAC on June 1, 1992, the wing was transferred to AMC. On January 1, 1994, the 22nd ARW moved without personnel or equipment to McConnell AFB, Kansas. March AFB continues as a KC-135 operating base with the 452nd Air Mobility Wing, Air Force Reserve and the 163rd Air Refueling Wing, California Air National Guard, still stationed at March AFB.

The 22nd Air Refueling Squadron was assigned to the 22nd Bomb Wing, operating as part of the wing from July 1, 1963, until the squadron was inactivated on December 1, 1989. The 22nd Air Refueling Squadron was activated on October 1, 1992, as the tanker squadron of the 366th Composite Wing based at Mountain Home AFB, Idaho.

The 909th Air Refueling Squadron was assigned to the 22nd Bomb Wing on June 25, 1966 and remained part of the 22nd Bomb Wing until the squadron moved to Kadena AB on July 1, 1971. The 909th ARS presently operates KC-135Rs as part of the 18th Wing based at Kadena AB, Okinawa.

KC-135A 55-3136, seen here in 22nd Bomb Wing markings, was configured similar to Combat Lightning aircraft, but with camera windows added to the forward fuselage. When in the aircraft had been used as a test resource for atomic weapons testing. (Terry Love Collection)

KC-135A 60-0316 of the 22nd Air Refueling Squadron, 22nd Bomb Wing was photographed in November, 1986. (Bob Bush)

MATHER AIR FORCE BASE, CALIFORNIA

Mather Air Force Base was located 12 miles east of Sacramento, California, was the home of the 320th Bomb Wing. KC-135As were first assigned to the base on March 1, 1959, as part of the 904th Air Refueling Squadron, 4134th Strategic Wing. The 320th Bombardment Wing Heavy replaced the 4134th SW during 1963. The 904th Air Refueling Squadron was inactivated on October 1, 1986.

RIGHT: KC-135A 63-8879 of the 320th Bomb Wing was photographed in September, 1985 on approach for landing. (Alan Winzerling)

KC-135A 63-8879 of the 320th Bomb Wing was photographed in September, 1983. (Alan Winzerling)

KC-135A 64-14836 with the tail stripe of the 320th Bomb Wing was photographed in July, 1985. (Alan Winzerling)

McCONNELL AIR FORCE BASE, KANSAS

McConnell Air Force Base, located in the southeast corner of Wichita, Kansas, is the home of the 22nd Air Refueling Wing. KC-135s have been based at McConnell since December 1, 1972. KC-135s were first assigned to the 91st Air Refueling Squadron. 384th Air Refueling Wing. The 384th Air Refueling Squadron was added to the 384th Air Refueling Wing on September 30, 1973.

The 91st Air Refueling Squadron was inactivated on July 1, 1987, to make room for the 28th Bomb Squadron, the future B-1B squadron. With the arrival of the B-1Bs in February, 1988, the 384th Air Refueling Wing was redesignated the 384th Bomb Wing. On January 1, 1994, the 22nd Air Refueling Wing was activated at McConnell, and the 384th Bomb Wing was redesignated as the 384th Bomb Group. On October 1, 1994, with the transfer of the B-1Bs to the 184th Bomb Group, Kansas Air National Guard, the 384th Bomb Group was inactivated.

The 22nd Air Refueling Wing presently operates KC-135R and KC-135T models, along with all the KC-135Rs equipped with air refueling receiver receptacles. The 931st ARG, AFRES augments the personnel of the 22nd ARW.

With the inactivation of SAC on June 1, 1992, the 384th Air Refueling Squadron was assigned to the 19th Operations Group, a part of the 19th Air Refueling Wing, AMC, at Robins AFB, Georgia. With the arrival of the 22nd ARW on January 1, 1994, the 384th ARS was reassigned to the 22nd ARW.

The tail of 63-8022, photographed at McConnell AFB on November 10, 1996, is marked as the 22nd Air Refueling Wing flagship. The tail stripe is made up of the four squadron colors, black for the 344th ARS, blue for the 349th ARS, red for the 350th ARS, and maroon for the 384th ARS. (Jerry Geer)

On January 1, 1994, the 349th and 350th Air Refueling Squadrons, both previously based at Beale AFB, were assigned to the 22nd Air Refueling Wing. The 344th Air Refueling Squadron, a KC-10A squadron at Seymour Johnson, was reassigned to the 22nd ARW at McConnell and began operation of KC-135 R and T models. The 22nd ARW, one of the tanker hub wings presently has four Air Refueling Squadrons assigned; the 344th, the 349th, the 350th, and the 384th.

This photo taken in June, 1973 shows the KC-135As of the 384th Air Refueling Wing lined up on the flightline at McConnell AFB. (Jerry Geer)

LEFT: KC-135A 57-1502 of the 384th ARW seen in this photo was photographed at Offutt AFB on April 10, 1981. (Don McGary) RIGHT: KC-135R 63-8024, of the 91st Air Refueling Squadron wears the tail stripe in the light blue and dark blue colors of the 384th Air Refueling Wing applied in the diamond pattern of the 19th Air Division, 8th Air Force.The 384th ARW was the first unit to be equipped with KC-135Rs. (Jerry Geer)

This photo taken in November, 1984 shows the KC-135As of the 384th Air Refueling Wing lined up on the flightline at McConnell AFB. (Jerry Geer)

KC-135R 59-1521 of the 91st Air Refueling Squadron, of the 384th Bomb Wing, on takeoff at McConnell AFB in March, 1989. The ARW changed to a Bomb Wing the arrival of B-1Bs in early 1988. (Don Logan)

KC-135R 61-0276 seen in flight on January 25, 1990. The "Keeper Of The Plains" art work of an Indian, is representative of a large statue on the Arkansas River in Wichita, Kansas, the location of McConnell AFB. (Keith Svendsen)

With the closing of SAC, the 384th Bomb Wing gave up its tankers, transferring them to the 19th Operations Group, which was assigned to the 19th Air Refueling Wing based at Robins Air Force Base, Georgia. The nose of 59-1521 seen here carries the black night markings of the 19th ARW. (Don Logan)

KC-135R 61-0276, of the 19th Operations Group (OG) was photographed on the McConnell AFB flight line on September 15, 1993. The tankers of the 19th OG carried a yellow tail stripe with BLACK KNIGHTS in black script. (Don Logan)

KC-135R 61-0310 in the new AMC light gray paint scheme on the McConnell AFB flight line in November, 1993. (Don Logan)

KC-135T 58-0089 carries the black band at the end of the yellow tail stripe indicating the aircraft is assigned to the 344th Air Refueling Squadron. (Don Logan)

KC-135R 58-0036 carries the blue band at the end of the yellow tail stripe indicating the aircraft is assigned to the 349th Air Refueling Squadron. (Don Logan)

KC-135R 63-8022 is the 22nd ARW flagship aircraft with a special serial number presentation and carrying tail markings made up of all four squadron's colors. (Jerry Geer)

KC-135R 61-0311 carries the red band at the end of the yellow tail stripe indicating the aircraft is assigned to the 350th Air Refueling Squadron. (Don Logan)

KC-135R 64-14828 carries the maroon band at the end of the yellow tail stripe indicating the aircraft is assigned to the 384th Air Refueling Squadron. (Don Logan)

RAF MILDENHALL, UNITED KINGDOM

RAF Mildenhall, located 30 miles northeast of Cambridge, England, is the home of the 100th Air Refueling Wing. The 100th ARW, US Air Forces in Europe (USAFE) was assigned to RAF Mildenhall on February 1, 1992. The KC-135 squadron, the 351st Air Refueling Squadron was activated on March 31, 1992, equipped with KC-135R models.

RIGHT: The 100 ARW marked 61-0312's tall in observance of the 50th Anniversary of the USAF. This photo was taken at RAF Mildenhall on May 24, 1997. (Alan Winzerling)

KC-135R 57-1499 of the 100th ARW was photographed at RAF Mildenhall on May 24, 1997. (Alan Winzerling)

KC-135R 62-3558 of the 100th ARW shows the difference between fresh and faded FS36081 dark gray used in the Shamu paint scheme. (Don Logan Collection)

MINOT AIR FORCE BASE, NORTH DAKOTA

Minot Air Force Base is located 13 miles north of Minot, North Dakota, and is the home of the 5th Bomb Wing. The 906th Air Refueling Squadron, flying KC-135As, was assigned to the 4136th Strategic Wing from June 1, 1959. The 450th Bomb Wing replaced the 4136th SW on February 1, 1963, and was replaced by the 5th Bomb Wing on July 25, 1968. With the inactivation of SAC on June 1, 1992, the 906th Air Refueling Squadron and its KC-135As were reassigned to 43rd Operations Group, AMC. The 5th Bomb Wing retained their B-52s and transferred to ACC. During 1993 the 906th Air Refueling Squadron converted to KC-135Rs. On January 30, 1994 the 906th Air Refueling Squadron was reassigned to the 319th Air Refueling Wing and moved to Grand Forks AFB.KC-135s are no longer assigned to Minot AFB.

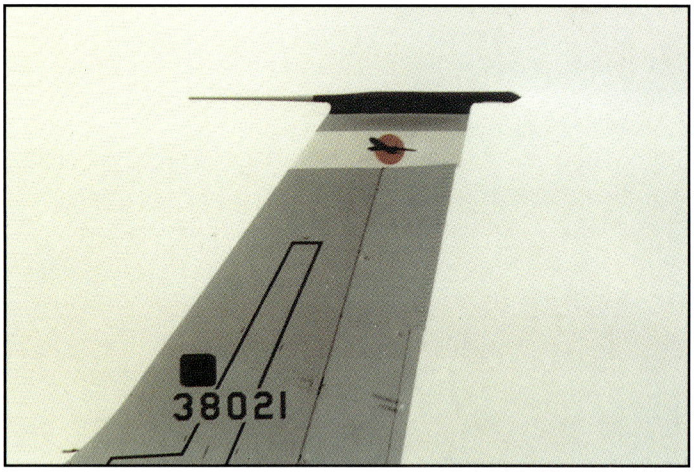

KC-135A 58-0098 photographed in June 1981, wears the 5th Bomb Wing insignia on the right side of the fuselage. (George Cockle)

KC-135A 63-8034 of the 906th Air Refueling Squadron, 5th Bomb Wing here, photographed on landing approach, September 13, 1990. (Don Logan Collection)

KC-135A 62-3497 assigned to the 43rd Operations Group (OG), attached to the 43rd ARW at Malmstrom AFB wore the light blue stripe of the 43rd ARW with the script MINOT in the stripe. (Don Logan)

KC-135A 60-0050, photographed on February 8, 1991 at Jeddah, Saudi Arabia, assigned, along with other tankers of the 5th Bomb Wing, to the 1709th Air Refueling Wing (Provisional) while taking part in Operation Desert Storm. (Brian C. Rogers)

KC-135A 63-8034 photographed on the ramp at Minot in August, 1989, is painted with the nose art of the "Silver Surfer." (Don Logan)

KC-135R 63-8024, photographed at Kadena AB during October 1993, was assigned to the 906th ARS, part of the 43rd OG. The 906th was transferred to the 319th ARW at Grand Forks AFB on January 30, 1994. (Alan Winzerling)

MOUNTAIN HOME AIR FORCE BASE, IDAHO

Mountain Home Air Force Base, located 10 miles southwest of Mountain Home, Idaho, is the home of the 366th Wing. The 22nd Air Refueling Squadron, the tanker unit of the composite wing, was assigned to the 366th Wing on October 1, 1992. The 22nd Air Refueling Squadron is equipped with KC-135Rs. The composite wing also has B-1B, F-15C/D, F-15E, and F-16 C/D squadrons assigned.

RIGHT: The nose of KC-135R 63-8004 is assigned to the 22nd Air Refueling Squadron, 366th Wing. The 22nd Air Refueling Squadron is the only KC-135 tanker squadron in Air Combat Command. (Brian C. Rogers)

KC-135R 63-8004 photographed at Langley AFB on July 21, 1993, wears the MO tail code of the 366th Wing and flagship markings for the 22nd Air Refueling Group (ARG). (Brian C. Rogers)

KC-135R 60-0365, photographed on August 7, 1996, in AMC light gray wears the MO tail code of the 366th Wing and ACC style serial number presentation. (Brian C. Rogers)

OFFUTT AIR FORCE BASE, NEBRASKA

Offutt Air Force Base, located 8 miles south of Omaha, Nebraska, is the home of the 55th Wing. The Wing has flown KC-135s in support of SAC headquarters and as flight crew training aircraft for the wing's reconnaissance squadrons.

RIGHT ABOVE: KC-135E 57-2589, photographed on October 4, 1995 at McChord AFB Washington, still is assigned to the 55th Wing and after reengining with JT3D engines is still used as a VIP transport for the units at Offutt AFB. (Don Abrahamson)

RIGHT: KC-135A 57-2589, photographed on December 14, 1980 at Offutt AFB, assigned to the 55th SRW, was used as the SAC commanders (CINCSAC) aircraft and flew using the callsign "Casey 01" (pronounced KC01). (Don McGary)

BELOW: KC-135A 58-0124, photographed at Offutt AFB July 1979, in was the first KC-135 tanker to have a refueling receptacle installed. It was assigned to the 55th Strategic Reconnaissance Wing (SRW) and used to train EC-135 and RC-135 pilots with using the more expensive specially equipped EC and RC aircraft. (Don Logan)

KC-135E 59-1514, the first KC-135E is assigned to the 55th wing and is used for pilot training, much the same as 58-0124 had been prior to being was converted to a KC-135R. (Jerry Geer)

PEASE AIR FORCE BASE, NEW HAMPSHIRE

Pease Air Force Base located in Portsmouth, New Hampshire, and was the home of the 509th Bomb Wing. The 34th Air Refueling Squadron flying KC-135As was assigned to the base from July 25, 1966, to March 31, 1976. The 509th Air Refueling Squadron was assigned to Pease on October 2, 1966, and was later reassigned to the 416th Bomb Wing at Griffiss AFB, New York.

On September 30, 1990, the 509th Bomb Wing moved to Whiteman AFB, Missouri to become the B-2 Bomb Wing. Pease, now an Air National Guard Base, continues as a KC-135 operating base with the 157th Air Refueling Wing, New Hampshire Air National Guard.

KC-135A 62-3529 displays the flying horse (similar to Mobil Oil Company's insignia) in the tail stripe of the 509th Air Refueling Squadron based at Pease AFB. (Jim Moseley Collection)

This closeup of the nose of 62-3538 photographed in October 1989, shows the "Valhalla Express" nose art. (Brian C. Rogers)

RIGHT: KC-135A 57-1474 photographed on October 28, 1986, wears the tail stripe in the red and royal blue colors of the 509th Bomb Wing applied in the diagonal stripe pattern of the 45th Air Division, 8th Air Force. (Brian C. Rogers)

KC-135A 60-0349 of the 509th Air Refueling Squadron, 509th Bomb Wing, photographed at Carswell AFB on August 25, 1988, wears the units flying horse tail stripe. (Brian C. Rogers)

PLATTSBURGH AIR FORCE BASE, NEW YORK

Plattsburgh Air Force Base was located adjacent to Plattsburgh, New York, and was the home of the 380th Bomb Wing. KC-135As of the 380th Air Refueling Squadron were the first KC-135s assigned to the base. They were assigned on July 1, 1964. The 310th Air Refueling Squadron was assigned to the 380th Bomb Wing on January 25, 1967. After the wing's FB-111s retired, the 380th Bomb Wing was redesignated, on July 1, 1991, as the 380th Air Refueling Wing. With the inactivation of SAC on June 1, 1992, the wing was transferred to AMC. The wing ceased flying operations on October 1, 1994, in preparation for the closing of the base.

The 310th and 380th Air Refueling Squadrons operated KC-135A and KC-135Q models until they converted to KC-135Rs during 1993. Both squadrons were inactivated on October 1, 1994.

As seen on KC-135A 59-1462, the 380th Bomb Wing used the "Big Apple" insignia on the tail of its tankers and bombers. (Jim Moseley Collection)

BELOW: KC-135Q 59-1467, photographed at Offutt AFB on May 2, 1981, shows a test tanker tail code system. The PBG standing for Plattsburg lasted only a short time. It's reported that the Generals at SAC headquarters, after seeing the tail code on this aircraft at its stopover at Offutt AFB, ordered the tail codes removed. Though SAC used unit tail markings, they never adopted alphabetical tail codes. (Don McGary)

KC-135A 62-3554 had special markings applied at one time during its assignment to the 380th Bomb Wing at Plattsburg AFB. (Don Logan Collection)

KC-135Q 58-0061 was photographed in Shamu paint scheme and 380th Bomb Wing markings at Forbes Field during March, 1993. (Jerry Geer)

KC-135Q 59-1510 was photographed on February 1, 1989 in 380th Bomb Wing markings. (Brian C. Rogers)

KC-135Q 57-1471 photographed on October 28, 1986, wears the tail stripe in the green and white colors of the 380th Bomb Wing applied in the diagonal stripe pattern of the 45th Air Division, 8th Air Force. (Brian C. Rogers)

KC-135R 63-8872 was photographed at McChord AFB in July, 1994, carries the green stripe of the 310th Air Refueling Squadron, 380th Air Refueling Wing. The other squadron, the 380th, carried maroon tail stripes. (Renato E. F. Jones)

RICKENBACKER AIR FORCE BASE, OHIO

Rickenbacker Air Force Base, was located 13 miles south of Columbus, Ohio, and was the home of the 301st Air Refueling Wing. The base was originally named Lockbourne AFB, but was renamed in May 1974, in honor of Capt. Eddie Rickenbacker, Americas leading World War I Ace. The wing operated KC-135s from April 1, 1963, until the wing was inactivated on September 30, 1979. The inactivation was in preparation for transfer of the base from SAC to the Ohio Air National Guard. Rickenbacker continues as a KC-135 operating base as the home of the 121st Air Refueling Wing, Ohio Air National Guard.

Four active duty SAC air refueling squadrons operated KC-135s from Rickenbacker. The 32nd Air Refueling Squadron was assigned to Rickenbacker from March 15, 1965, until September 30, 1979. The 91st Air Refueling Squadron was assigned to Rickenbacker from June 15, 1964, until July 1, 1971. The 301st Air Refueling Squadron was assigned to Rickenbacker from September 30, 1973, until December 31, 1975, and the 321st Air Refueling Squadron was assigned to Rickenbacker from April 1, 1963, until March 15, 1965.

BELOW: KC-135A 63-7982 of the 301st Air Refueling Wing photographed at Barksdale AFB in November, 1974, carries the text "PRIDE OF COLUMBUS OHIO CAPTAIN EDDIE" on the fuselage side below the cargo door. (Tom Brewer Collection)

ROBINS AIR FORCE BASE, GEORGIA

Robins Air Force Base, located 15 miles southeast of Macon, Georgia, at Warner-Robins, is the home of the 19th Air Refueling Group. KC-135s have been based at Robins since December 1, 1961, first assigned to the 912th Air Refueling Squadron of the 4137th Strategic Wing, The 465th Bomb Wing replaced the 4137th SW on February 1, 1963. The 465th BW was replaced by the 19th BW on July 25, 1968. The 19th BW was redesignated the 19th Air Refueling Wing on October 1, 1983. It became the 19th Air Refueling Group on July 1, 1997, to make room on the ramp for the E-8 JointSTARS aircraft.

The 99th Air Refueling Squadron was assigned to the 19th Air Refueling Wing on October 1, 1983. With the inactivation of SAC on June 1, 1992, the 19th Air Refueling Wing was transferred to SAC to AMC. On April 1, 1994, the 912th Air Refueling Squadron was reassigned to the 319th Air Refueling Wing at Grand Forks AFB, North Dakota, and was replaced at Robins AFB by the 712th Air Refueling Squadron. Both the 19th ARW's Air Refueling Squadrons, the 99th and 712th operated the KC-135R. The 712th was inactivated on July 1, 1997.

The 19th Air Refueling Wing markings on the tail of KC-135R 3530 are made up of the black knight's head and the tail stripe of a map of the state of Georgia being pierced by a Sword. The black knights head was also applied to KC-135Rs at McConnell while McConnell's tankers were assigned to the 19th Operations Group, then part of the 19th Air Refueling Wing. (Brian C. Rogers)

KC-135A 58-0066, photographed at Barksdale in November, 1974, was at that time assigned to the 912nd Air Refueling Squadron, 19th Bomb Wing based at Robins AFB. (Tom Brewer Collection)

This side view of KC-135A 57-1454, taken at Offutt AFB on June 8, 1981, shows off the 19th Bomb Wing insignia on the right side of the fuselage. (Don McGary)

KC-135R 63-7977, in 19th Air Refueling Wing markings, was photographed at Forbes Field, Kansas in April 1990. (Jerry Geer)

KC-135R 62-3530, in the "Shamu" camouflage was photographed at Robins AFB on March 21, 1992. (Brian C. Rogers)

KC-135R 63-7995, photographed at McChord AFB in July, 1994 during the Airlift Rodeo wearing white chalk celebration markings. (Ben Knowles)

KC-135R 62-3554 on March 21, 1992, with the nose art it wore while part of the 19th Air Refueling Wing. This aircraft set 16 Time to-Climb world records on October 19, 1988. "Cherokee Rose" was flown by several flight crews during the day. (Brian C. Rogers)

KC-135R 63-7977 on March 21, 1992, with the nose art it wore while part of the 19th Air Refueling Wing. (Brian C. Rogers)

KC-135R 57-2597 on March 21, 1992, with the nose art it wore while part of the 19th Air Refueling Wing. (Brian C. Rogers)

KC-135R 62-3569 on March 21, 1992, with the nose art it wore while part of the 19th Air Refueling Wing. (Brian C. Rogers)

SEYMOUR-JOHNSON AIR FORCE BASE, NORTH CAROLINA

Seymour-Johnson Air Force Base, located in the city of Goldsboro, North Carolina, was the home of the 68th Air Refueling Wing. KC-135s were assigned to the 911th Air Refueling Squadron. The 911th was part of the 4241 Strategic Wing from December 15, 1958, until replaced by the 68th Bomb Wing April 15, 1963. The 68th Bomb Wing was redesignated the 68th Air Refueling Wing on October 1, 1982, and was inactivated in 1985. The 916th ARW, 77th ARS, AFRES, presently operates KC-135Rs at Seymour-Johnson.

KC-135A 57-2591 carried this nose art of the Wright Brother's aircraft at the SAC Bombing and Navigation Competition at Barksdale AFB in November, 1974. (Tom Brewer Collection)

KC-135A 59-1483 of the 911th Air Refueling Squadron, 68th Bomb Wing, was photographed at Offutt AFB on May 6, 1980. (Don McGary)

TRAVIS AIR FORCE BASE, CALIFORNIA

Travis Air Force Base, located 50 miles northeast of San Francisco at Fairfield, California, was the home of the 5th Bombardment Wing from September 1, 1959, until the 5th BW moved to Minot AFB on July 25, 1968. The 307th Air Refueling Group was activated on July 15, 1977.

KC-135s were assigned to the 916th Air Refueling Squadron, and was component of the 5th Bomb Wing. After the 5th BW moved to Minot, the 916th was a direct reporting unit of the 47th Air Division. The 916th became part of the 307th Air Refueling Group on July 15, 1977. The 916th was inactivated on October 13, 1983.

KC-135A 58-0100 of the 916th Air Refueling Squadron was photographed at RAF Mildenhall on September 9, 1974. (Tom Brewer Collection)

KC-135A 60-0330 was photographed at Travis AFB on June 2, 1975. (Tom Brewer Collection)

WURTSMITH AIR FORCE BASE, MICHIGAN

Wurtsmith Air Force Base was located 3 miles northwest of Oscoda, Michigan, and was the home of the 379th Bomb Wing. KC-135As of the 920th Air Refueling Squadron were first assigned to Wurtsmith on June 15, 1960, as part of the 4026th Strategic Wing. The 379th Bombardment Wing replaced the 4026th on January 9, 1961. With the inactivation of SAC on June 1, 1992, the KC-135s were reassigned to 305th Operations Group, AMC. The 379th Bomb Wing retained their B-52s and transferred to ACC. As a result of the planned closing of the base, the 379th Bomb Wing was inactivated on June 15, 1993.

The 920th Air Refueling Squadron was assigned to the 379th Bomb Wing, operating as part of the wing from June 15, 1960, until SAC's demise on June 1, 1992. From June 1, 1992, until its inactivation on September 30, 1992, the 920th Air Refueling Squadron was assigned to the 305th Operations Group part of the 305th Air Refueling Wing at Grissom AFB, Indiana.

KC-135A 59-1515 of the 920th Air Refueling Squadron, 379th Bomb Wing was photographed at Offutt AFB on May 30, 1991. (Don McGary)

BELOW: KC-135A 59-1516, photographed on October 3, 1986, assigned to the 920th Air Refueling Squadron, wears the tail stripe in the red and yellow colors of the 379th Bomb Wing applied in the vertical stripe pattern of the 40th Air Division, 8th Air Force. (Brian C. Rogers)

KC-135A 62-3559, photographed on August 19, 1987, shows the new tail stripe of the 920th Air Refueling Squadron, a stylizes hawk head. (Brian C. Rogers)

KC-135R 62-3512, photographed in flight on October 24, 1990, seen painted in "Shamu" camouflage with the triangle K tail markings on the tail. (Alan Winzerling)

KC-135A 64-14839 was photographed on September 28, 1988 in "Shamu" camouflage. (Brian C. Rogers)

KC-135A 64-14837, photographed on June 25, 1990, wears the triangle K tail marking adopted by the 379th Bomb Wing for their KC-135s and B-52s. (Brian C. Rogers)

KC-135A 60-0317, photographed on approach, carries the 920th Air Refueling Squadron tail stripe. (Mike Grove)

AIR FORCE RESERVE TANKER BASES

434 AIR REFUELING WING
GRISSOM AIR RESERVE BASE, INDIANA

The 72nd Air Refueling Squadron, 434th Air Refueling Wing, AFRES is based at Grissom Air Reserve Base, near Kokomo, Indiana. The 72nd Air Refueling Squadron operating out of Grissom, was initially assigned to the 931st Air Refueling Group (ARG) which was a part of the 452nd Air Refueling Wing. During 1987, 72nd Air Refueling Squadron started receiving KC-135Es and the 931st ARG was replaced by the 434th after the 434th converted from A-10As. During summer of 1993, the 72nd picked up KC-135Rs from the active duty 305th ARW, also at Grissom. With the receipt of the KC-135Rs, the 72nd's KC-135Es were transferred to the 63rd Air Refueling Squadron, 927th Air Refueling Group, at Selfridge Air National Guard Base, Michigan.

As the 305th drew down, a second KC-135 Air Refueling Squadron, the 74th ARS, was activated at Grissom on August 1, 1992.

KC-135E 61-0307 carries the 434 Air Refueling Wing stripe in red of the 74th Air Refueling Squadron. 72nd Air Refueling Squadron Aircraft wear a blue stripe. (Randy Walker)

KC-135A 58-0013 photographed at Carswell AFB on April 12, 1985 wears the blue and white AFRES tail stripe of the 72nd Air Refueling Squadron. (Brian C. Rogers)

KC-135E 58-0013, of the 72nd Air Refueling Squadron, was photographed at Forbes Field Kansas during October, 1990. (Jerry Geer)

KC-135R 60-0322, of the 72nd Air Refueling Squadron was photographed at Nellis AFB during September, 1995. (Alan Winzerling)

KC-135R 58-0015, of the 74th Air Refueling Squadron was photographed at Dyess AFB on November 14, 1995. (Alan Winzerling)

KC-135R 61-0272, in "Shamu" paint was photographed on August 7, 1994, wearing the blue stripe of the 74th Air Refueling Squadron. (Brian C. Rogers)

452 AIR MOBILITY WING
MARCH AIR FORCE BASE, CALIFORNIA

The 336th Air Refueling Squadron, 452nd Air Mobility Wing, AFRES is based at March Air Force Base, 9 miles southeast of Riverside, California. The 452nd operated KC-135s since beginning conversion from C-130B during January, 1976. During 1985 the 452nd traded its KC-135As for KC-135Es. In 1996 the unit transitioned to KC-135Rs.

BELOW: This KC-135A 58-0052 was photographed at March AFB, California in May 1983. This aircraft has since been modified to a KC-135E, and then to a KC-135R, all the while being assigned to March AFB. (Don Logan Collection)

KC-135E 57-2598, in 366th Air Refueling Squadron markings, was photographed June, 1987. (Don Logan Collection)

KC-135E 57-1512, "KUKAI MARU" photographed on August 6, 1989, later served in Desert Storm. (Pat Martin)

ABOVE: KC-135E 57-2598, photographed in October 1995 at March, and painted in AMC gray is still assigned to the 452nd Air Mobility Wing (AMW). (Roger Messick)

RIGHT: As seen here on the ruddervators of a 452nd AMW KC-135, the markings left no doubt to the pilots in the receiver aircraft the unit which had just refueled them. (Roger Messick)

507 AIR REFUELING WING
TINKER AIR FORCE BASE, OKLAHOMA

The 465th Air Refueling Squadron, 507th Air Refueling Wing, AFRES is based at Tinker Air Force Base in Oklahoma City, Oklahoma. The 465th Fighter Squadron received KC-135Rs and was redesignated as the 465th Air Refueling Squadron on April 1, 1994. Prior to operating KC-135Rs, the unit had been a Fighter unit for 20 years. In those 20 years the 465th operated the F-105D, F-4C, and F-16A/B aircraft.

The KC-135Rs of the 507th wear the unofficial 507th insignia of an Indian shield with OKIES below. (Jerry Geer)

BELOW: KC-135R 63-8880, photographed at Tinker AFB on December 1, 1994, was one of the 507th's first KC-135s. (Don Logan)

KC-135R 58-0079, photographed on December 1, 1994, in AMC gray paint had recently arrived at Tinker AFB, and had not yet had the AFRES insignia added to the nose. (Don Logan)

916 AIR REFUELING WING SEYMOUR-JOHNSON AIR FORCE BASE, NORTH CAROLINA

The 77th Air Refueling Squadron, 916th Air Refueling Wing, AFRES is based at Seymour Johnson, operates KC-135Rs. The unit changed from KC-10As to KC-135Rs starting in October, 1995.

RIGHT: KC-135R 62-3556 was one of the first KC-135Rs assigned to the 916th Air Refueling Wing. (Jerry Geer)

BELOW: KC-135R 62-3556 was assigned to the 916th ARW following the change over of the 916th from KC-10As to KC-135Rs. (Jerry Geer)

927 AIR REFUELING WING SELFRIDGE AIR NATIONAL GUARD BASE, MICHIGAN

The 63rd Air Refueling Squadron, 927th Air Refueling Wing, AFRES is based at Selfridge Air National Guard Base at Mt. Clemens, Michigan. The 927th operated KC-135Es since beginning conversion from C-130Es in August, 1992. During the summer 1993, the 63rd received additional KC-135Es from the 72nd ARS at Grissom AFB.

BELOW LEFT: The 63rd Air Refueling Squadron carries a purple tail stripe. (Brian C. Rogers)

BELOW: KC-135E 61-0270 the "Spirit Of Selfridge", photographed on August 2, 1996, carries a map of Michigan on its nose. (Brian C. Rogers)

KC-135E 59-1447 of the 63rd Air Refueling Squadron, 927th Air Refueling Wing was photographed at Selfridge on August 2, 1996. (Brian C. Rogers)

KC-135E 59-1477, photographed in July 1994, is seen here on takeoff. (Ben Knowles)

940 AIR REFUELING WING
McCLELLAN AIR FORCE BASE, CALIFORNIA

The 314th Air Refueling Squadron, 940th Air Refueling Wing, AFRES, is based at McClellan Air Force Base, in Sacramento California. The 940th operated KC-135As since beginning conversion from C-130Bs during 1976. At the same time, during 1976, the unit moved from McClellan AFB to Mather AFB. While at Mather the 940th replaced its KC-135As with KC-135Es. In July, 1993 the unit moved back to McClellan in preparation for the closing of Mather AFB.

BELOW: KC-135A 58-0053 of the 341th Air Refueling Squadron is seen here is aluminum paint on July 7, 1984. (Brian C. Rogers)

KC-135A 58-0096 is seen here is gloss gray at Castle AFB on July 7, 1984.

KC-135E 58-0064 in gloss gray was photographed at Luke AFB on June 10, 1988. (Douglas Sloviak Vortex Photographics)

KC-135E 58-0096 in "Shamu" paint was photographed in June of 1993. (David F. Brown)

KC-135E 61-0268 in AMC gray was photographed at March AFB in August 1993. (Roger Messick)

AIR NATIONAL GUARD TANKER BASES

ALABAMA AIR NATIONAL GUARD
BIRMINGHAM INTERNATIONAL AIRPORT

The 106th Air Refueling Squadron, 117th Air Refueling Wing, Alabama Air National Guard is based at Birmingham International Airport, Birminghan, Alabama. The 117th Tactical Reconnaissance Wing received KC-135Rs and was redesignated as the 117th Air Refueling Wing on October 1, 1994. Prior to operating KC-135Rs, the unit had been equipped with RF-4Cs, for over 23 years, since February, 1971. The RF-4Cs had replaced RF-84Fs which the 177th had operated since May of 1957.

LEFT: KC-135R 58-0106, "The Spirit Of Birmingham" is the flagship of the 117th Air Refueling Wing. (Don Logan)

BELOW: KC-135R 58-0106 was photographed at Birmingham International Airport on August 14, 1995. (Don Logan)

KC-135R 57-1453 also photographed on August 14, 1995, was the 117th only "Shamu" tanker. (Don Logan)

ALASKA AIR NATIONAL GUARD
EIELSON AIR FORCE BASE, FAIRBANKS

The 168th Air Refueling Squadron, 168th Air Refueling Group, Alaska Air National Guard is based at Eielson Air Force Base, near Fairbanks, Alaska. In October, 1986, the 168th received four KC-135Es. By July 1990, with the receipt of all four of the TF33-P-102 re-engined KC-135Ds, the unit doubled its number of aircraft to eight. The unit operated these eight aircraft until they were replaced with KC-135Rs during mid 1995.

LEFT: KC-135R 59-1521 was one of the KC-135Rs the 168th received during 1995. (Alan Winzerling)

BELOW: KC-135E 57-1448 of the 168th Air Refueling Squadron, 176th Composite Wing was photographed on January 31, 1987. (Don McGary)

KC-135E 62-3566 was photographed at Phoenix Sky-Harbor airport on April 14, 1994. (Douglas Sloviak Vortex Photographics)

ARIZONA AIR NATIONAL GUARD
SKY-HARBOR INTERNATIONAL AIRPORT, PHOENIX, ARIZONA

The 197th Air Refueling Squadron, 161st Air Refueling Wing, Arizona Air National Guard is based at Sky-Harbor International Airport, Phoenix, Arizona. The Unit has operated KC-135s since converting from Boeing KC-97Ls to KC-135As in October of 1977. The unit was the first to convert to re-engined KC-135E tankers, receiving their first KC-135E (57-1496) on July 28, 1982. The unit operated two of the KC-135Ds for a short period of time during late summer and early fall of 1995.

KC-135A 57-1433, in aluminum paint, was photographed on September 8, 1979. (Brian C. Rogers)

KC-135E 55-3143, in gloss gray, was photographed on June 5, 1983. The 161st Air Refueling Wing was the first unit to be equipped with KC-135Es. (Douglas Sloviak Vortex Photographics)

KC-135E 61-0281, in "Shamu" was photographed on April 10, 1991. (Douglas Sloviak Vortex Photographics)

KC-135E 55-3143, with the emblem of the Arizona Rattlers on the nose, was photographed on January 9, 1994. (Douglas Sloviak)

KC-135E 57-1426 is seen here with the new tail stripe added in mid 1995. (Douglas Sloviak Vortex Photographics)

KC-135E 57-3143 wears the emblem of the Arizona Rattlers Indoor (Arena) Football Team. (Douglas Sloviak Vortex Photographics)

KC-135E 57-1475 wears the emblem of the Phoenix Cardinals Football Team. (Don Logan)

KC-135E 61-0281 wears the emblem of the Phoenix Suns Basketball Team. (Don Logan)

ARKANSAS AIR NATIONAL GUARD
LITTLE ROCK AIR FORCE BASE

The 154th Air Refueling Squadron, 189th Air Refueling Group, Arkansas Air National Guard was based at Little Rock Air Force Base, near Little Rock, Arkansas. On January 1, 1976, the 154th gave up its RF-101s and received KC-135As. During 1984, the unit exchanged the KC-135As for re-engined KC-135Es. On October 1, 1986, the 154th was redesignated as a Tactical Airlift Squadron when the 154th squadron gave up its tankers and received Lockheed C-130Es.

KC-135A 57-1426 was photographed on October 13, 1980. (Don McGary)

KC-135A 57-1465 of the 154th Air Refueling Squadron, 189th Air Refueling Group was photographed on April 27, 1978. (Brian C. Rogers)

KC-135A 57-1448, in gloss gray, was photographed at Phoenix on July 10, 1983. (Douglas Sloviak Vortex Photographics)

CALIFORNIA AIR NATIONAL GUARD
MARCH AIR FORCE BASE, RIVERSIDE

The 196th Air Refueling Squadron, 163rd Air Refueling Wing, California Air National Guard is based at March Air Force Base, 9 miles southeast of Riverside, California, along with KC-135Es of the U. S. Air Force Reserve's 452nd Air Mobility Wing. The 163rd Tactical Reconnaissance Group received KC-135Es and was designated as the 163rd Air Refueling Wing on October 1, 1993. The unit operated one of the KC-135Ds for a short period of time during late summer and early fall of 1995. The unit transitioned to KC-135Rs during late 1996 and early 1997. Prior to operating KC-135Es, at March AFB, the unit had been equipped with RF-4Cs.

RIGHT: A version of this tail stripe was also carried on other 196th Squadron aircraft such as the F-102, O-2, and RF-4C. (Douglas Sloviak Vortex Photographics)

KC-135E 57-1428 when photographed on September 17, 1994 was carrying a drogue basket on the boom. (Brian C. Rogers)

KC-135R 59-1505 was one of the 163rd ARWs first KC-135E to KC-135R conversions. (Roger Messick)

KC-135E 57-1459, in AMC gray, was photographed at NAS Pt Mugu on September 23, 1995. (Craig Kaston)

HAWAII AIR NATIONAL GUARD
HICKAM AIR FORCE BASE, HONOLULU

The 203rd Air Refueling Squadron, 154th Wing, Hawaii Air National Guard is based at Hickam Air Force Base, Honolulu, Hawaii. The 203rd Air Refueling Squadron was activated on January 16, 1993, equipped with KC-135Rs as part of the 154th Operations Group. The 199th Fighter Squadron, flying F-15s, is also a member of the 154th Wing.

KC-135R 62-3514, photographed in July, 1994, lifts off at McConnell AFB. (Conrad Youngblum)

KC-135R 61-0290 of the 154th Wing, Hawaiian Air National Guard was photographed at Phoenix on February, 1994. (Douglas Sloviak Vortex Photographics)

ILLINOIS AIR NATIONAL GUARD
O'HARE INTERNATIONAL AIRPORT, CHICAGO

The 108th Air Refueling Squadron, 126th Air Refueling Wing, Illinois Air National Guard is based at O'Hare International Airport, Chicago, Illinois. The Unit has operated KC-135s since converting from Boeing KC-97Ls to KC-135As in December of 1976. The unit converted to KC-135Es, receiving their re-engined aircraft during 1983.

RIGHT: KC-135A 58-0031 of the 108th Air Refueling Squadron, 126th Air Refueling Wing was photographed at Offutt AFB on July 12, 1981. (Don McGary)

KC-135A 58-0020 of the 108th Air Refueling Squadron, 126th Air Refueling Wing was photographed on September 28, 1978. (Brian C. Rogers)

KC-135E 58-0003 of the Illinois Air National Guard, photographed on May 13, 1993, carried a large sunburst on its tail only for a short time. (Norris Graser)

KC-135E 57-1441 carried the yellow Illinois tail stripe. (Douglas Sloviak Vortex Photographics)

KC-135E 59-1487 photographed in September, 1995 carried the white tail stripe presently used by the Illinois ANG. (Jerry Geer)

KC-135E 58-0057, photographed on August 7, 1993, carries the emblem of the Chicago Cubs Baseball Team. (Norris Graser)

KC-135E 59-1487, photographed on August 7, 1993, carried the emblem of the Chicago Bears Football Team and Desert Storm Markings. (Norris Graser)

KANSAS AIR NATIONAL GUARD
FORBES FIELD, TOPEKA

The 117th Air Refueling Squadron, 190th Air Refueling Wing, Kansas Air National Guard is based at Forbes Field, Topeka, Kansas. The 190th Defense Systems Evaluation Group traded its EB-57Bs for KC-135As and was redesignated as the 190th Air Refueling Group on July 8, 1978. The unit received KC-135Es during 1984. Prior to operating KC-135s, the unit had been equipped with various models of the Martin B-57 for over 30 years. The 190th ARW now operates all four of the USAF's KC-135Ds.

BELOW: KC-135A 56-3641 of the 117th Air Refueling Squadron, 190th Air Refueling Group, Kansas Air National Guard was photographed on February 1, 1981. (Brian C. Rogers)

The Kansas Air National Guard's 190th Air Refueling Group (ARG) operated both KC-135As and KC-135Es. (Jerry Geer)

KC-135E 57-1482 of the 190th ARG was photographed in April 1987, taxiing at its home base Forbes Field. (Jerry Geer)

KC-135E 56-3658, in "Shamu" paint was photographed at Forbes Field on July 16, 1993. (Don Logan)

KC-135E 57-1482 is seen here at Forbes Field, photographed in August, 1984. 57-1482, like other Kansas ANG KC-135s carries nose art. (Jerry Geer)

KC-135D, 63-8059, was painted with the "Minuteman Jack" tail in June of 1997. The markings were only on the tail ashort time and were removed by the end of summer 1997. (Jerry Geer)

KC-135E 56-3626 of the 117th Air Refueling Squadron, 190th Air Refueling Group photographed in August, 1994. (Jerry Geer)

KC-135E 56-3641 of the 117th Air Refueling Squadron, 190th Air Refueling Group photographed in May, 1993. (Jerry Geer)

KC-135E 57-1460 of the 117th Air Refueling Squadron, 190th Air Refueling Group photographed in August, 1994. (Jerry Geer)

KC-135E 57-1460 of the 117th Air Refueling Squadron, 190th Air Refueling Group photographed in April, 1992. (Jerry Geer)

KC-135E 57-1429 of the 117th Air Refueling Squadron, 190th Air Refueling Group photographed in August, 1994. (Jerry Geer)

KC-135E 57-1463 of the 117th Air Refueling Squadron, 190th Air Refueling Group photographed in August, 1994. (Jerry Geer)

KC-135E 57-1463 of the 117th Air Refueling Squadron, 190th Air Refueling Group photographed in August, 1994. (Jerry Geer)

KC-135E 57-1482 of the 117th Air Refueling Squadron, 190th Air Refueling Group photographed in August, 1994. (Jerry Geer)

MAINE AIR NATIONAL GUARD BANGOR INTERNATIONAL AIRPORT

The 132nd Air Refueling Squadron, 101st Air Refueling Wing, Maine Air National Guard is based at Bangor International Airport, Bangor, Maine. The 101st Fighter Interceptor Group ended 29 years of flying fighters when they traded their F-101Bs for KC-135As and were redesignated as the 101st Air Refueling Group on April 1, 1976. With the receipt of the KC-135s, the "Maine Bangors" as they were called changed their nickname to the "Maineiacs." The unit received KC-135Es during 1985.

KC-135E 57-1505, in AMC gray, was photographed on October 1, 1996. (Jerry Geer)

KC-135E 56-3640, Maine Air National Guard, was photographed on September 26, 1988 during a visit to Carswell AFB, Texas. (Brian C. Rogers)

KC-135E 57-1450, of the Maine Air National Guard, in "Shamu" paint was photographed at Forbes Field, Kansas in July, 1989. (Jerry Geer)

KC-135A 57-1443 of the 132nd Air Refueling Squadron, 101st Air Refueling Wing, was photographed at Phoenix on December 8, 1983. (Brian C. Rogers)

MISSISSIPPI AIR NATIONAL GUARD KEY FIELD, MERIDIAN

The 153th Air Refueling Squadron, 186th Air Refueling Wing, Mississippi Air National Guard is based at Key Field, Meridian, Mississippi. The 186th Tactical Reconnaissance Group, after receiving its first two KC-135Rs, was redesignated as the 186th Air Refueling Group on April 1, 1992.

ABOVE: This sign, attached to the safety rail in the cargo door opening of the 186th Air Refueling Wing tankers, welcomes passengers on board. (Don Logan)

BELOW: KC-135R 57-1418, photographed on August 15, 1995, in AMC gray, seen parked at the 186th ARW's new facility at Key Field, Meridian, Mississippi. (Don Logan)

KC-135R 59-1455, photographed on August 15, 1995, was the 186th ARWs only "Shamu" painted KC-135R. (Don Logan)

NEBRASKA AIR NATIONAL GUARD LINCOLN MUNICIPAL AIRPORT

The 173rd Air Refueling Squadron, 155th Air Refueling Wing, Nebraska Air National Guard is based at Lincoln Municipal Airport, Lincoln, Nebraska. The 155th Tactical Reconnaissance Group received KC-135Rs and was redesignated as the 155th Air Refueling Group on January 1, 1994. Prior to operating KC-135Rs, the unit had been equipped with RF-4Cs for over 22 years. The RF-4Cs had replaced RF-84Fs which the 155th had operated since May, 1964.

KC-135R 63-8015 photographed on June 12, 1994, was one of the 155th ARWs KC-135s. (Don Logan)

KC-135R 59-1461 was photographed in July, 1995. The 155th transitioned to KC-135Rs after flying reconnaissance fighters for over 30 years. (Jerry Geer)

NEW HAMPSHIRE AIR NATIONAL GUARD
PEASE AIR NATIONAL GUARD BASE, PORTSMOUTH

The 133rd Air Refueling Squadron, 157th Air Refueling Wing, New Hampshire Air National Guard is based at Pease Air National Guard Base, Portsmouth, New Hampshire. The Unit has operated KC-135s since converting from Lockheed C-130As to KC-135As in the summer of 1975. The unit then converted to KC-135Es, receiving their re-engined tankers during 1984. During 1994, the 157th exchanged their KC-135Es for KC-135Rs.

KC-135A 56-3645 was photographed on September 23, 1981, in aluminum paint. (Brian C. Rogers)

KC-135A 58-0068 with "The Albatross" on the crew entry door of the 157th Air Refueling Wing New Hampshire Air National Guard was photographed in August, 1981. (James Goodall)

KC-135E 59-1499 was photographed in May, 1988. (Lionel Paul)

KC-135E 59-1450, in "Shamu" paint is seen in October, 1992 at Byrd Field, Richmond International Airport, returning from a mission refueling F-16Cs of the 149th Fighter Squadron, Virginia Air National Guard. (Don Logan)

KC-135R 62-3576 of the 133rd Air Refueling Squadron, 157th Air Refueling Wing was photographed on September 27, 1996. (Jerry Geer)

KC-135R 58-0092 of the 133rd Air Refueling Squadron, 157th Air Refueling Wing was photographed on September 27, 1996. The New Hampshire ANG like many other KC-135 units carries unit markings on their engine inlet covers. (Jerry Geer)

NEW JERSEY AIR NATIONAL GUARD McGUIRE AIR FORCE BASE, TRENTON

The 141st and 150th Air Refueling Squadrons, 108th Air Refueling Wing, New Jersey Air National Guard are based at McGuire Air Force Base, near Trenton, New Jersey. The 141st operated KC-135s since beginning conversion from McDonnell/Douglas F-4Es to KC-135Es in September, 1991.

The 150th Air Refueling Squadron, 170th Air Refueling Group has been operating KC-135s since early 1977, when the unit exchanged its C-7s for KC-135As. During 1983, the 150th converted to KC-135Es. On October 1, 1993, the 150th Air Refueling Squadron was reassigned from the 170th to the 108th Air Refueling Wing.

KC-135E 59-1456 of the 141st Air Refueling Squadron "Tigers" was painted with what was probably the largest nose art put on an U.S. Air Force aircraft. (Don Spering/AIR)

KC-135E 59-1456 had the nose art applied for the Battle of Britain Air Show held on September 15 through 19, 1995 at RAF Leuchars, Scotland. It was removed shortly after returning to New Jersey. (Don Spering/AIR)

KC-135E 58-0044, photographed in April 1992, "Prime Beef" was one of the 141st "Tigers" tankers. (Paul Hart)

KC-135E 59-1456 flew back to England for the Royal International Air Tatoo at RAF Fairford at the end of July 1997. The Tiger Tanker paint scheme had been improved with additional fuselage and tail markings. (Martin von Wartburg)

KC-135E 58-0111, photographed on March 12, 1992 unofficially wore NJ tail codes left over from their F-4Es for a short time. (Tom Kaminiski)

ABOVE RIGHT AND TWO BELOW: Throughout 1992 the 141st "Tigers" experimented with tail marking variations as seen here on KC-135Es 58-0111, 58-0044, and two versions on 55-3146. (Paul Hart)

KC-135E 59-1903, photographed on October 26, 1992, carries yet a different tail marking, a tiger head. (Tom Kaminiski)

KC-135E 59-1456 of the 150th Air Refueling Squadron, was photographed on April 8, 1994. (Brian C. Rogers)

KC-135A 58-0078 of the 150th Air Refueling Squadron, 170th Air Refueling Group, of the New Jersey Air National Guard was photographed in June 1981. (David F. Brown)

KC-135A 58-0078 was photographed in June, 1983. (Don Logan Collection)

KC-135E 58-0087 was photographed in November, 1983 at McGuire AFB, New Jersey. (David F. Brown)

KC-135E 58-0087 of the 170th Air Refueling Squadron, seen here in "Shamu" paint on December 10, 1991, carried "Jersey Girl" nose art. (Paul K. Withers)

NEW YORK AIR NATIONAL GUARD
NIAGARA FALLS INTERNATIONAL AIRPORT

The 136th Air Refueling Squadron, 107th Air Refueling Wing, New York Air National Guard is based at Niagara Falls International Airport, Niagara Falls, New York. The 136th Fighter Squadron received KC-135Rs and was redesignated as the 136th Air Refueling Squadron on July 1, 1994. Prior to operating KC-135Rs, the unit had been a Fighter unit for over 40 years. In those 40 years the 136th operated the F-51H, F-86H, F-94B, F-100C/F, F-101B/F, F-4C, and F-16A/B ADF aircraft.

KC-135R 64-14839, "Maid Of The Mist" is the 107th Air Refueling Wing's flagship aircraft, photographed here in October, 1995. (Jerry Geer)

KC-135R 63-7981 was painted in "Shamu" when photographed at Niagara Falls International Airport in October, 1995. (Jerry Geer)

KC-135R 60-0358 of the 136th Air Refueling Squadron, 107th Air Refueling Wing was photographed at Niagara Falls International Airport in October, 1995. (Jerry Geer)

OHIO AIR NATIONAL GUARD RICKENBACHER AIR NATIONAL GUARD BASE, COLUMBUS

The 145th and 166th Air Refueling Squadrons, 121st Air Refueling Wing, Ohio Air National Guard are based at Rickenbacher Air National Guard Base, near Columbus, Ohio. The 166th operated KC-135Rs since beginning conversion from LTV A-7D/Ks in January, 1993.

The 145th Air Refueling Squadron, 160th Air Refueling Group has been operating KC-135s since April, 1975 when the unit exchanged its Boeing KC-97Ls for KC-135As. During 1984 the 150th converted from KC-135As to KC-135Es, and in 1992 from KC-135Es to KC-135Rs. On October 1, 1993, the 145th Air Refueling Squadron was reassigned from the 160th ARG to the 121st Air Refueling Wing.

The 121st Air Refueling Wing carries an Ohio tail stripe, The stripe for the 145th Air Refueling Squadron is red, and the 166th Air Refueling Squadron tail stripe, seen here, is blue. (Brian C. Rogers)

KC-135A 5-3146, of the 145th Air Refueling Squadron, seen here in June 1982, carried the black stripe and "Ohio Air Guard" text which was a carry over from the units KC-97L markings. (James Goodall)

KC-135E 56-3611, of the 145th Air Refueling Squadron, was photographed on August 25, 1986. (Don McGary)

KC-135R 60-0341 when photographed in March, 1994 in the "Shamu" paint, carried the "Ohio" red stripe of the 145th Air Refueling Squadron. (Ben Knowles)

KC-135R 58-0083 of the 166th Air Refueling Squadron was photographed during a stopover at Langley AFB on February 14, 1994. (Brian C. Rogers)

KC-135R 63-7992 was photographed at McChord AFB on June 17, 1994. (Renato E. F. Jones)

KC-135R 59-1458 of the 166th Air Refueling Squadron, 121st Air Refueling Wing was photographed at Forbes Field, Kansas in June, 1996. (Jerry Geer)

PENNSYLVANIA AIR NATIONAL GUARD
PITTSBURGH INTERNATIONAL AIRPORT

The 146th and 147th Air Refueling Squadrons, 171st Air Refueling Wing, Pennsylvania Air National Guard are based at Pittsburgh International Airport, near Pittsburgh, Pennsylvania. The 146th Air Refueling Squadron as part of the 112th Air Refueling Group, operated KC-135Es since beginning conversion from LTV A-7D/Ks in the summer of 1991. On October 1, 1993, the 146th Air Refueling Squadron was reassigned from the 112th Air Refueling Group to the 171st Air Refueling Wing.

The 147th Air Refueling Squadron, 171st Air Refueling Wing, has been operating KC-135s since July 1977, when the unit exchanged its Boeing KC-97Ls for KC-135As. During 1983 the 147th converted from KC-135As to KC-135Es.

KC-135A 59-1499 of the 147th Air Refueling Squadron, 171st Air Refueling Wing, was photographed at Forbes Field during July, 1980. (Jerry Geer)

KC-135E 59-1479 of the 146th Air Refueling Squadron, 171st Air Refueling Wing, was photographed in June, 1994. As part of the 171st Air Refueling Wing, the 146th ARS has black tail stripes with yellow letters, while the 147th has a yellow stripe with black letters. (Jerry Geer)

KC-135E 58-0024 of the 146th Air Refueling Squadron is caught on approach during March, 1994. (Mike Grove)

KC-135E 59-1447 was photographed in May, 1996, at Forbes Field, Kansas. (Jerry Geer)

KC-135A 57-1509 of the 147th Air Refueling Squadron was photographed on February 20, 1982, in gloss gray. (Douglas Sloviak Vortex Photographics)

KC-135E 57-2607 was photographed at Tinker AFB during PDM (Programmed Depot Maintenance), in October, 1993. The desert storm markings are visible aft of the crew entry door. (Don Logan)

KC-135E 59-1484 of the 147th Air Refueling Squadron was photographed on September 11, 1993 at Pease AFB, New Hampshire. (Gilles Auliard)

KC-135E 59-1457 of the 147th Air Refueling Squadron was photographed on October 9, 1985. (Douglas Sloviak Vortex Photographics)

KC-135E 57-2595 in AMC gray is seen in this photograph taken in June, 1993. (David F. Brown)

TENNESSEE AIR NATIONAL GUARD
McGHEE TYSON AIRPORT, KNOXVILLE

The 151st Air Refueling Squadron, 134th Air Refueling Wing, Tennessee Air National Guard is based at McGhee Tyson Airport, near Knoxville, Tennessee. The unit has operated KC-135s since converting from Boeing KC-97Ls to KC-135As in summer of 1976. The unit converted to re-engined KC-135E tankers in 1982.

KC-135E 57-1485, of the 151st Air Refueling Squadron, waits with its boom extended, for the receiver aircraft to move into contact position. (Don Spering/AIR)

KC-135E 56-3607, of the 151st Air Refueling Squadron in aluminum paint, was photographed on March 26, 1983 shortly after receiving its TF-33 engines. (Brian C. Rogers)

KC-135E 56-3609 in "Shamu" paint was photographed at McGhee-Tyson Airport in Knoxville Tennessee on August 14, 1995. (Don Logan)

KC-135E 56-3643 of the 134th Air Refueling Wing at McGhee-Tyson Airport on August 14, 1995. (Don Logan)

KC-135E 59-1492 of the 134th Air Refueling Wing at McGhee-Tyson Airport on August 14, 1995. (Don Logan)

UTAH AIR NATIONAL GUARD
SALT LAKE CITY INTERNATIONAL AIRPORT

The 191st Air Refueling Squadron, 151st Air Refueling Wing, Utah Air National Guard is based at Salt Lake City International Airport, Salt Lake City, Utah. The unit has operated KC-135s since converting from Boeing KC-97Ls to KC-135As in April, 1978. The unit converted to re-engined KC-135E tankers in 1982.

ABOVE: KC-135E 57-1510 of the 191st Air Refueling Squadron, 151st Air Refueling Wing, Utah Air National Guard in "Shamu" paint scheme was photographed at Forbes Field, Kansas during September, 1989. (Jerry Geer)

LEFT: KC-135E 58-0006 photographed in October, 1988. (James Goodall)

BELOW: KC-135E 59-1489 of the 191st Air Refueling Squadron, 151st Air Refueling Wing, Utah Air National Guard was photographed at Forbes Field, Kansas during May, 1988. (Jerry Geer)

KC-135E 59-1489, of the 191st Air Refueling Squadron in AMC gray, was photographed in September, 1995. (Jerry Geer)

WASHINGTON AIR NATIONAL GUARD
FAIRCHILD AIR FORCE BASE, SPOKANE

The 116th Air Refueling Squadron, 141st Air Refueling Wing, Washington Air National Guard is based at Fairchild Air Force Base, near Spokane, Washington. The Unit has operated KC-135s since converting from F-101B/Fs to KC-135As in Summer of 1976. The unit began converting to re-engined KC-135E tankers in 1984, receiving their last E model in March of 1986.

KC-135A 58-0032 of 116th Air Refueling Squadron, 141st Air Refueling Wing was photographed at Phoenix on November 14, 1982. (Douglas Sloviak Vortex Photographics)

KC-135E 59-1445 of the 116th Air Refueling Squadron was photographed at Elmendorf AFB, Alaska, in June, 1989. (James Goodall)

KC-135E 57-1501 of the 116th Air Refueling Squadron was photographed during April, 1990, in "Shamu" paint scheme, at Forbes Field, Kansas. (Jerry Geer)

WISCONSIN AIR NATIONAL GUARD GENERAL MITCHELL INTERNATIONAL AIRPORT, MILWAUKEE

The 126th Air Refueling Squadron, 128st Air Refueling Wing, Wisconsin Air National Guard is based at General Mitchell International Airport, Milwaukee, Wisconsin. The Unit has operated KC-135s since converting from Boeing KC-97Ls to KC-135As starting in December, 1977. The unit began converting to re-engined KC-135E tankers in 1983. In 1992, the 126th Air Refueling Squadron converted to KC-135Rs.

KC-135A 58-0111 of 126th Air Refueling Squadron, 128th Air Refueling Wing is seen at General Mitchell International Airport in Milwaukee during June, 1982. (James Goodall)

KC-135A 57-2600 of the 126th Air Refueling Squadron was photographed at Offutt AFB on April 17, 1981. (Don McGary)

KC-135A 59-1485 of the Wisconsin ANG, was photographed, in gloss gray paint, on February 1, 1983, at Davis-Monthan AFB. (Brian C. Rogers)

KC-135R 58-0130 Taxis out for takeoff at General Mitchell International Airport on June 15, 1994. (Don Logan)

ABOVE: KC-135R 57-1470, seen here at Phoenix, burned on the ramp at General Mitchell International Airport on December 10, 1992. 1470 is the only KC-135R to have been lost to date. (Douglas Sloviak Vortex Photographics)

RIGHT: This nose art was carried by KC-135R 57-1470. (Norris Graser)

FOREIGN C-135s

C-135F/C-135FR

France became the first and only foreign government to order new C-135s when, in 1962, they ordered 12 of the tanker version of the C-135A from Boeing. The C-135F tankers, as they were designated differed from the USAF version. The French aircraft have a metal cargo floor (instead of the plywood floor of the KC-135), two air conditioning packs rather than one, and originally no upper deck fuel tank. The flying boom was the same high speed model as that used on the SAC tankers, and was normally fitted with the drogue system for refueling the probe equipped French fighters.

French C-135 Tanker Serial Numbers (12):

63-8470	63-12735
63-8471	63-12736
63-8472	63-12737
63-8473	63-12738
63-8474	63-12739
63-8475	63-12740

On July 1, 1972 the only French tanker (63-8473) to be lost crashed after take-off from an island air field in the South Pacific. The aircraft lost power on engine number three, and as the crew turned back to attempt a landing, power was lost on engine number four. The aircraft crashed a short time later, killing the crew of four.

The French government purchased twelve C-135F tankers. (Boeing)

The French tankers were all delivered with J-57 engines. (Joe Bruch Collection)

As a result of the favorable outcome of the USAF KC-135R re-engine program, which used the CFM56/F-108 turbofan engine manufactured by a U.S./French consortium of CFM International, the French government decided, in 1981, to re-engine their remaining eleven C-135Fs with the CFM56 engine. The re-engining was accomplished at Boeing's Wichita plant, on the same mod line performing the USAF KC-135 re-engining. The first CFM56 powered aircraft (63-12736), redesignated as the C-135FR, was delivered back to the Armee de l' Air in August of 1985.

Aircraft	Delivery Date
63-12736	August 1985
63-12735	September 1985
63-12739	November 1985
63-8471	February 1986
63-8470	August 1986
63-8474	October 1986
63-8475	January 1987
63-8472	September 1987
63-12740	November 1987
63-12738	January 1988
63-12737	April 1988

The French aircraft avionics differ from the USAF versions, with European manufactured flight director, air data computer, and dual INS systems.

The next major modification of the French tankers, once again accomplished by Boeing at Wichita, was the installation of wing tip refueling pods. In addition to the pod system, an upper deck tank was installed. This occurred during 1993 and 1994. With the original boom drogue system the tanker could only refuel one fighter at a time. Now, with two pods, the tanker could refuel two fighters, one on each wing. There is however, not enough clearance to allow the refueling of an aircraft on the boom while a fighter is refueling from one of the pod drogues.

Prototype installation and testing of the pod system was accomplished at Boeing's Wichita facility. Installation of the kits on the remaining ten French tankers was accomplished in France.

During the Pod modification the USAF temporarily loaned three KC-135R tankers to the French Air Force. During December, 1992, 57-1439, 62-3516, and 63-8033 were sent to France. When flight test of the pod installation was complete, C-135FR 63-12736, the prototype aircraft returned to France, and KC-135R 57-1439 returned to the USAF.

The French tankers are painted in a different scheme than U.S. Air Force tankers. (Boeing)

All 11 remaining C-135F tankers were re-engined into C-135FR between August, 1985 and April, 1988. (Boeing)

Boeing Manufactured installation kits and preformed flight testing for wing tip drogue air refueling pods manufactured by Flight Refueling Limited of England. (Boeing)

ABOVE: A F-100 from Flight Systems Incorporated was used by Boeing to test the pod refueling system. (Boeing)

RIGHT AND TWO BELOW: Three U.S. Air Force KC-135Rs were loaned to the French government, they were 57-1439, 62-3516, and 63-8033. (Randy Walker)

FUTURE FOREIGN TANKERS

The French government and Turkish government have purchased a total of 10 KC-135As from storage at AMARC and is having them converted to KC-135R configuration. In addition the Government of Singapore is purchasing four of the additional ten to twelve KC-135As at AMARC capable of being converted to KC-135Rs. Many KC-135E's may be available in the next few years which could be purchased by other foreign governments.

The Turkish government has contracted for seven aircraft, and the French have contracted for three. As with the French, the Turkish government has received KC-135R's on loan until their aircraft are delivered. USAF KC-135R 62-3512 and 62-3568 were loaned to the Turkish Air Force.

The deliveries of the first 10 (3 French and all 7 Turkish aircraft) commenced in June 2, 1997 with the delivery of 62-3525 to France.

TURKEY	FRANCE	SINGAPORE
57-2609	62-3497	59-1454
58-0110	62-3525	61-0325
60-0325	62-3574	63-8009
60-0326		63-8016
62-3539		
62-3563		
62-3567		

62-3512, one of the KC-135Rs loaned to Turkey, was photographed at RAF Mildenhall in July, 1996. (Ben Knowles Collection)

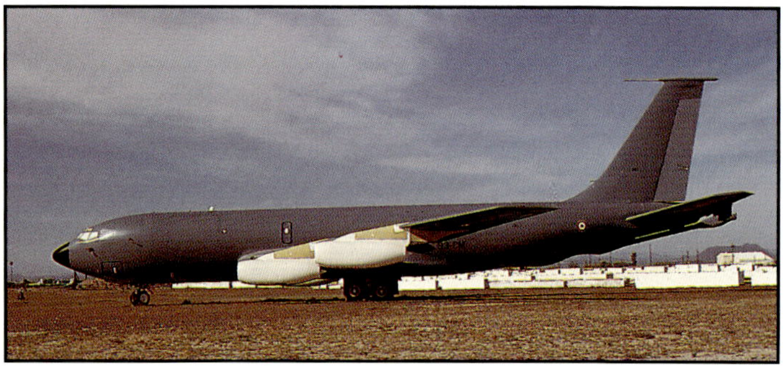

The KC-135As purchased by the foreign governments were removed from storage at AMARC and flown to Tinker AFB were they went through Programmed Depot Maintenance (PDM) and were repainted. They then went back to AMARC to await their turn to be reengined at Boeing's Wichita, Kansas facility. 62-3497, is seen here at AMARC, after returning from PDM at Tinker AFB. (Norris Graser)

This KC-135R, 58-0110, sits on the ramp at AMARC on September 27, 1997 awaiting final delivery to Turkey. (Kevin Patrick)

CHAPTER THREE

Reconnaissance Aircraft

The KC-135/C-135 family served as the basis for a number of reconnaissance aircraft which played significant roles in USAF intelligence gathering operations for over thirty years. Until taken over by ACC, all the RC-135s and their mission responsibilities (with the exception of the RC-135As which were operated by MATS/MAC) came under the control of SAC. Since transfer of the aircraft to ACC. In 1992 the operational control of the reconnaissance aircraft was transferred to the theater commanders.

RC-135s were primarily used for intelligence gathering missions while flying around the borders of the former Soviet Union and other potential aggressor nations. RC-135s have been used for Signal intelligence (SIGINT) gathering, Side-Looking Airborne Radar (SLAR) reconnaissance, and visual inspection/tracking of reentry vehicles from Soviet ballistic missile tests.

Signal intelligence (SIGINT) is the RC-135s primary means of intelligence collecting. Under SIGINT are additional sub classes of intelligence. Communications intelligence (COMINT) is the interception and processing of radio, TV, telephone, or other types of electromagnetic communications. Electronic intelligence (ELINT) is intelligence including frequencies, signal strength, and other specifications derived from noncommunication electromagnetic sources such as radars and electronic warfare equipment. Telemetry intelligence (TELINT) is the collection of intelligence from electromagnetic emissions associated with the testing and operational deployment of foreign aerospace systems, either military or civilian.

The size of the KC-135/C-135 allowed large amounts of interior equipment to be installed, with the cargo door allowing easy change and removal of the equipment. Much of the

This view of the Offutt AFB flightline in the late 1960s shows seven RC-135Cs. Two RB-47 are visible at the end of the line. (Joe Bruch Collection)

internal electronic equipment is carried forward in the cabin, while the crew positions are in the aft fuselage.

RC-135s may differ internally from others of the same model, as reconfigurations for specific mission requirements can easily be made.

All RC-135 assets presently are assigned to the 55th Wing at Offutt AFB, Nebraska. In order to support intelligence gathering world wide, there have been several forward bases used by the RC-135 fleet. These included: RAF Mildenhall in the United Kingdom, Hellenikon AB in Greece, and Kadena AB on Okinawa.

All current RC-135s are powered by TF33 turbofan engines. The addition of air refueling receiver receptacles gave the RC-135s greatly extended range and endurance. Antenna installations are extensive and varied. Many different types of aerials, fairings and radomes can be seen on RC-135s. One common modification is an extended thimble shaped nose radome, known as the hog nose, which encloses a larger nose radar.

RC-135s were active during the Vietnam War, U.S. military actions against Libya during 1986 and Operation DESERT STORM.

Re-engining of the RC-135V and Ws, using the F108(CFM56) got underway at Boeing's Product Support Division in Wichita, Kansas, with the production of two re-engining kits for the RC-135 occuring during 1997. The kits will be installed during 1998.

KC-135R RECONNAISSANCE AIRCRAFT

Four KC-135As were modified into KC-135R reconnaissance aircraft at various points in time. Not to be confused with the much later KC-135R re-engined tanker, the initial KC-135R model was the first KC-135 aircraft to be configured for reconnaissance duties. Some features seen on later RC-135s, such as the hog nose radome and the rear fuselage teardrop radome, were first installed on KC-135Rs. Only 58-0126 had the hog nose radome installed. These aircraft were unofficially called RC-135Rs.

Aircraft 55-3121 became a KC-135R in 1971, Aircraft 59-1514 was converted into a KC-135R in 1963, while 58-0126 became a KC-135R in 1970. 59-1465 was converted by 1964 into a reconnaissance KC-135A, and redesignated as a KC-135R in June 1967.

A wingtip integral probe was installed on the left wingtip and a fence like antenna was installed along the top fuselage centerline. Two thin antennas were placed in the fuselage mid section along the top centerline, and a large flat sided, tear drop shaped antenna was located forward of the horizontal stabilizer on the left fuselage. The KC-135Rs had four small camera ports on the left side of the fuselage aft of the cargo door. All four aircraft were powered by J-57 engines and had air refueling receiver receptacles installed.

59-1465, on July 19, 1967, crashed while taking off from Offutt AFB for an air crew training mission.

With the advent of more sophisticated RC-135s, the three remaining KC-135Rs were phased out of service. 55-3121 was converted to the sole RC-135T and lost as result of a crash on February 25, 1985. 58-0126 and 59-1514 were converted back to KC-135A tankers, 1514 in 1973 and 0126 in 1976. 59-1514 in 1981 became the prototype KC-135E and was later assigned to the 55th Wing at Offutt as an aircrew proficiency trainer.

KC-135R Reconnaissance Serial Numbers (4):

55-3121	59-1465
58-0126	59-1514

This photograph of 55-3121 shows the antenna fence and the first set of four camera windows on the right side of the forward fuselage. (Boeing)

In This photograph of 55-3121, taken on March 26, 1981, a set of three more camera windows can be seen on the forward fuselage over the "U.S." (Don McGary)

RC-135A PACER SWAN

Among the last C-135s built (and the last to be delivered) were four J-57 powered aircraft modified for photographic reconnaissance under the designation RC-135As (Boeing Model 739-700). Nine aircraft had originally been ordered to replace 16 RB-50s assigned to unclassified aerial mapping and geodetic survey duties. The five RC-135As assigned serial numbers 63-8062 through 63-8066 were never built.

The four RC-135As were delivered to MATS in 1965-1966. A camera compartment replaced the normally installed forward body fuel tank. Two 30-inch diameter by 25-inch thick optically ground camera windows were mounted in the bottom of the camera compartment. An external, track-mounted door slid aft to expose the camera windows. The RC-135As were originally used by MATS/MAC for photographic and geodetic surveying work, and were assigned to the 1370th Photo Mapping Wing, Air Photographic and Cartographic Service (APCS), MATS, Turner AFB, Georgia in September of 1965, and moved to Forbes AFB, Kansas, in August 1967.

63-8058, the first of the RC-135As, was assigned to the 1st Air Cartographic and Geodetic Squadron (ACGS) at Forbes Air Force Base, Kansas when this photograph was taken in October, 1971. (Tom Brewer Collection)

The entire group was converted to the tanker configuration during the late 1970s and redesignated KC-135Ds.

RC-135A Serial Numbers (4):

63-8058	63-8060
63-8059	63-8061

63-8062 thru 63-8066 were cancelled.

BELOW: 63-8059 in seen here on June 5, 1969, in Military Airlift Command markings during a stopover at Andrews AFB. The modified boom pod area is clearly visible in this photograph. (Tom Brewer Collection)

RC-135A 63-8058, in SAC markings, was photographed on April 7, 1976. (Don McGary)

RC-135B/C

The RC-135B was the first C-135 specifically built by Boeing for use as a reconnaissance platform and was powered by TF33-P-9 turbofan engines. The aircraft had air refueling receiver receptacles during manufacture. Ten were produced during 1964-1965 with the Boeing designation Model 739-445B. The RC-135B was the last of the C-135 series off the production line and became the basis for numerous future ELINT conversions.

The ten aircraft were delivered directly from Boeing to the Glenn L. Martin Co. in Baltimore, Maryland, where they were placed in long-term storage. Equipment was installed under the BIG TEAM conversion program. Following this modification the aircraft were redesignated as RC-135Cs, with the first, 63-9792, delivered to the 55th SRW at Offutt AFB on January 27, 1967.

All ten RC-135Cs were operated by the 55th Strategic Reconnaissance Wing (SAC), Offutt AFB, Nebraska, replacing the Wing's RB-47Hs.

The boom operator's compartment was converted into a camera compartment. TF33 engines powered the RC-135Cs. Large cheeks containing various antennas were installed on the forward fuselage of these airplanes, Two additional HF probe antennas were installed, one on each wingtip. The HF probes on the wingtips were identical to the probe on the vertical fin. A fuel dump tube was installed in place of the refueling boom.

Two of these 10 aircraft are now RC-135Us, and the other eight are RC-135Vs.

RC-135B/C Serial Numbers (10):

63-9792	64-14845
64-14841	64-14846
64-14842	64-14847
64-14843	64-14848
64-14844	64-14849

A RC-135C photographed on takeoff, the radome behind the nose gear and tear drop antenna below the flight deck are clearly visible. (Boeing)

RC-135C 64-14844 carries no unit markings, only the serial number and standard U. S. Air Force national markings were on the aircraft when photographed. (Joe Bruch Collection)

RC-135D RIVET BRASS

Three KC-135As became RC-135Ds during 1966 and 1967. The Rivet Brass RC-135Ds had a number of antennas fitted in cylinder-shaped fairings on both sides of the forward fuselage, beginning at the wing roots (a similar configuration was tested on NKC-135A (55-3132). The RC-135Ds were also modified with hog nose radomes and were air refueling receiver capable, being modified with the LTV (E-System) receiver system.

One RC-135D (60-0362) modified as Rivet Brass 3 was equipped with a prototype phased array Multi-Beam Antenna System (MBAS) located under the fuselage forward of the wing.

RC-135Ds participated in the Vietnam conflict, occasionally flying Combat Apple missions.

The RC-135Ds were converted to KC-135As by E-Systems with the conversion of 60-0357 and 60-0362 being accomplished in 1976 and conversion of 60-0356 in 1978. They retained their air refueling receiver receptacles. All three were later converted to KC-135Rs.

RC-135D Serial Numbers (3):

60-0356 60-0362
60-0357

The cylindrical antenna fairings forward of the wing root are clearly visible in this photo of 60-0362. (Joe Bruch Collection)

As seen in this photograph of 60-0362, the cylindrical fairings have been removed and a large antenna fairing has been added to the bottom of the fuselage behind the nose gear. (Joe Bruch Collection)

RC-135E RIVET AMBER/LISA ANN

One of the most unusual RC-135 variants, the RC-135E was a conversion of a C-135B (62-4137). It had a major portion of the forward fuselage structure removed and replaced by a unique fiberglass radome housing a Hughes SLAR antenna. Cameras were installed to allow photography of missile reentry vehicles, and an external pod was mounted under each wing. One pod contained a heat exchanger and the other an electrical power generator, both needed for operation of the SLAR.

Used by the 6th SW, the Lisa Ann, as the RC-135E was code named, was lost on June 5, 1969 during a flight over the Bering Strait. The crash was believed to be caused by the failure of the radome structure. No trace of the aircraft or crew of 19 was ever found.

RC-135E Serial Number (1):

62-4137

This takeoff photograph of the RC-135E (62-4137) shows the large radome built in to the right side of the forward fuselage. The right hand pod is barely visible under the right wing next to the fuselage. (Boeing)

This view of the left side of 62-4137 shows the left hand pod under the wing. (Tom Brewer Collection)

RC-135M RIVET CARD

Six C-135Bs were converted to RC-135Ms during 1967-1968. These aircraft were powered by TF33-P-5 turbofan engines with thrust reversers, and were air refueling receiver capable, being modified with the LTV (E-System) receiver system. The aircraft were used to collect SIGINT. As part of the modification they received hog nose radomes and tear-drop shaped rear fuselage fairings. Antenna arrays were installed in the faired-over boom position. Originally assigned to the 82nd SRS and deployed to the 4252nd SW, the RC-135Ms saw extensive use during the Vietnam War, flying Combat Apple ELINT missions out of Kadena AB, Okinawa. The RC-135Ms were later used by the 55th SRW, flying out of Offutt AFB and deploying to world wide locations such as RAF Mildenhall. These aircraft were extensively rebuilt under the BIG SAFARI program during the early 1980s and re-designated as Rivet Joint RC-135Ws.

RC-135M Serial Numbers (6):

62-4131	62-4135
62-4132	62-4138
62-4134	62-4139

RC-135M 62-4135 in aluminum paint was photographed on the runway slowing down with thrust reversers deployed. (Joe Bruch Collection)

RC-135M 62-4132, photographed at Offutt AFB on June 30, 1981, highlights the left side tear drop shaped antenna located on the tail. (Don McGary)

RC-135M 62-4131 was photographed at Offutt AFB on December 20, 1978. (Don McGary)

RC-135S RIVET BALL/COBRA BALL

Used by the 6th SW, the first RC-135S was a conversion of KC-135A 59-1491 to the Telemetry Intelligence (TELINT) role to gather information on Soviet missile tests. The first RC-135S was lost on January 13, 1969 on landing when it failed to stop and ran off the runway at Shemya AFB. Shemya AFB is located in Alaska at the western end of the Aleutian Islands. In order to replace 59-1491, two C-135Bs (61-2663 and 2664) were modified to RC-135S configuration under BIG SAFARI during 1969. After the crash of 61-2664 at Shemya on March 15, 1981, another C-135B, 61-2662, was modified by E-Systems and delivered to the 6th SW at Eielson AFB on November 2, 1983.

The RC-135Ss were developed from C-135Bs. The airplanes have hog noses, and were air refueling receiver capable, being modified with the LTV (E-System) receiver system. An integral probe antenna was installed at each wingtip. In addition to the two flat-sided aft fuselage antennas carried by the RC-135Ms, two similar antennas are mounted between the base of the vertical stabilizer and the other flat-sided antennas. One probe antenna is mounted to the lower part of the main cargo door. Three similar probe antennas are mounted on the right side of the fuselage forward of the wing. Prior to 1972, both airplanes had a small round window located between the upper and middle HF probe antenna on the right side of the fuselage. The middle antenna was installed with the aft end higher, apparently for aerodynamic reasons.

59-1491, the WANDA BELLE RC-135S was operated out of Shemya during the same time period as the RC-135Ds, it was mistakenly assumed to be a fourth RC-135D.

In 1972, airplane 61-2664 had been modified to have the middle HF probe antenna installed parallel to the other two antennas. The single round window was replaced by three large round windows. Subsequently, airplane 61-2663 was modified in a similar manner. In addition, a large rectangular sliding door was installed over the forward large window on the right side of the fuselage. When the sliding door was installed, the upper HF probe antenna was deleted. The 1972 modifications resulted in the upper right wing and the inboard surfaces of the number 3 and 4 engine struts and pods being painted black for anti-glare purposes.

In 1997 the sole RC-135X, 62-4128, was modified to RC-135S configuration.

The RC-135S aircraft were operated by the 24th Strategic Reconnaissance Squadron, SAC, Eielson AFB, Alaska with a detachment at Shemya AB, in the Aleutian Islands.

RC-135S Serial Numbers (5):

59-1491	61-2664
61-2662	61-4128
61-2663	

This boom pod view of RC-135S 61-2663 shows the black paint on the right wing. This paint cuts prevents sun light from being reflected into the camera lenses. (Alan Winzerling)

59-1491 was the first RC-135S and was operated out of Shemya AFB as a "RIVET BALL" aircraft. It crashed at Shemya AFB, January 13, 1969. There were no fatalities in this mishap. (Tom Brewer Collection)

RC-135S 61-2663 is pictured here on the ramp at Offutt AFB in April, 1982. (George Cockle)

RC-135S 61-2663 of the 45th Reconnaissance Squadron, 55th Strategic Reconnaissance Wing, wearing the wing's OF tail code was photographed at Langley AFB on March 30, 1994. (Brian C. Rogers)

This view of RC-135S 61-2662, photographed at Offutt AFB in May, 1993, shows the black right wing and the camera windows on the right forward fuselage. (Joe Bruch)

RC-135T

As a result of the crash of KC-135R (Reconnaissance) 59-1465 on a training flight, the need of an aircraft dedicated for use as a RC air crew training aircraft was recognized.

In July 1973 another KC-135R (Reconnaissance) 55-3121 was modified into a trainer, with the air refueling receiver receptacle being retained. The RC-135T was used to provide initial and recurring air crew training eliminating the need to use one of the expensive and much in demand reconnaissance airframes for routine training missions. For a short time the aircraft was unofficially referred to as a KC-135T.

During January, 1982, 55-3121 was re-engined with TF33-PW-102 airline engines at Boeing, Wichita as part of the KC-135E re-engine program. The RC-135T crashed near Valdez, Alaska on February 25, 1985, while on a training mission practicing instrument approaches.

RC-135T Serial Number (1):

55-3121

This left side view of RC-135T was photographed after reengining with TF33-PW-102 airliner engines. (George Cockle)

55-3121, the lone RC-135T, was 1 of 4 KC-135R (reconnaissance) models. In this photograph the forward set of camera windows are visible, with the second set further aft covered over. It crashed near Valdez, Alaska during a snowstorm on February 25, 1985. The 3 crew members were killed in the crash. (Joe Bruch Collection)

RC-135U COMBAT SENT

Three RC-135Cs became RC-135Us during 1971. Initially, the RC-135U conversion was minor, consisting of an extended tailcone. The aircraft retained its air refueling receiver capability.

RC-135Us were later modified with a number of new features, becoming the most radically modified type of RC-135 presently in service. A chin radome was added behind and below the standard nose radome, a second radome was added below the forward fuselage, two rabbit ear antennas were mounted above each cheek fairing installation and the boom position was faired over (in a more angular fashion than with similar installations on other RC-135s).

The RC-135Us flew Combat Sent missions during the later stages of the Vietnam War. One aircraft (63-9792) was reconfigured during 1976, becoming redesignated as an RC-135V. The two remaining aircraft are still in active service as RC-135Us.

RC-135U Serial Numbers (3):

63-9792	64-14849
64-14847	

RC-135U 64-14849, photographed from the boom pod of a KC-135A, approaching pre-contact position. (Boeing)

As seen here on 64-14849, in addition to the cheek fairing and the chin fairing, the RC-135Us also have a small round radome on the bottom of the aircraft aft of the nose gear. (Joe Bruch Collection)

RC-135U 64-14849 was photographed at Offutt AFB on November 3, 1979. (Don McGary)

RC-135U 64-14847, when photographed at Offutt AFB on May 24, 1981, was wearing temporary nose art of a crow on the left side. The crow is the mascot of electronic warfare system operators. (Don McGary)

This photo of RC-135U 64-14847 shows the individual antenna covers in the cheek fairing. (Don McGary)

RC-135U 64-14847 was wearing a sharkmouth when photographed on July 19, 1991 at Offutt AFB. (Brian C. Rogers)

RC-135V RIVET JOINT

As a result of a modification of seven RC-135C airframes and one RC-135U (63-9792), the RC-135V is currently the most numerous RC-135 variant in service. These aircraft generally perform SIGINT missions. The RC-135V was the first variant to incorporate both cheek antenna fairings and the hog nose radome. Additionally, there are four large blade antennas mounted under the center section of the fuselage with another three blade antennas mounted further back under the fuselage. Two long wire antennas are installed between the vertical fin and the fuselage. A retrofit introduced even more ventral antennas, similar to the RC-135W configuration.

The RC-135Vs have operated in the Mediterranean and Middle East regions flying out of Hellenikon AB, Greece. During Desert Shield/Desert Storm, the RC-135Vs flew missions from Riyadh, Saudi Arabia.

During most of Operation Desert Shield three USAF RC-135s were based at Riyadh in Saudi Arabia from the Strategic Air Command's 55th Strategic Reconnaissance Wing at Offutt AFB, Nebraska. Other RC-135s may have operated along the Turkey- Iraq border.

The RC-135 Rivet Joint aircraft allowed allied commanders to electronically watch the Iraqi air defenses in action. As an example, it was Rivet Joint produced information that showed that Iraqi air-defense radars would shut down as soon as they detected F-4G Wild Weasels switching on their systems, proving the effectiveness of the Weasel mission.

RC-135V Serial Numbers (8):

63-9792	64-14844
64-14841	64-14845
64-14842	64-14846
64-14843	64-14848

RC-135V 64-14845 is seen here in SAC markings. (Joe Bruch Collection)

RC-135V 63-9792, previously a RC-135U, was photographed on December 26, 1980 on the ramp at Offutt AFB. The overwing escape hatch has been removed and replaced with a heater hose attachment. The heater is used to keep the main cabin warm during operations in Alaska, or in Omaha, Nebraska during the cold winter. (Don McGary)

RC-135V 64-14844, photographed in April, 1993, is seen in ACC markings which include the OF tail code of the 55th Strategic Reconnaissance Wing, and the fighter style serial numbers. (Joe Bruch)

RC-135V 64-14843 banks away showing off the antennas on the bottom of the fuselage. (Joe Bruch Collection)

RC-135W RIVET JOINT

All six of the RC-135Ms underwent a rebuilding and update to Rivet Joint Block III standards during the early 1980s being redesignated as RC-135Ws. These aircraft are equipped to a standard close to that of the RC-135V.

The primary difference between the RC-135V and the RC-135W is the engines; the RC-135W engines have thrust reversers, the RC-135V engines do not.

Like the RC-135V, the RC-135W has a hog nose and the E-Systems installed cheeks. They also have the four large mushroom shaped MUCELS antennae on the bottom of the fuselage forward of the main wheel well, and three large blade antennae aft of the main wheel well.

Conversion is underway modifying 62-4125, 62-4128, and 62-1430 to RC-135Ws.

RC-135W Serial Numbers (9):

62-4125	62-4131	62-4135
62-4128	62-4132	62-4138
62-4130	62-4134	62-4139

Three RC-135Ws of the 55th Strategic Reconnaissance Wing photographed on March 15, 1981, are lined up on the ramp at Offutt AFB. (Don McGary)

RC-135W 62-4134, in ACC markings, was photographed on takeoff with the main landing having just retracted and the main gear doors just starting to close. (Mike Grove)

RC-135W 62-4135 was photographed on the ramp at Offutt AFB on December 26, 1980. Like the RC-135Vs, the RC-135Ws use external heaters to warm up the aircraft before flight. (Don McGary)

RC-135W 62-4138, of the 38th Reconnaissance Squadron, was photographed on July 24, 1994 in ACC markings. (Brian C. Rogers)

RC-135W 62-4132 was photographed at Nellis AFB on July 20, 1990. (Keith Svendsen)

RC-135X COBRA EYE

One EC-135B (62-4128) was rebuilt and redesignated as the RC-135X Cobra Eye. This aircraft is associated with the Optical Airborne Measurements Program. The aircraft was intended to gather imagery of Soviet missile tests for the SDI "Star Wars" program.

The COBRA EYE aircraft equipment was designed to optically identify and discriminate ballistic missile reentry vehicles in midcourse. The COBRA EYE program was jointly sponsored by the U.S. Army and Air Force.

E-Systems began converting the EC-135B into RC-135X configuration in July, 1983. After a six year development program, the aircraft was delivered to the 24th SRS, 6th SRW at Eielson AFB on July 16, 1989. It operated from Shemya AFB, routinely observing Soviet ballistic missile tests.

On February 22, 1993, the RC-135X was withdrawn from operational use and flown to E-Systems Majors Field facility at Greenville, Texas. The sophisticated equipment has been removed and the aircraft is in long term storage.

The airplane has a hog nose, but lacks any cheeks. The aircraft has an LTV air refueling receiver receptacle system. A large sliding door on the right side of the fuselage covers the sensor bay, with the upper surface of the right wing painted black to reduce glare on the mission optical sensors. Since the aircraft was modified originally from a C-135B, it is powered by TF33-P-5 engines. The USAF modified 4128 to RC-135S configuration.

RC-135X Serial Number (1):

62-4128

The large sliding door on the right side of the fuselage forward of the wing which covers the sensors can be seen in this photo of the single RC-135X (62-4128), The right wing an the inboard side of the engine nacelles were painted black to protect the sensors from unwanted reflections. (Boeing)

62-4128 is seen here on takeoff. (Joe Bruch Collection)

WC-135W

61-2666 is equipped to a standard close to that of the RC-135W, with 61-2666 adding Rivet Joint external equipment, and now resembling the RC-135W. 61-2666 was used as a flying test bed for much of the new RC-135 equipment developed by E-Systems. It was also used as a proficiency trainer for Air Force flight crews assigned at E-Systems. 61-2666 is assigned to AFMC and based at Majors Field, Greenville, Texas. 2666 carries a MF (Majors Field) tail code.

The single TC-135B (61-2667) underwent a modification program during the early 1994 at E-Systems and in May, 1995 was redesignated as WC-135W. The only visible modification is the air scoops added aft of the overwing escape hatches on both sides of the aircraft. These scoops are used to obtain air samples in an effort to detect and identify nuclear explosions. 65-2667 is assigned to the 55th Wing based at Offutt AFB, before being retired in late 1997 due to airframe corrosion.

WC-135W Serial Number (2):

61-2666 61-2667

61-2666, a former WC-135B was modified into WC-135W configuration at E-Systems. The resulting aircraft looked quite similar to a RC135V or W. (Joe Bruch Collection)

TC-135B 61-2667 was redesignated as a WC-135W in May, 1995. The only visible difference on 2667, photographed at Offutt AFB during July, 1995, was the addition of an air sampling scoop aft of the overwing escape hatch. (Don Logan)

OC-135B OPEN SKIES

Three WC-135B aircraft have been modified into OC-135B Open Skies. These aircraft are scheduled to be used to verify compliance with the Open Skies treaty with the former Soviet Union. The aircraft are assigned to the 45th RS, 55th Wing at Offutt AFB.

The treaty allows the Open Skies aircraft to be "loaned" along with U.S. Air Force flight crews to other nations to collect data on compliance with the treaty. This data would then be available to any signatory of the treaty.

61-2674 is presently in storage at AMARC.

OC-135B Serial Numbers (3):

61-2670 61-2674
61-2672

ABOVE LEFT: The number 1 Open Skies aircraft OC-135B 61-2670 was a WC-135B prior to its modification to the open skies mission with its tail markings advertising its mission. (Joe Bruch)
ABOVE RIGHT: OC-135B 61-2672, also converted from a WC-135B, has a different style serial presentation than aircraft number 1. Number 2s serial number includes OF, the tail code of the 55th Wing. (Randy Walker)

The OC-135Bs have camera windows in the cargo door and also in the fairing below the tail where the boom pod on a tanker is located. (Mike Grove)

The number 2 aircraft carries a side looking radar antenna contained in a small radome on the fuselage bottom aft of the nose gear. The markings on the two aircraft differ slightly. (Jerry Geer)

55th WING TRAINING AIRCRAFT

Following the loss of 59-1465 during an air crew training mission, aircraft, originally C-135Bs, were modified to the external configuration of reconnaissance platforms. This modification allowed the air crews to complete their initial and proficiency training without "tying up" a valuable mission aircraft. Since the aerodynamic configurations of the C-135 reconnaissance aircraft differed, three aircraft were converted to the TC-135B, TC-135S, and TC-135W trainer aircraft for the 55th Wing.

TC-135B

The TC-135B was used for flight crew proficiency training of EC-135, OC-135B and WC-135B aircrews. The aircraft was redesignated during mid-1995 and was designated as a WC-135W, before being retired in late 1997.

TC-135B Serial Number (1):

61-2667

TC-135S

To replace the lost RC-135T, an EC-135B (62-4133) was converted to the role of aircrew training as the TC-135S. The aircraft was given the external configuration of an RC-135S. It is assigned to the 55th Wing at Offutt AFB.

TC-135S Serial Number (1):

62-4133

TC-135W

An C-135B (62-4129) was converted to the role of aircrew training as the TC-135W. The aircraft was given the external configuration of a RC-135W. It is assigned to the 55th Wing at Offutt AFB.

TC-135W Serial Number (1):

62-4129

From left to right, the TC-135B (61-2667) , the first KC-135E (59-1514), and the TC-135W (62-1429) are lined up on the Offutt flightline in this photograph taken in July, 1993. (Joe Bruch)

TC-135B 62-2667, converted from a WC-135B, and used for flight crew proficiency training, was photographed at Offutt AFB in October, 1993. (Joe Bruch)

ABOVE: TC-135S 62-4133, converted from an EC-135B, was photographed at Offutt AFB during March, 1993. (Joe Bruch)

RIGHT: TC-135S 62-4133 wore the nose art called "North Star" when photographed in March, 1993. (Joe Bruch)

BELOW: TC-135W 62-4129, a former C-135B, was photographed at Offutt AFB during May, 1993. (Joe Bruch)

TC-135W 62-4129 wore nose art called "Road Warrior" when photographed at Ellsworth AFB on December 31, 1990. (Brian C. Rogers)

TC-135W 62-4129 wore nose art called "Greyhound" when photographed at McConnell AFB on September 17, 1988. (Don Logan)

TC-135W 62-4129, in SAC markings, was photographed at McConnell AFB on September 17, 1988. (Don Logan)

CHAPTER FOUR

EC-135 Series Aircraft

EC-135 aircraft are of two types, Airborne Command and Control aircraft and Test Range support aircraft. The Airborne Command and Control aircraft include the following:

EC-135A	SAC
EC-135C	SAC
EC-135G	SAC-ALCC/
EC-135H	CINCLANT/USAFE
EC-135J	PACAF/NCA
EC-135K	TAC/ACC
EC-135L	SAC Relay
EC-135N	CINCCENT (Non ARIA)
EC-135P	PACAF/CINCLANT
EC-135Y	CINCCENT

The Range Support Aircraft include the following:

EC-135B	T/RIA
EC-135E	ARIA
EC-135N	ARIA

EC-135C 63-8046, the EC-135C "Looking Glass" , with 14 aircraft of the type, was the most numerous of the EC-135s. (Joe Bruch Collection)

AIRBORNE COMMAND POST/ COMMUNICATIONS AIRCRAFT

In the event of nuclear war, most U.S. land-based military command and communication facilities would probably be targeted and destroyed in the opening stages. During the cold war, SAC operated the Post Attack Command Control System (PACCS), an airborne command, control, and communications (C3) system that mainly used KC-135/C-135 derivatives with the capability to take over command and control from destroyed ground installations. The command function of this system is carried out by various types of Airborne Command Post (ABNCP) aircraft.

The most numerous of the ABNCPs were fourteen SAC EC-135C Airborne Command Posts. During the Cold War an EC-135 ABNCP was airborne at all times. Designed to take over for CINCSAC (Strategic Air Command Commander) headquartered at Offutt AFB, Omaha, Nebraska, the ABNCPs could relay U.S. nuclear strike orders from the President to bombers, ICBM launch control facilities and nuclear missile submarines at sea.

In addition to the SAC ABNCPs, there were several airborne command post versions for use by the various area Commanders in Chiefs including CINCPAC, CINCLANT, and CINCCENT. Tying together the various ABNCPs and any surviving ground stations in wartime would be the job of a fleet of radio relay aircraft, which were conversions of KC-135As. The EC-135G and EC-135L relay aircraft could also serve as an Airborne Launch Control Center (ALCC), able to launch SAC's ICBMs if ground control centers were disabled. EC-135As and EC-135Cs also had ALCC equipment installed. The EC-135 ABNCP and relay variants were well equipped for communications, with numerous radios and a large number of antennas. They all have refueling receptacles on the upper fuselage just back of the cockpit which allowed flights of up to 96 hours duration, the limiting factor being engine oil supplies. All still had the refueling boom and, if required, could use the boom in reverse to draw fuel from receivers. This capability was required if tankers were not available, as well might be the case in wartime. Some J57-powered variants were re-engined with the more fuel efficient and powerful JT3D/TF33 turbofan engines.

EC-135C 62-3582. (Joe Bruch Collection)

EC-135A AIRBORNE LAUNCH CONTROL SYSTEM

The first Stratotanker relay derivatives for PACCS were six KC-135As converted to EC-135As in 1965. These aircraft had inflight refueling capability and extra antennas added, and retained the J57 engines.

The primary mission of SAC's EC-135As was to provide an airborne launch capability for the Minuteman and Peacekeeper ICBM force. This mission, and the equipment installed on board the EC-135As, was called Airborne Launch Control System (ALCS).

Until they were retired in 1992, as many as three EC-135As were on continuous ground alert at Ellsworth AFB, South Dakota, and Minot AFB, North Dakota. From those bases, they could launch and be in position within minutes to provide an airborne launch capability for five of SAC's six Minuteman ICBM wings.

Additional HF probe antennas were mounted over each wingtip. The EC-135As were flown by the 4th ACCS flying from Ellsworth AFB, South Dakota.

One EC-135A, (61-0293), after being converted back to KC-135A configuration in the 1970s, was converted to the first CFM56 equipped (KC-135R) aircraft.

The remaining five EC-135As have been retired. 61-0262 is displayed at the South Dakota Air and Space Museum at Ellsworth AFB, 61-0287 is displayed at Offutt AFB, and the remaining three (61-0278, 61-0289, and 61-0297) are presently stored at AMARC.

EC-135A Serial Numbers (6):

61-0262	61-0289
61-0278	61-0293
61-0287	61-0297

EC-135A 61-0278 of the 28th Bomb Wing at Ellsworth AFB was photographed at Ellsworth AFB, taxiing out for takeoff in September, 1987. (Don Logan)

ABOVE: EC-135A 61-0262, photographed on October 16, 1988, wears the then new Mount Rushmore tail cap of the 28th Bomb Wing. (Keith Snyder)

RIGHT: EC-135A 61-0262 wore nose art called "Rollin Thunder" when photographed on May 12, 1989. (Don McGary)

BELOW: EC-135A 61-0278 was photographed on the ramp at Ellsworth AFB on March 13, 1991. (Brian C. Rogers)

EC-135C LOOKING GLASS

Fourteen KC-135Bs were built as airborne command posts for use by SAC. Later designated as EC-135Cs, they were equipped with extensive communications equipment and air refueling receiver capability which allowed them to function as ABNCPs for SAC, replacing KC-135As used in that role.

The EC-135Cs were originally assigned to SAC's numbered Air Forces (NAFs); the 2nd Air Force at Barksdale AFB, 8th Air Force at Westover AFB, and 15th Air Force at March AFB. They were operated for the NAFs by the 913 AREFS at Barksdale, the 99 AFRES at Westover, and the 22 AREFS at March. They were later operated by both the 2nd ACCS, SAC, Offutt AFB, Nebraska and the 4th ACCS, SAC, Ellsworth AFB, South Dakota.

Powered by the TF33-P-9, these aircraft were equipped with both inflight refueling receptacles and booms. There were additional HF probe antennas installed at each wingtip. Two wire antennas extended from the vertical fin to the mid and forward fuselage areas. A trailing wire antenna was housed in the fairing on the lower fuselage, right of the centerline, and forward of the main wheel well. Five blade antennas were installed along the belly, while six were located along the upper fuselage centerline.

MILSTAR and its identifying radome on the top of the fuselage has been added to some the EC-135Cs.

Until 1990, at least one EC-135C was airborne at all times, flying eight-hour missions that ended when another EC-135C was on station and ready to take over. Nine EC-135Cs were assigned to the 2nd ACCS, 55th SRW at Offutt AFB, while four were assigned to the 4th ACCS of the 28th Bomb Wing at Ellsworth AFB. 62-3584 was converted to an EC-135J.

Eight EC-135Cs; 62-3581, 62-3582, 62-3585, 63-8046, 63-8048, 63-8052, 63-8053, and 63-8054 were assigned to the 55th Wing at Offutt AFB. 62-3581, 62-3585, 63-8046, and 63-8054 had MILSTAR antennas. 63-8053 was attrited after a very hard landing at Pope AFB on September 2, 1997. The last of the eight aircraft was scheduled for retirement in late 1997. The Navy E-6 took over the mission of the EC-135Cs.

63-8050 had the EC-135C equipment removed and was redesignated as a NKC-135B. 8050 is assigned to the 412th test wing at Edwards AFB. 62-3584 was converted to an EC-135J and crashed at Pope AFB on May 29, 1992. 63-8049 is on display at Offutt AFB Nebraska, and the other three EC-135Cs were retired to AMARC.

EC-135C Serial Numbers (14):

62-3581	63-8048
62-3582	63-8049
62-3583	63-8050
62-3584	63-8051
62-3585	63-8052
63-8046	63-8053
63-8047	63-8054

Visible on this photograph of EC-135C 62-3581 is the white MILSTAR radome and the weathered black AFSATCOM antenna. (Bruch Collection)

EC-135C 62-3583 was photographed on the 55th Strategic Reconnaissance Wing flightline on July 12, 1980. (Don Logan)

EC-135C 62-3582 was photographed waiting to take the runway for takeoff at Ellsworth AFB during September, 1988. (Don Logan)

EC-135C 63-8047 was wearing nose art called "Night Hawk" when photographed in August, 1988. (Mike Grove)

EC-135C 62-3581 with the MILSTAR radome, was photographed on the 55th SRW flightline on July 19, 1991. (Brian C. Rogers)

EC-135C 62-3582 was photographed in the ACC markings of the 7th Airborne Command and Control Squadron (ACCS), 55th Wing on August 7, 1994. (Brian C. Rogers)

LEFT: The EC-135C aircraft carried trailing wire antenna systems for the low frequency (LF) and very low frequency (VLF) radios. (Joe Bruch) RIGHT: The EC-135Cs had part of the forward fuselage fuel tank removed and replaced with an electronics compartment. These vents are used to cool the equipment if the modified forward compartment. This aircraft also has the MILSTAR system installed as indicated by the large radome on the top of tho fuoclagc. Four EC-135Cs (62-3581, 62-3585, 63-8046, and 63-8054) received this modification. (Joe Bruch)

This underside view of EC-135C 63-8052 shows the location of the trailing wire antenna system. (Mike Grove)

EC-135G

Four EC-135Gs, converted from KC-135As were also used in the radio relay role. In addition to their relay capability, these aircraft could, while airborne, command launch ICBMs in the ALCS role. All four aircraft, conversions of KC-135A airframes, retained their refueling booms and were equipped with inflight refueling receptacles (ARRs). Eight blade antennas were placed on the upper fuselage. Six blade antennas were installed on the belly. HF probe antennas are mounted our each wingtip. Two wire antennas run from the vertical fin to the forward fuselage.

The EC-135Gs were assigned to the 4th ACCS, 28th Bomb Wing at Ellsworth AFB, and the 70th AREFS at Grissom AFB Indiana.

The Ellsworth airplanes were primarily employed in the ALCS role, while those assigned to Grissom primarily supported the Radio Relay mission. For most of the SAC years, three EC-135G were assigned to Ellsworth and one was assigned to Grissom.

All four aircraft have been retired and are stored at AMARC.

EC-135G Serial Numbers (4):

62-3570	63-7994
62-3579	63-8001

The first EC-135G, 62-3570 was still unpainted in its natural metal finish when this photograph was taken just prior to delivery to the USAF. (Boeing)

EC-135G 62-3579 of the 4th ACCS, 28th Bomb Wing banks over the badlands of South Dakota. (USAF)

EC-135G 63-7994 of the 3rd ACCS was photographed at McCoy AFB on November 21, 1971. (Tom Brewer Collection)

EC-135G 63-7994, with nose art called "Dina-Might" of the 4th ACCS taxis out for takeoff at Ellsworth AFB during September, 1988. (Don Logan)

EC-135G 62-3579, accelerates for takeoff with water injection smoke pouring from the J-57 engines. (Don Logan)

EC-135G 63-8001 was assigned to the 70th Air Refueling Squadron at Grissom AFB, Indiana, when photographed at McConnell AFB in September, 1988. (Don Logan)

EC-135H

Five KC-135As were converted to EC-135Hs during 1968. An inflight refueling receptacle was installed and the refueling boom was retained. Six blade antennas were installed along the aircraft belly and two along the top of the fuselage. HF probe antennas were installed on each wingtip. A saddle-shaped antenna was located on the top of the fuselage aft of the overwing exit hatches. Two wire antennas were installed from the vertical fin to the forward fuselage top. A trailing wire antenna pod was located on the belly, forward of the right main gear wheel well.

61-0274 was used by CINCLANT (Commander In Chief Atlantic) and operated by the 6th ACCS at Langley AFB Virginia. The other four were assigned to the 10th ACCS and flew out of RAF Mildenhall used by USAFE (US Air Forces Europe) to serve as airborne command posts for the United States Commander-In-Chief Europe (USCINCEUR).

All five EC-135Hs were re-engined with TF33-PW-102 engines as part of the airline re-engine program.

61-0274 was converted to an EC-135P in 1988.

The remaining four aircraft have been retired.

EC-135H Serial Numbers (5):

(CINCLANT) SCOPE LIGHT
61-0274

(USAF Europe) SILK PURSE

61-0282	61-0286
61-0285	61-0291

EC-135H 61-0285. (Joe Bruch Collection)

EC-135H 61-0285 is seen here at AMARC in ACC markings. The FF tail code, standing for First Fighter the F-15 wing based at Langley, was carried by the 6th ACCS aircraft until they were retired to AMARC. (Randy Walker)

EC-135H 61-0274, flown by the 6th ACCS at Langley AFB for CINCLANT was photographed at Langley AFB on July 29, 1978. (Ray Leader)

EC-135H 61-0285 was one of four EC-135H flown by the 10th ACCS for U.S. Air Forces Europe. (Joe Bruch Collection)

EC-135H 61-0282 of the 10th ACCS was photographed on April 25, 1970, at RAF Mildenhall. (Tom Brewer Collection)

EC-135J

The EC-135Js were converted from KC-135Bs. These aircraft had both an inflight refueling receptacle and a refueling boom. Two wire antennas ran from the forward fuselage to the vertical fin. HF probe antennas were installed over each wingtip, with a fairing for a VLF trailing wire antenna installed on the bottom of the fuselage. A saddle antenna was installed over the mid fuselage. The aircraft were TF33 powered.

The EC-135Js were initially delivered to Andrews AFB outside Washington DC as the Night Watch National Emergency Airborne Command Post (NEACP) aircraft. The EC-135Js were replaced as NEACP by the E-4A.

They were then reassigned to Hickam AFB where they replaced PACAF's EC-135Ps serving as airborne command posts and operated under the "Blue Eagle" program for the Commander-In-Chief Pacific (CINCPAC).

62-3584, originally an EC-135C, was converted to an EC-135J and was destroyed at Pope AFB, North Carolina when it ran off the end of the runway on May 29, 1992.

The three remaining EC-135Js were retired to AMARC, with 63-8057 being towed across the highway and put on display at the Pima Air and Space Museum in Tucson, Arizona.

EC-135J Serial Numbers (4):

62-3584	63-8056
63-8055	63-8057

EC-135J 63-8056. (USAF)

EC-135J 63-8055 of the 1st ACCS was photographed at Andrews AFB on March 1, 1974. (J. Morris via Tom Brewer)

EC-135J 63-8057 of the 1st ACCS was also photographed at Andrews AFB on March 1, 1974. (J. Morris via Tom Brewer)

EC-135J 63-8056 of the 9th ACCS, 15th Air Base Wing at Hickam AFB, Hawaii, was photographed at Carswell AFB on December 7, 1984 (Brian C. Rogers)

EC-135J 63-8055, assigned to the 55th Wing at Offutt AFB was photographed at Altus AFB, Oklahoma, on June 6, 1993. (Randy Walker)

EC-135K

Two KC-135As, 55-3118 (first C-135 production aircraft, "City of Renton") and 62-3536 were converted to serve as Tactical Air Command and later Air Combat Command (ACC) airborne command posts under the designation EC-135K. The aircraft were modified into the EC-135K configuration under the "Oxeye Daisy" program. The aircraft are no longer tanker capable, because the boom was been replaced with a fuel-dump pipe similar to those on C-135 aircraft and do not have air refueling receiver capability.

Aircraft 62-3536, the second to become an EC-135K, had served with NASA as Zero G trainer for the astronauts. EC-135K 62-3536 was destroyed when it hit a mountain on climbout from Kirtland AFB, New Mexico on September 14, 1977. It was replaced by 59-1518, converted from a KC-135A. 59-1518 had started its life as an FAA aircraft FAA-N96 "Ol Smoky."

Both remaining EC-135Ks were re-engined with commercial JT3D engines (redesignated as TF33-PW-102) as part of the airline re-engining program. HF probe antennas were installed on each wingtip and two wire antennas were installed over the fuselage. A third wire was installed in 1966.

EC-135Ks accompany tactical aircraft on long deployments to provide communication links and accurate navigational data. While serving as the TAC airborne command posts, the airplanes were operated by the 18th Air Command and Control Squadron (ACCS), TAC, Seymour-Johnson AFB, North Carolina. The aircraft were assigned to the 8th TDCS (Tactial Deployment Control Squadron) of the 552nd Air Control Wing (ACW) at Tinker AFB, Oklahoma until early 1996 when they were transferred to the 89th Airlift Wing based at Andrews AFB outside of Washington D.C. During the summer of 1996 55-3118 was retired, modified back to KC-135A configuration, and put on display at McConnell AFB during spring 1997. 59-1518 was reassigned, also during the summer of 1996, to the 65th Airlift Squadron, 15th Air Base Wing at Hickam AFB Hawaii.

EC-135K Serial Numbers (3):

55-3118 62-3536
59-1518

The first EC-135K 55-3118 is seen here with a short tail and in its da-glo orange paint scheme was photographed at Nellis AFB in the early 1960s. (Dave Menard Collection)

EC-135K 62-3536 of the 18th ACCS was photographed at Seymour-Johnson AFB on August 9, 1972. (Tom Brewer Collection)

EC-135K 55-3118 of the 8th TDCS, was photographed at Carswell AFB on May 3, 1985. (Brian C. Rogers)

EC-135K 59-1518 was photographed Luke AFB on April 27, 1991. (Douglas Sloviak Vortex Photographics)

EC-135K 55-3118 assigned to the 8th TDCS, was photographed on takeoff at Tinker AFB during September, 1993. (Steve Link)

EC-135K 59-1518 of the 8th TDCS, was photographed on takeoff at Tinker AFB during October, 1994. (Steve Link)

EC-135L

Eight KC-135As were converted to SAC radio relay aircraft during 1965 and designated EC-135L. The refueling boom was retained and an inflight refueling receptacle (ARR) system was installed in five of the eight aircraft. Nine blade antennas were installed on the top of the fuselage with six blade antennas on the belly. A red and white radiation hazard warning band was applied near the refueling boom pod.

These aircraft were primarily operated by the 70th AREFS Grissom AFB, Indiana, standing SAC alert at Grissom AFB and Rickenbacker AFB, Ohio. One aircraft was later assigned to the 4th ACCS, SAC, Ellsworth AFB, South Dakota.

Three aircraft; 61-0281, 61-0288, and 61-0302 were reconfigured to KC-135A tankers. Aircraft 61-0281 is presently flying as a KC-135E, 61-0288 and 61-0302 are presently KC-135Rs. 61-0269 is on display at Grissom AFB and the remaining four, 61-0261, 61-0263, 61-0279, and 61-0283 are stored at AMARC.

EC-135L Serial Numbers (8):

61-0261	61-0281
61-0263	61-0283
61-0269	61-0288
61-0279	61-0302

EC-135L Southeast Asia

When modification of additional KC-135As to the Combat Lightning configuration was delayed, Headquarters SAC sent two EC-135Ls of its PACCS fleet to U-Tapao in mid-May, 1967, in order to expand radio relay coverage as planned. Starting at the end of May, the four Combat Lightning aircraft began 24-hour coverage in the Gulf of Tonkin orbit. Three additional KC-135As joined the Combat Lightning fleet in the first part of October. In addition to carrying regular radio relay equipment, these aircraft were outfitted with a secure voice communications equipment. The original Combat Lightning aircraft required the secure voice modification as well as a regularly scheduled wing fatigue retrofit, so the EC-135Ls could not be returned to the PACCS fleet immediately.

The modification of the original Combat Lightning aircraft was completed by the end of 1967, and the EC-135Ls returned to their PACCS duties.

EC-135L Desert Storm

Two EC-135Ls from the 305th Air Refueling Wing (Grissom AFB) were deployed to King Khalid International Airport in Riyadh Saudi Arabia, and assigned to the 1703rd Air Refueling Wing (Provisional). The aircraft were used to relay communications between satellites and ground stations to speed up transmission of SCUD missile detection information. The two aircraft returned to Grissom on March 7, 1991.

BELOW: EC-135L 61-0261 of the accelerates for takeoff at Forbes Field, Kansas during January, 1991. (Jerry Geer)

EC-135L 61-0269 was photographed at Offutt AFB on August 9, 1980. (Don McGary)

EC-135L 61-0269 of the 4th ACCS, 28th Bomb Wing at Ellsworth AFB was photographed during January, 1991. (Jerry Geer)

EC-135L 61-0283 of the 70th Air Refueling Squadron, Grissom AFB, was photographed at McConnell AFB in September, 1991. (Jerry Geer)

EC-135N CINCCENT

61-0327 still carries the designation EC-135N, however it has been modified with the ARIA systems removed and JT3D engines added as part of the airline re-engining program. It now serves as an airborne command post. It was assigned to the 19th ARW at Robins AFB Georgia, flying along with EC-135Y 55-3125 for use as an Airborne Command Post by CINCCENT (Central Command). Both aircraft transferred to the 91st Air Refueling Squadron, part of the 6th Air Refueling Wing at McDill AFB, during summer, 1997.

EC-135N CINCCENT Serial Number (1):

61-0327

EC-135N 61-0327, the last aircraft to still carry the designation of EC-135N is seen here on March 21, 1992, at Robins AFB, Georgia. (Brian C. Rogers)

EC-135Y CINCCENT

The EC-135Y was a converted during 1988 from NKC-135A 55-3125 for use as an Airborne Command Post by CINCCENT (Central Command) during 1984.

An LTV air refueling receiver receptacle was added. The aircraft was re-engined with JT3D as part of the airline re-engine program.

The aircraft along, with EC-135N 61-0327, was assigned to the 19th ARW at Robins AFB, Georgia, moving to the 91st ARS, 6th ARW in summer, 1997.

EC-135Y Serial Number (1):

55-3125

EC-135Y 55-3125, shares CINCCENT duties with EC-135N 61-0327. 55-3125 was photographed at Robins AFB, Georgia in November, 1994. (Peter Becker)

EC-135P

There were five ex-KC-135As (the original KC-135A Looking Glass aircraft) modified as Airborne Command Posts under the designation EC-135P. The refueling boom was retained, and an inflight refueling receptacle (ARR) system was installed. Two HF probe antennas were installed on the wingtips. A pair of wire antennas extended from the vertical fin to the forward fuselage. Seven blade antennas were installed on the top of the fuselage, with five blade antennas on the belly. A trailing wire antenna fairing was located on the belly, forward of the right main wheel well. A red and white radiation hazard warning band was applied near the refueling boom pod. A saddle antenna was located on the fuselage top in a line with the wing root leading edge.

These aircraft were initially used to support SAC and CINCPAC.

Aircraft 58-0007, 58-0011, and 58-0018 were operated by the 9th ACCS, PACAF, Hickam AFB, Hawaii, as a command post for CINCPAC.

When the EC-135Js were assigned to PACAF at Hickam, the EC-135P models went to Langley AFB, Virginia and were operated by the 6th ACCS as command posts for CINCLANT.

In 1988, 61-0274 was converted to a EC-135P from a TF33-PW-102 re-engined EC-135H.

55-3129, 58-0019, and 58-0022 were re-engined with TF33-PW-102 engines as part of the airline re-engine program.

58-0007 burned on the ramp at Langley AFB on January 30, 1980. 58-0011 and 58-0018 were re-converted to KC-135A tanker configuration and then re-engined with F108(CFM56) engines as KC-135Rs. The other four are in storage at AMARC.

EC-135P Serial Numbers (7):

(PACAF) BLUE EAGLE

58-0007	58-0018
58-0011	

(CINCLANT) SCOPE LIGHT

55-3129	58-0022
58-0019	61-0274

EC-135P 58-0022, seen here at Boeing's Wichita, Kansas facility prior to being reengined with TF33-PW-102 engines. (Boeing)

EC-135P 58-0019, on the ramp at Wichita was also reengined at Boeing Wichita. (Boeing)

EC-135P 58-0022 was photographed on July 29, 1978. (Ray Leader)

EC-135P 61-0274, was a reengined EC-135H when it was converted to a EC-135P. Assigned to the 7th ACCS, 1 TFW, it was photographed at Langley AFB on June 1, 1991. (Gilles Auliard)

EC-135P 58-0019, in 7th ACCS, 1 TFW markings was photographed in March, 1992. (Bob Shane)

RANGE SUPPORT (ARIA) AIRCRAFT

EC-135B

Two of the C-135B T/RIAs were put to use in the ARIA role during 1978-1979 as EC-135Bs. Of these two, 62-4133 later became the TC-135S, while 62-4128 became the RC-135X.

EC-135B Serial Numbers (2):

62-4128 62-4133

EC-135B 62-4128, seen here with the radome off exposing the ARIA antenna, was photographed in March, 1980. (Tom Brewer Collection)

EC-135E 60-374, took over some of the ARIA duties from EC-18's retired to be used as E-8C Joint STARS airframes. (USAF)

EC-135B 62-4133, seen here on the ramp at Wright-Patterson, was photographed on April 18, 1980. (Don McGary)

EC-135E

This designation refers to four EC-135Ns that were re-engined with TF33-PW-102 engines. The aircraft were replaced in the ARIA role by EC-18Bs and EC-18Ds (707 conversions). When four of the EC-18 ARIAs were de-moded to be used as E-8 Joint STARS airframes, the EC-135Es were brought back into ARIA service. Three aircraft, 60-0374, 61-0326, and 61-0330 are now assigned to the 452nd Flight Test Squadron, 412 Test Wing at Edwards AFB, California. 61-0329 has been retired and is located at Tinker AFB, being used as a battle damage repair trainer.

EC-135E Serial Numbers (4):

60-0374	61-0329
61-0326	61-0330

EC-135E 61-0326 was photographed on the PDM line at Tinker AFB on January 22, 1994. (Randy Walker)

EC-135E 61-0329 was photographed at Edwards AFB on April 12, 1995. (Don Logan)

EC-135E 61-0330 was photographed at Edwards AFB on April 12, 1995.

EC-135N ARIA

To support the Apollo lunar-landing program, eight C-135As were modified by Douglas Aircraft Company's Modification Division in Tulsa, Oklahoma during 1967 as Apollo Range Instrumentation Aircraft (ARIA). They were given a large 10- foot long nose radome housing a 7-foot diameter parabolic dish steerable antenna. Four were modified with the Northrop A-LOTS (Airborne Lightweight Optical Tracking System), first tested on NKC-135A (55-3123). The A-LOTS was housed in a pod mounted forward on the left side of the fuselage. Operated by the 6549th Test Squadron at Patrick AFB, the EC-135Ns provided tracking and communications relay capability during the Apollo flights. After the Apollo program ended, the EC-135Ns were redesignated Advanced Range Instrumentation Aircraft keeping the acronym ARIA.

Of the eight original EC-135Ns, four aircraft (60-0374, 61-0326, 61-0329, and 61-0330) have been re-engined with TF33 engines and fly as ARIA EC-135Es. 61-0328 crashed while still in the EC-135N configuration at Walkersville, Maryland during May 1981. 60-0372 and 60-0375 have been modified to C-135E configuration.

EC-135N 61-0327 was photographed at Patrick AFB, Florida, on April 12, 1975. (Ken Buchanan via Tom Brewer)

61-0327 kept the EC-135N designation after the ARIA equipment was removed. It now flies as an airborne command post for CINCCENT along with the one EC-135Y (55-3125)

EC-135N Serial Numbers (8):

60-0372	61-0327
60-0374	61-0328
60-0375	61-0329
61-0326	61-0330

EC-135N 60-0375 was photographed on October 1, 1976. (Mick Roth)

EC-135N 61-0326 was photographed at Wright-Patterson AFB on April 18, 1980. (Don McGary)

CHAPTER FIVE

Transport C-135s

C-135A

Fifteen C-135A Stratolifters were procured by the U. S. Air Force for use as long range logistic transports. The aircraft did not have a refueling boom, and therefore could not be used as tankers. They had metal floors for carrying cargo, and two air conditioning packs required proper pressurization and cooling/heating when in the passenger configuration.

These airplanes were assigned to MATS. The 18th and 41st Air Transport Squadrons, 1611th Air Transport Wing, MATS operated the Eastern Transport Air Force (EASTAF) routes from McGuire AFB, New Jersey. Thirteen C-135As were based at McGuire. The 44th Air Transport Squadron, 1501st Air Transport Wing, MATS flew the Western Transport Air Force (WESTAF) routes from Travis AFB, California. One C-135A was used by the 44th ATS. Two C-135As, serial numbers 60-0376 and 60-0377, were operated alternately by the 44th ATS and the Los Alamos Scientific Laboratories, Los Alamos, New Mexico.

60-0356, 60-0357, and 60-0362, though originally built as KC-135As, were designated C-135As before they were modified into the KC-135Ds.

60-0377 was the last C-135A still flying and still had J57 engines. It was operated as an NC-135A by ASD in support of the B-2 program until retired to the Edwards AFB Museum in 1996.

60-0373 was lost on June 25, 1965, when after taking off at night from MCAS El Toro, California, it hit a mountain peak 4 miles away from the field. 60-0369 was retired to Chanute AFB where it served as a ground maintenance trainer.

C-135A 60-0376 seen here was photographed in June, 1980, assigned to the 55th wing at Offutt AFB. It was later reengined to C-135E configuration, and served as a VIP transport for U.S. Space Command. (James Goodall)

60-0374, 61-0326, 61-0329, and 61-0330 were modified to EC-135Ns and then with the addition of TF33 engines, redesignated as EC-135Es. They are presently assigned to the 452nd Flight Test Squadron at Edwards AFB.

With the addition of TF33 engines, 60-0372, 60-0375, 60-0376 were converted to C-135Es.

60-0370, 60-0371, and 60-0378 have all been retired. 60-0378 was used as the battle damage repair training aircraft at Tinker AFB, and then used as the paint removal test aircraft for the Large Aircraft Robotic Paint System (LARPS) paint stripper at Tinker AFB. 60-0370 has been scrapped.

C-135A Serial Numbers (15):

60-0369	60-0374	61-0326
60-0370	60-0375	61-0327
60-0371	60-0376	61-0328
60-0372	60-0377	61-0329
60-0373	60-0378	61-0330

C-135A 60-0378, which served with NASA as Weightless Wonder III between July, 1969 and May, 1973, was photographed as a member of the 55th wing at Offutt AFB on March 11, 1979. (Don McGary)

BELOW: C-135A 60-0376 was assigned to the 55th Strategic Reconnaissance Wing when photographed at Offutt AFB on July 5, 1981. (Don McGary)

C-135A 60-0378 was photographed at Offutt AFB in 55th wing markings in June, 1993, shortly before the aircraft was retired to Tinker AFB to be used for battle damage repair training. (Joe Bruch)

C-135B

Thirty C-135B Stratolifter versions of the C-135A, powered by TF33 engines with thrust reversers, were procured by the U. S. Air Force and assigned to MATS for use as long range logistic transports. The 18th and 41st Air Transport Squadrons, 1611th Air Transport Wing, MATS operated the Eastern Transport Air Force (EASTAF) routes from McGuire AFB, New Jersey. Fifteen C-135Bs were based at McGuire. The 44th Air Transport Squadron, 1501st Air Transport Wing, MATS flew the Western Transport Air Force (WESTAF) routes from Travis AFB, California. Fifteen C-135Bs were used by the 44th ATS.

The C-135s were replaced by the C-141s as the mainstay of the MAC airlift force.

61-0331 was a special purpose C-135B. It crashed into the Pacific Ocean on June 13, 1971.

61-0332 crashed at Clark AB, The Philippines on May 11, 1964. 62-4136 crashed on approach to Guantanamo Bay NAS, Cuba on October 23, 1962.

61-2662, 61-2663, and 61-2664 were converted into RC-135S aircraft.

62-4125, 62-4126, 62-4127, 62-4129 and 62-4130 were converted to VC-135Bs. Four were converted back to C-135B configuration, 62-4126 is assigned to the 108 ARW, New Jersey ANG at McGuire AFB and 62-4127 assigned to the 65th AS, 15 Air Base Wing at Hickam AFB, Hawaii. 62-4125 and 62-4130 are presently at E-Systems, Majors Field, Greenville, Texas.

Ten; 61-2665, 61-2666, 61-2667, 61-2668, 61-2669, 61-2670, 61-2671, 61-2672, 61-2673, and 61-2674 were converted to WC-135B Weather Reconnaissance aircraft, and later to OC-135Bs and WC-135Ws.

62-4137 was modified into the only RC-135E. It crashed into Bering Sea on June 5, 1969.

62-4131, 62-4132, 62-4134, 62-4135, 62-4138, and 61-4139 were modified into RC-135Ws.

61-2662, 61-2663 and 61-2664 were converted to the RC-135S model. 61-2664 crashed at Shemya AB, Alaska March 15, 1981.

62-4128 was modified into the one RC-135X.

62-4133 was modified into the TC-135S and 62-4129 was modified into the TC-135W.

There are four remaining C-135Bs. 62-4125, and 62-4130 are assigned to E-Systems, and rumored to be designated RC-135Js. 62-4126 is assigned to 108th Air Refueling Wing at McGuire AFB, New Jersey. 62-4127 is assigned to the 15th Air Base Wing at Hickam AFB, Hawaii.

Conversion of 62-4125, 62-4127, and 62-4130 to RC-135Ws is underway at E Systems, leaving 62-4126 as the only operational C-135B.

C-135B Serial Numbers (30):

61-0331	61-2670	62-4130
61-0332	61-2671	62-4131
61-2662	61-2672	62-4132
61-2663	61-2673	62-4133
61-2664	61-2674	62-4134
61-2665	62-4125	62-4135
61-2666	62-4126	62-4136
61-2667	62-4127	62-4137
61-2668	62-4128	62-4138
61-2669	62-4129	62-4139

C-135B 61-2663 is seen in Military Air Transport Service (MATS) markings. (Joe Bruch Collection)

RIGHT: C-135B 62-4131 of the 1611th Airlift Wing of the Military Air Transport Service was photographed at McGuire AFB. (Tom Brewer Collection)

BELOW: C-135B 62-4130 in Military Airlift Command (MAC) markings was photographed during March, 1967 at Tan Son Nhut Air Base in what was then Saigon, South Vietnam. (Tom Brewer Collection)

BELOW RIGHT: C-135B 62-4129 assigned to the 55th wing was photographed at Offutt AFB on March 25, 1979. (Don McGary)

C-135B 62-4130 when photographed in June, 1993 at Offutt AFB, was wearing the 55th Wing's ACC markings. 62-4130 has since transferred to the E-Systems facility at Majors Field, Texas. (Joe Bruch)

C-135B 62-4126, in airline type markings is seen on takeoff during the summer of 1996, at McGuire AFB in New Jersey. (USAF)

VC-135B

The VC-135B is a Special Air Mission VIP transport conversion. Five C-135Bs were given VIP interiors and assigned to the 89th MAW. Most were used as staff transports for high level officials.

Five C-135Bs were converted to VC-135Bs and were assigned to the 89th Military Airlift Wing, Andrews AFB, Maryland for special mission operations.

62-4125, 62-4126, 62-4127, and 62-4130 have had their designations changed back to C-135Bs. 62-4129 was converted to the TC-135W.

VC-135B Serial Numbers (5):

62-4125	62-4129
62-4126	62-4130
62-4127	

VC-135B 62-4127 seen in Special Air Mission markings while assigned to the 89th Military Airlift Wing at Andrews AFB. (Boeing)

VC-135B 62-4127 was photographed at Elmendorf AFB, Alaska, during April, 1970. (Norm Taylor via Tom Brewer)

VC-135B 62-4130 was photographed at Offutt AFB on December 20, 1978. (Don McGary)

VC-135B 62-4127 was photographed at Andrews AFB on August 2, 1976. (Robert J. Mills)

VC-135B 62-4126 assigned to the 1st Military Airlift Squadron, 89th Military Airlift Group at Andrews AFB was photographed at Offutt AFB on May 6, 1982. (Don McGary)

VC-135B 62-4129 was assigned to the 1st Military Airlift Squadron, 89th Military Airlift Group at Andrews AFB when photographed at Offutt AFB on May 16, 1986. (Don McGary)

C-135C

Three WC-135Bs were re-converted to the transport role under the designation C-135C. These aircraft retained the air refueling receiver capability and are the only C-135 transports to have this feature. 61-2668 was used by Detachment One of the 89th MAW, and was later assigned to the 65th AS, 15 Air Base Wing, Hickam AFB Hawaii. During a PDM (Programmed Depot Maintenance) inspection at Tinker AFB 61-2668 was found to have extensive corrosion and was retired from service. 61-2669 is operated by the 412th Test Squadron, 412th Test Wing at Edwards AFB. 61-2669 carries the nickname "Speckled Trout" and is used as a VIP transport for the USAF Chief of Staff and in the avionics testing role at Edwards AFB. 61-2669 was badly damaged on September 19, 1997 when the number four engine exploded after a full stop landing at NAS Point Mugu.

The third C-135C, 61-2671, has been retired and is on display as the gate guard at Tinker AFB, Oklahoma.

C-135C Serial Numbers (3):

61-2668	61-2671
61-2669	

C-135C 61-2668 in Special Air Mission paint scheme was photographed on takeoff. (Ben Knowles Collection)

C-135C 61-2668 assigned to Detachment 1 of the 89th Military Airlift Wing, used for support of CINCPAC missions was photographed at Offutt AFB on August 7, 1980. (Don McGary)

C-135C 61-2669 seen here taxiing past the north end of Boeing's Wichita Aircraft Modification Center. (Boeing)

C-135C 61-2671 received a tail from an American Airlines 720 before being placed on display at the front gate of Tinker AFB. (Randy Walker)

C-135C 61-2669 was photographed on takeoff at Tinker AFB on August 5, 1994. A short time later the aircraft was reassigned to the 412th Test Squadron at Edwards AFB. (Don Logan)

C-135C 61-2671 is seen here on its final resting place as the gate guard at Tinker AFB. (Alan Winzerling)

C-135E

Three C-135As were re-engined using Pratt & Whitney TF33-PW-102 and redesignated as C-135Es. 60-0372 and 60-0375 are assigned to the 452nd Test Squadron, 412th Test Wing at Edwards AFB, California.

60-0376 was assigned to the 8th ACCS of the 552 ACW at TINKER AFB, Oklahoma, flying personnel and transport missions in support of U.S. Space Command requirements.

During early 1996 60-0376 was transferred to the 89th Airlift Wing at Andrews AFB, and then during the summer of 1996 reassigned to the 15th Air Base Wing, Hickam AFB, Hawaii.

C-135E Serial Numbers (3):

60-0372	60-0376
60-0375	

C-135E 60-0376 is seen here on the Boeing Wichita flightline shortly after being reengined with TF33-PW-102 airline engines. (Boeing)

BELOW: C-135E 60-0375 is seen here in AFMC (Air Force Materiel Command) markings at Wright-Patterson AFB. (Tom Brewer Collection)

C-135E 60-0376 photographed at Tinker AFB in November 1993 while assigned to the 552nd ACW. (Don Logan)

CHAPTER SIX

Special Purpose Aircraft

WC-135B WEATHER RECONNAISSANCE

Ten C-135Bs were modified to the WC-135B configuration, although none of the aircraft have remained in this configuration. These airplanes were operated by MAC for weather reconnaissance. Originally delivered in 1962, these airplanes were converted to WC-135Bs in 1965. The airplanes were operated alternately by the 55th Weather Reconnaissance Squadron, McClellan AFB, California and the 56th Weather Reconnaissance Squadron, Yokota AB, Japan. All WC-135Bs are currently operated by the 45th Reconnaissance Squadron of the 55th Wing at Offutt AFB Nebraska.

The WC-135Bs were powered by four TF33-P-5 turbofan engines. An Boeing air refueling receiver (ARR) system was installed on these airplanes. Being a C-135B originally, no refueling boom was ever installed; however, a fuel dump tube was located under the aft fuselage. These airplanes were equipped with U-1 foils on each side of the fuselage, used to trap air particles for air sampling studies. External stiffeners were installed on the fuselage sides in the area of the foils.

None of these aircraft still active are designated as WC-135Bs, three (61-2670, 61-2672, and 61-2674) were converted to OC-135B Open Skies aircraft, 61-2665 was retired to AMARC on September 11, 1996, 61-2666 was converted to a WC-135W, and 61-2667 was converted to the TC-135B and then in mid-1995, after being re-equipped with special filters and air samplers, was redesignated as a WC-135W.

61-2669 was modified into a VIP transport, a C-135C, named "Speckled Trout." The aircraft is used for avionics testing at Edwards AFB and as a transport by the Air Force Chief of Staff. 61-2668 was converted to a C-135C, 61-2671 is on display as the gate guard at Tinker AFB, and 61-2673 is stored at AMARC.

WC-135B Serial Numbers (10)

61-2665	61-2669	61-2672
61-2666	61-2670	61-2673
61-2667	61-2671	61-2674
61-2668		

WC-135B 61-2673 is seen here on takeoff roll in natural metal finish and Military Airlift Command (MAC) Weather markings. (Joe Bruch Collection)

WC-135B 61-2668, assigned to the 55th Weather Reconnaissance Squadron, photographed during May, 1972 in MAC Weather markings. (Tom Brewer Collection)

WC-135B 61-2668 was photographed at McClellan AFB, Sacramento, California during March, 1980. (Tom Brewer Collection)

WC-135B 61-2674 is seen here in gloss gray paint at McClellan AFB on March 15, 1981. (Don Logan Collection)

WC-135B 61-2673 photographed in July, 1991, in new gloss gray and white paint scheme. (Keith Snyder)

WC-135B 61-2670 photographed in October, 1993, in the markings of the 45th Reconnaissance Squadron, 55th Wing, with ACC OF tail code and fighter style serial numbers. (Joe Bruch)

C-135B T/RIA

Four Military Airlift Command fan-engined C-135B aircraft were modified into Telemetry/Range Instrumented Aircraft (T/RIA) by the Douglas Aircraft Company's Tulsa Division in 1967, and later designated EC-135Bs. These airplanes had the same duckbill platypus nose as the EC-135N aircraft, These airplanes did not have A-LOTS provisions. Air Force Systems Command operated these planes out of Patrick AFB, Florida to provide communications support for the space program.

61-0331 was a special purpose C-135B with the ARIA nose removed and assigned to the 4950th Test Wing at Wright Patterson AFB. It crashed into the Pacific Ocean on June 13, 1971.

61-2664 was converted to an RC-135S and later crashed. 62-4128 was converted to the single RC-135X. 62-4133 was converted to the TC-135S.

C-135B T/RIA Serial Numbers (4):

61-0331	62-4128
61-2664	62-4133

C-135B T/RIA 62-4128 was photographed at Wright-Patterson AFB on June 4, 1971. This aircraft was later modified into the lone RC-135X. (Tom Brewer Collection)

KC-135A PACER CLERK (FEDERAL AVIATION ADMINISTRATION)

The FAA operated two KC-135As to certify high altitude jet routes, flight check the high altitude jet routes, and perform regular flight check operations, The aircraft allocated to the FAA were 59-1481 (N98) and 59-1518 (N96). N96 was assigned to Hickam AFB, Hawaii in 1966 to check the Pacific navigational aids, N98 was transferred to NASA and N96 returned to FAA, Oklahoma City to resume its flight check operations. Eventually N96 was returned to the Air Force. The FAA KC-135s did not carry refueling booms

59-1481 flew as NASA's Weightless Wonder IV and was retired in mid-1996. 59-1518 is presently operational as an EC-135K, presently assigned to the 65th Airlift Squadron, 15th Air Base Wing, Hickam Hawaii.

FAA Number	USAF Serial Number
N98	59-1481
N96	59-1518

KC-135A 59-1518, FAA N96, carried the name "OL SMOKY." (Don Logan Collection)

BELOW: KC-135A 59-1481, FAA N98, was photographed during September, 1995. (Tom Brewer Collection)

KC-135A 59-1518, seen here during April, 1976 with the FAA markings removed, was stored at Tinker AFB before being converted to an EC-135K. (Jerry Geer)

KC-135A (NATIONAL AERONAUTICS AND SPACE ADMINISTRATION)

Stratotankers have also contributed to the U.S. space program, with the type being used to simulate the weightless condition of space by flying parabolic trajectories. This technique has been used for astronaut training and various microgravity experiments. The current "Weightless Wonder" (nicknamed "Vomit Comet") aircraft is 63-7998 Weightless Wonder V, which are operated by NASA from Ellington AFB, Texas. 59-1481, Weightless Wonder IV was retired in the summer of 1996 after having operated with the civil registration number N930NA. NKC-135s 55-3129 and 62-3536, and C-135A 60-0378 have also been used in this role.

55-3129 Weightless Wonder I was converted to an EC-135P and is now stored at AMARC.

62-3536 was converted to an EC-135K, and was lost when it crashed on September 14, 1977, departing Kirtland AFB, New Mexico.

60-0378 served as a C-135A and is now used for battle damage repair at Tinker AFB.

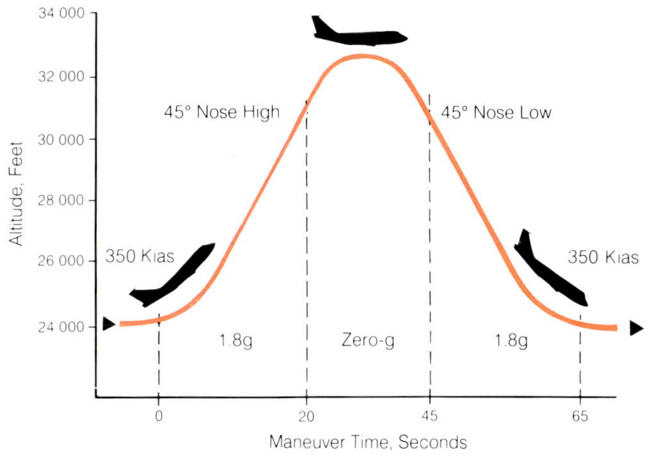

The above diagram shows a typical zero-g maneuver. However, the maneuver can be modified to provide any level of g force less than one g. Some typical g-levels used on different tests and the corresponding time for each maneuver are as follows:

Negative-g (-0.1g)	Approximately 15 seconds
Zero-g	Approximately 25 seconds
Lunar-g (one-sixth g)	Approximately 30 seconds
Martian-g (one-third g)	Approximately 40 seconds

BELOW: Weightless Wonder IV, N930NA, (59-1481) is seen early NASA markings in a 45 degree nose high entry to the zero G maneuver. (NASA)

After used for filming the weightless sequences for the movie Apollo 13, 59-1481 has been retired and still located at Ellington Field, Texas.

NASA Serial Numbers (5):

55-3129	Weightless Wonder I
62-3536	Weightless Wonder II
60-0378	Weightless Wonder III
59-1481	Weightless Wonder IV
63-7998	Weightless Wonder V

AIRCRAFT ZERO G MANEUVERS SUMMARY (DATA THROUGH MAY 26, 1995)

Aircraft	Dates	Hours	Maneuvers
55-3129	1/60 – 6/68	2012	12347
56-3536	1/67 – 5/70	1069	9946
60-0378	7/69 – 5/73	1120	11795
59-1481	8/73 – 5/95	5296	57667
63-7998	11/94 – 5/95	5	0

Weightless Wonder IV, N930NA, wore these NASA markings at the end of its career.(NASA)

Weightless Wonder II 62-3536, in standard aluminum paint finish, carried da-glo nose and da-glo tail stripes. After service as a Weightless Wonder, the aircraft was converted to a EC-135K. It crashed outside Albuquerque, New Mexico, on September 14, 1977. (Joe Bruch Collection)

This photo of Weightless Wonder IV was taken on November 15, 1973, three months after arriving at Ellington AFB, Texas. (Tom Brewer Collection)

U.S. NAVY NKC-135A

The U.S. Navy operated two NKC-135As (55-3134, 56-3596), on loan from the USAF to equip the Fleet Electronic Warfare Support Group. These aircraft have not been given Bureau Numbers (Navy Serial Numbers), but display the USAF serial numbers 553134 (55-3134) and 563596 (56-3596), respectively. The Navy used the NKC-135As for ECM/ECCM training and testing, along with general Electronic Warfare research.

Both aircraft have been retired to AMARC. 56-3596 retired on June 26, 1995, with 55-3134 arriving at AMARC on February 20, 1996.

Navy Serial Numbers (2):

55-3134 56-3596

Navy NKC-135A 55-3134, photographed in April, 1994, has a large antenna canoe on the forward fuselage bottom and a smaller tear drop radome in front of the boom pod. (Mike Grove)

This view of 55-3134 was taken in November, 1994. (Don Logan Collection)

55-3134 was the last J-57 powered -135 type operated by the U.S. military flying for the last time on February 20, 1996. (Vance Vasquez)

ABOVE: The antenna configuration on 56-3596 differed slightly from its sister ship with a tear drop radome on the top of the forward fuselage. The aircraft's operating base in Waco, Texas is represented by the black map of Texas on the forward fuselage. (Douglas Sloviak Vortex Photographics)

RIGHT: 56-3596 carried this nose art during its service with the U.S. Navy. (Douglas Sloviak Vortex Photographics)

BELOW: The U.S. Navy NKC-135As carried the full serial number on the tail. (Douglas Sloviak Vortex Photographics)

NKC-135/NC-135 FLIGHT TEST AIRCRAFT

The test fleet has included aircraft which were derived from KC-135As, KC-135B, C-135As and C-135Bs. For the most part, these aircraft came under the jurisdiction of the Air Force Systems Command (AFSC), though many were operated by other organizations.

NKC-135A Serial Numbers (14):

55-3119	55-3125	55-3132
55-3120	55-3127	55-3134
55-3122	55-3128	55-3135
55-3123	55-3129	56-3596
55-3124	55-3131	

NKC-135B Serial Number (1):

63-8050

NKC-135E Serial Numbers (2):

55-3132 (has an air refueling receiver receptacle)
55-3135

NC-135A Serial Numbers (6):

60-0369	60-0371	60-0376
60-0370	60-0372	60-0377

NC-135B Serial Number (1)

61-2662

NC-135E Serial Number (2)

60-0372 60-0375

A number of KC-135As have been used extensively in the test-bed role under the designation NKC-135A During the 1960s, a number of Stratotankers were designated as JKC-135As to serve as temporary test-beds. These were later replaced by fourteen KC-135As which were re-designated as NKC-135As for use as permanent test aircraft.

There is no standard configuration for the NKC-135A since each have been put through a number of different modification programs. Some configurations retain the boom, while others have fuel-dump pipes or other alterations in the boom area. Some of the many programs undertaken by the NKC-135A fleet include: High Energy Laser (HEL) and Airborne Laser Laboratory (55-3123), Winglet testing (55-3129), SLAR testing (55-3132), celestial navigation testing (55-3134), "Big Crow" ICBM vulnerability program (55-3132) and A-LOTS testing (55-3123).

The Airborne Lightweight Optics Tracking System (A-LOTS), originally tested in 55-3132 was later used on the EC-135N ARIA aircraft. The A-LOTS pod was carried on struts mounted on the cargo door. The sighting blister was a hemisphere 30 inches in diameter. A fairing could be installed over the sighting dome when the A-LOTS was not required for the mission. At that time, the A-LOTS was the worlds largest airborne telescope. It had a 22-inch telescope with a focal length in excess of 200 inches, A high speed 70-millimeter motion picture camera and two television cameras were attached to the telescope.

63-8050, a former EC-135C, was converted back to tanker configuration, had its EC-C equipment removed and is now used for flight test support, being assigned to the 412th Test Wing at Edwards AFB.

A MAC WC-135B, serial number 61-2669, became an AFSC avionics test bed under the project "Speckled Trout." These aircraft have been used for ionispheric research, infrared/optical flying laboratories, airborne laser laboratories, ECM testing, weightless tests, nuclear readiness testing, Apollo program support, and satellite communications (SATCOM) testing. Some of these aircraft have been called piccolo tubes because of the large number of windows which have been added.

In 1964, the three NC135As, 60-0359, 60-0370, and 60-0371 were primarily allocated for weapons test diagnostics should above ground nuclear tests be resumes. When not used for support of atomic tests, these aircraft were used to view solar eclipses, comet photography, or cosmic ray studies. These airplanes were then assigned to the Atomic Energy Commission and used by Lawrence Livermore Laboratory, Los Alamos Scientific Laboratory, and Sandia Laboratories. Originally assigned to the Lawrence Livermore Laboratory, AF 60-0370 was modified with all special observation windows on the left side. This configuration allowed the aircraft to fly a counter-clockwise track or fly parallel tracks with 60-0369 and 60-0371 in order to obtain simultaneous views from opposite sides.

NKC-135A 55-3120, photographed on June 14, 1974, was used by the Air Force Special Weapons Center at Kirtland AFB as a flying Infra-red laboratory under the program name "Project Hula Hoop." (Ben Knowles)

Starting in the early 1970s, NKC-135A 55-3123 was used as the Airborne Laser Laboratory (ALL). This program, which eleven years was used in an experiment which proved a high energy laser could be operated in an aircraft and used against airborne targets. (Jim Moseley Collection)

The view of 55-3123, photographed at Kirtland AFB on June 14, 1973, shows an early ALL configuration. (Ben Knowles)

This photograph of 55-3123, taken on April 18, 1980, shows a later configuration of the upper fairing. During the eleven year program, 3123 destroyed five AIM-9 Sidewinder air to air missiles and one BQM-34A target drone with its laser. The aircraft was retired to the USAF Museum at Wright Paterson AFB in May, 1988. (Don McGary)

NKC-135A 55-3124, photographed at Edwards AFB in November, 1977, was used to test the KC-10 boom, which is readily visible under the tail. (Don Logan Collection)

NKC-135A 55-3124, photographed on October 11, 1990, carries nose fairings and the wing tip pods which indicate this aircraft was used to test ECM systems. (Mick Roth Collection)

NKC-135A 55-3127 was used at Patrick AFB, next to Cape Canaveral, for airborne optical and infra-red tracking of ballistic objects. (Tom Brewer Collection)

NKC-135A 55-3128 was the last J-57 powered -135 aircraft flown by the U.S. Air Force. It was used for icing tests, spraying water out of a modified boom. The large radome on the nose of was left from earlier testing of the AMSA (Advanced Manned Strategic Aircraft) radar. (Don Logan Collection)

NKC-135A 55-3129 was photographed at Wright-Patterson on August 12, 1974 was used for general test duties. (Mick Roth)

LEFT: This modified boom nozzle on NKC-135A 55-3128 sprayed water in a fine spray to induce icing on aircraft following behind the boom. (Don Logan)

NKC-135A 55-3129, photographed at Edwards AFB during November, 1980, was used for testing of the winglets on the wingtips. (Mick Roth)

NKC-135A 55-3131, photographed at Wright-Patterson on April 18, 1980, was used as an airborne Infra-red laboratory. (Don McGary)

NKC-135A 55-3132, photographed at Wright-Patterson on March 18, 1972, was used for testing of antenna "cheeks" later used on RC-135s. (Tom Brewer Collection)

NKC-135A 55-3132, photographed at Nellis AFB, February 4, 1980, was used in the Big Crow Project. (Kirk Minert)

NKC-135A 55-3135, photographed at Edwards AFB in July, 1976, was used as an instrumented tanker. (Mick Roth)

NKC-135A 56-3596 was used for testing the Airborne Lightweight Optical Tracking System (ALOTS) pod. (Ben Knowles)

This front view of 56-3596, photographed on June 14, 1974, shows the struts which attach the ALOTS pod to the cargo door. (Ben Knowles)

NKC-135A 56-3596, photographed at NAS Moffett in December, 1975, in an early U.S. Navy configuration. This aircraft received additional ECM mods and was later repainted in U.S. Navy markings. (Mike Grove)

NC-135A 60-0371, photographed at NAS Pt. Mugu during August, 1986, was used as an airborne diagnostic aircraft (photo patterns painted on the side of the fuselage) for the Airborne Laser Laboratory. (Bruce Trombecky)

63-8050, formerly an EC-135C, had its main cabin equipment removed, and is now designated as the single NKC-135B. It is flown by the 452nd Test Squadron at Edwards AFB and used for inflight refueling support. (Don Logan)

RIGHT: NC-135A 60-0369, photographed at Nellis AFB in March, 1975 was used for spectral testing to CTTC. (Don Logan)

BELOW: NC-135A 60-0372 was used as a testbed for AFSATCOM (Air Force Satellite Communications) testing. (Jerry Geer)

BELOW RIGHT: NC-135A 60-0376, nicknamed the "Flying Piccolo," was assigned to the Air Force Special Weapons Center at Kirtland AFB and used for nuclear weapons testing support. (Tom Brewer Collection)

NC-135A 60-0377, photographed with a black fuselage top on August 31, 1970, was used for infra-red testing under project IWATCH. (Tom Brewer Collection)

NC-135A 60-0377 used for B-2 avionics and radar testing was retired to the Edwards AFB Museum on December 15, 1995. (USAF)

CHAPTER SEVEN

Aircraft Description

C-135 AIRCRAFT FAMILY TREE

AIRCRAFT DESIGNATIONS					AIR REFUELING	
PRODUCTION	PRESENT	AIRFRAME	ENGINES	STABILIZER	BOOM	RECEIVER
C-135A	C-135A	A	J57-43/59	Short	No	No
	C-135E		TF33-PW-102	Long		
	EC-135E		TF33-PW-102	Long		
	EC-135N		TF33-PW-102	Long		
C-135A	NC-135A	A	J57-43	Short	No	No
C-135B	C-135B	A	TF33-P-5	Long	No	Yes
	C-135C					
	RC-135S					
	RC-135W					
	RC-135X					
	TC-135B					
	TC-135S					
	TC-135W					
C-135B	WC-135B	A	TF33-P-5	Long	No	Yes
KC-135A	KC-135A	(K)A	J57-43/59	Short	Yes	No
	EC-135A		J57-59	Short		Yes
	EC-135G		J57-59	Short		Yes
	EC-135H		TF33-PW-102	Long		Yes
	EC-135K		TF33-PW-102	Long		No
	EC-135L		J57-59	Short		Yes
	EC-135P		TF33-PW-102	Long		Yes
	EC-135Y		TF33-PW-102	Long		No
	KC-135E		TF33-PW-102	Long		A
	KC-135Q		J57-59	Short		No
	KC-135R		F108-CF-100	Long		B
	KC-135T		F108-CF-100	Long		No
	NKC-135A		J57-43	Short		No
KC-135A	NKC-135E	(K)A	TF33-PW-102	Long	Yes	No
KC-135B	EC-135C	(K)A	TF33-P-9	Long	Yes	Yes
KC-135B	EC-135J	(K)A	TF33-P-9	Long	Yes	Yes
RC-135A	KC-135D	A	TF33-PW-102	Long	Yes	No
RC-135B	RC-135U	(K)A	TF33-P-9	Long	No	Yes
RC-135B	RC-135V	(K)A	TF33-P-9	Long	No	Yes

A 59-1514 IS ONLY KC-135E RECEIVER AIRCRAFT.

B 58-011, 58-018, 58-124, 58-126, 60-356, 60-357, 60-362, AND 61-293 ARE ONLY KC-135R RECIEVER AIRCRAFT.

AIRCRAFT DIMENSIONS

AIRCRAFT ENGINE / AIRCRAFT COMPONENT	J57-43 J57-59 TURBOJET	TF33-P-5 TF33-P-9 TF33-PW-102 TURBOFAN	F108-CF-100 TURBOFAN
General			
Span	130 ft 10 in.	130 ft 10 in.	130 ft 10 in.
Overall Length (not including boom)	134 ft 6 in.	135 ft 1 in.	135 ft 1 in.
Height	41 ft 9 in.	41 ft 9 in.	41 ft 9 in.
Height (fin folded)	19 ft 7 in.	19 ft 7 in.	19 ft 7 in.
Inboard Nacelle Clearance (average)	33 in.	29 in.	21.1 in.
Outboard Nacelle Clearance (average)	57 in.	53 in.	45.7 in.
Maximum Gross Weight – Taxi			
C-135A	279,500 lbs.		
EC-135A/G/L, KC-135A/Q, NC-135A, NKC-135A	301,600 lbs.		
C-135B/C, RC-135S/W, TC-135 B/S/W, WC-135B		277,500 lbs.	
C-135E, EC-135E/N		279,500 lbs.	
EC-135C/E/H/J/K/P, KC-135D/E, NKC-135E, RC-135U/V/X		301,600 lbs.	
KC-135R/T			322,500 lbs.
Wing			
Type	Low	Low	Low
Airfoil Section	BAC 310, 311, 312, 313	BAC 310, 311, 312, 313	BAC 310, 311, 312, 313
Chord at Root	337.8 in.	337.8 in.	337.8 in.
Chord Near Tip	112.0 in.	112.0 in.	112.0 in.
Mean Aerodynamic Chord	241.88 in.	241.88 in.	241.88 in.
Incidence	2 degrees	2 degrees	2 degrees
Dihedral	7 degrees	7 degrees	7 degrees
Sweepback (at 1/4 chord)	35 degrees	35 degrees	35 degrees
Aspect Ratio	7.035	7.035	7.035
Stabilizer			
Span	39 ft 8 in.	43 ft 0 in.	43 ft 0 in.
Maximum Chord	208.00 in.	214.24 in.	214.24 in.
Incidence (normal)	8 degrees	8 degrees	8 degrees
Dihedral	7 degrees	7 degrees	7 degrees

AIRCRAFT DIMENSIONS

AIRCRAFT ENGINE / AIRCRAFT COMPONENT	J57-43 J57-59 TURBOJET	TF33-P-5 TF33-P-9 TF33-PW-102 TURBOFAN	F108-CF-100 TURBOFAN
Fin			
Height	25 ft	25 ft	25 ft
Base Chord	20 ft 2 in.	20 ft 2 in.	20 ft 2 in.
Angle of Sweepback (leading edge)	36 deg 10 min	36 deg 10 min	36 deg 10 min
Fuselage			
Maximum Width	12 ft	12 ft	12 ft
Maximum Height	17 ft 10 in.	17 ft 10 in.	17 ft 10 in.
Overall Length	128 ft 10 in.	128 ft 10 in.	128 ft 10 in.
Height of Entry Door Above Ground	5 ft 4 in.	5 ft 4 in.	5 ft 4 in.
Dimensions of Entry Door			
Height	40 in.	40 in.	40 in.
Width	49 in.	49 in.	49 in.
Height of Cargo Door Above Ground	10 ft	10 ft	10 ft
Dimensions of Cargo Door			
Height	6 ft 6 in.	6 ft 6 in.	6 ft 6 in.
Width	9 ft 9 in.	9 ft 9 in.	9 ft 9 in.
Areas			
Wings (less ailerons)	2313.4 sq ft	2313.4 sq ft	2313.4 sq ft
Wing (with flaps extended)	2754.4 sq ft	2754.4 sq ft	2754.4 sq ft
Ailerons (total)	119.6 sq ft	119.6 sq ft	119.6 sq ft
Flaps (total)	361.6 sq ft	361.6 sq ft	361.6 sq ft
Stabilizers (including elevators)	500.0 sq ft	545.0 sq ft	545.0 sq ft
Elevators (total including tab)	125.6 sq ft	125.6 sq ft	125.6 sq ft
Elevator Tabs (total)	11.0 sq ft	11.0 sq ft	11.0 sq ft
Fin (including rudder)	337.0 sq ft	337.0 sq ft	337.0 sq ft
Rudder (including tabs)	102.8 sq ft	102.8 sq ft	102.8 sq ft
Rudder Tabs (total)	7.29 sq ft	7.29 sq ft	7.29 sq ft

J57 POWERED AIRCRAFT

AIRCRAFT WITH J57-43 OR J57-59 TURBOJET ENGINES

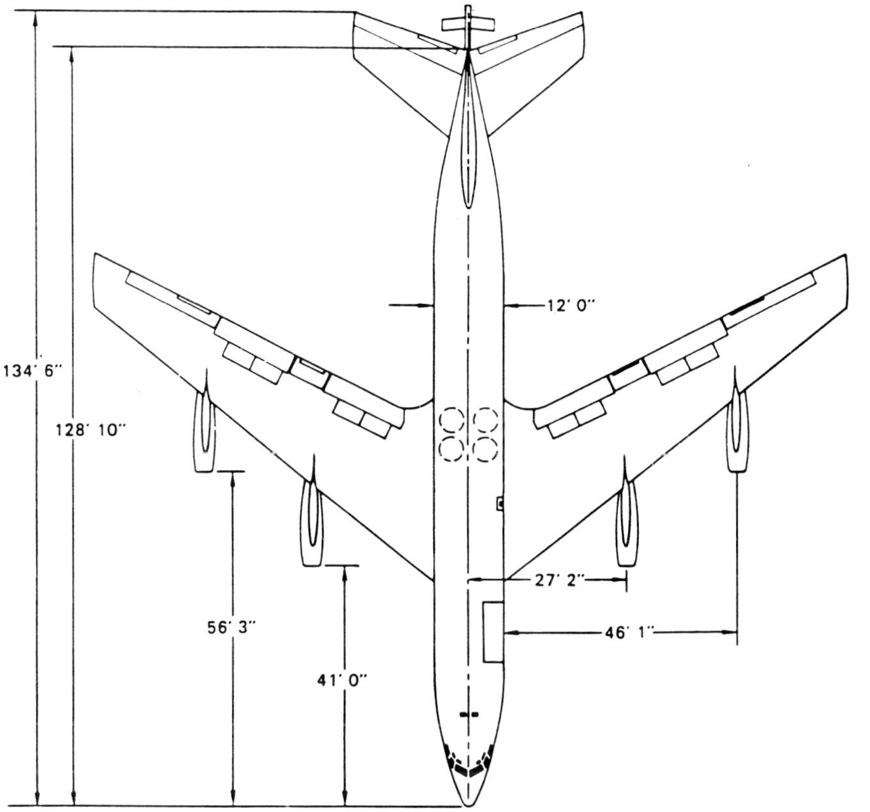

PLAN VIEW

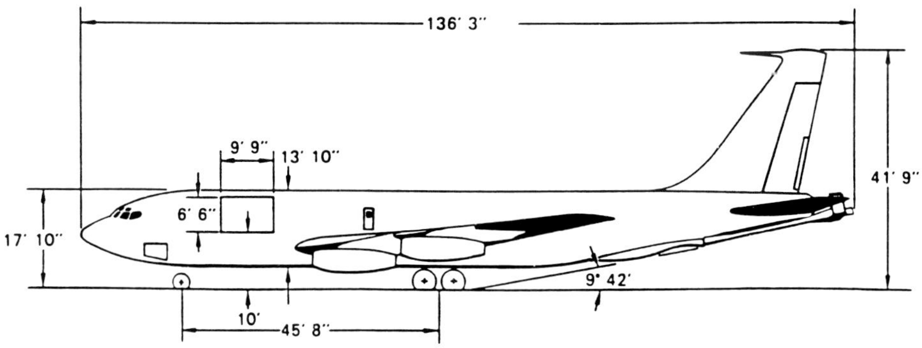

SIDE VIEW

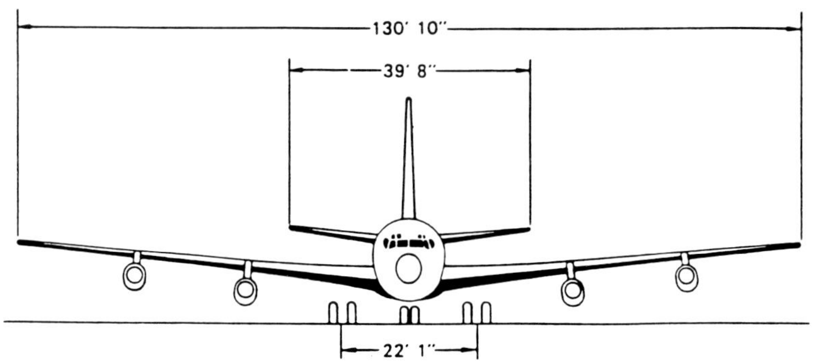

FRONT VIEW

TF33 POWERED AIRCRAFT

AIRCRAFT WITH TF33-P-5, TF33-P-9, AND TF33-PW-102 TURBOFAN ENGINES

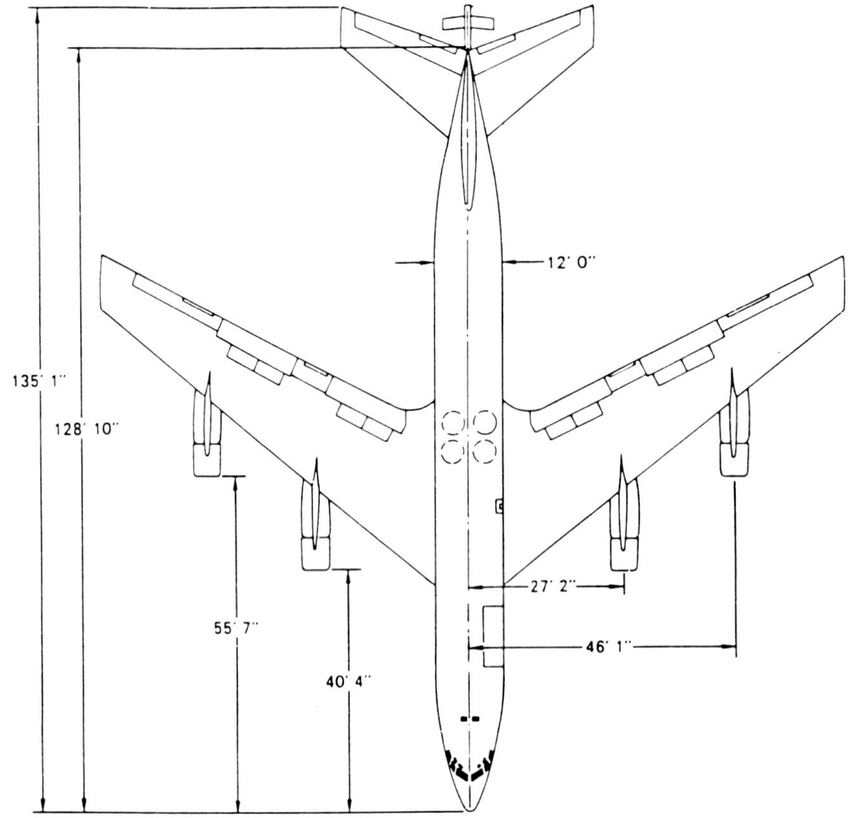

PLAN VIEW

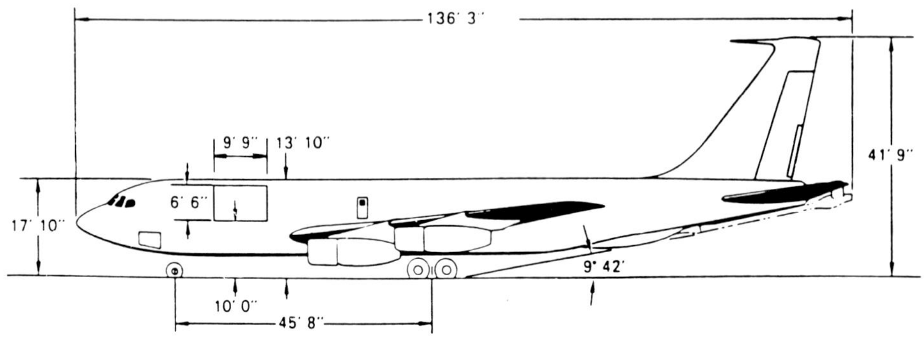

SIDE VIEW

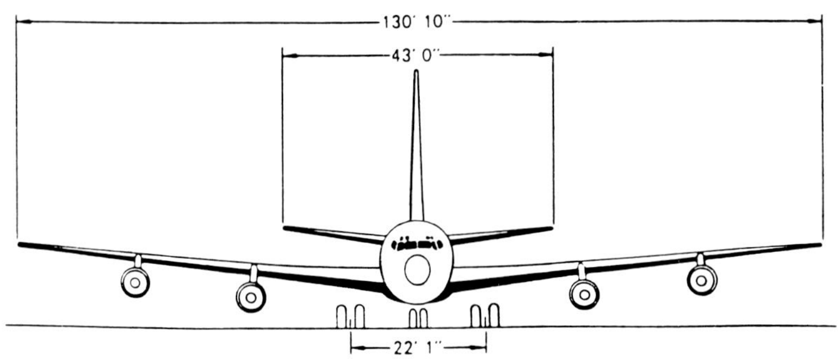

FRONT VIEW

F108-CF-100 (CFM56) POWERED AIRCRAFT

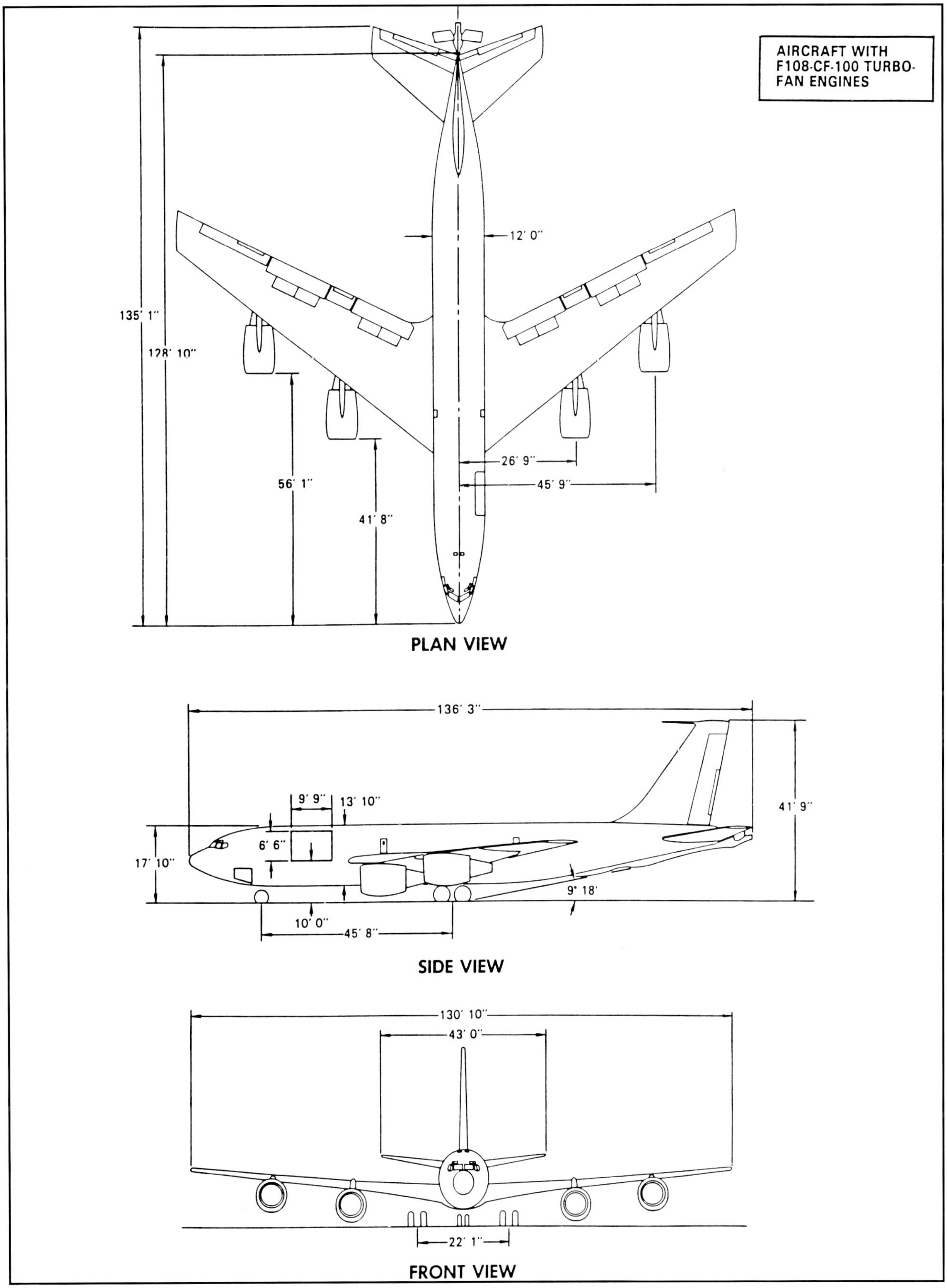

Appendices

C/KC-135 AIRCRAFT WITH AIR REFUELING RECEIVER (ARR) CAPABILITY

	BOEING	LTV
KC-135R		
58-0011	X	
58-0018	X	
58-0124		X
58-0126		X
60-0356		X
60-0357		X
60-0362		X
61-0293	X	
KC-135E		
59-1514		X
NKC-135E		
55-3132		X
C-135C		
61-2668	X	
61-2669	X	
61-2671	X	
EC-135A		
61-0262	X	
61-0278	X	
61-0287	X	
61-0289	X	
61-0297	X	
EC-135C		
62-3581	X	
62-3582	X	
62-3583	X	
62-3585	X	
63-8046	X	
63-8047	X	
63-8048	X	
63-8049	X	
63-8050	X	
63-8051	X	
63-8052	X	
63-8053	X	
63-8054	X	
EC-135G		
62-3570	X	
62-3579	X	
63-7994	X	
63-8001	X	
EC-135H		
61-0282	X	
61-0285	X	
61-0286	X	
61-0291	X	
EC-135J		
63-8055	X	
63-8056	X	
63-8057	X	
EC-135L		
61-0261	X	
61-0263	X	
61-0269	X	
61-0279	X	
61-0283	X	
EC-135N		
61-327		X
EC-135P		
55-3129	X	
58-0007	X	
58-0019	X	
58-0022	X	
61-0274	X	
EC-135Y		
55-3125		X
OC-135B		
61-2670	X	
61-2672	X	
61-2674	X	
WC-135B		
61-2673	X	
WC-135W		
61-2665	X	
61-2666	X	
61-2667	X	
RC-135S		
61-2662		X
61-2663		X
61-2664		X
62-4128		X
RC-135T		
55-3121		X
RC-135U		
64-14847	X	
64-14849	X	
RC-135V		
63-9792	X	
64-14841	X	
64-14842	X	
64-14843	X	
64-14844	X	
64-14845	X	
64-14846	X	
64-14848	X	
RC-135W		
62-4125		X
62-4130		X
62-4131		X
62-4132		X
62-4134		X
62-4135		X
62-4138		X
62-4139		X
TC-135S		
62-4133		X
TC-135W		
62-4129		X

KC-135Rs 61-0288 and 61-0302, and KC-135E 61-0281 have disabled ARR Systems. These aircraft at one time in their service life were included in EC-135L PACCS Radio Relay Fleet and had the Boeing system like the current EC-135L aircraft. These aircraft are not currently refuelable tankers.
LTV (Ling-Temco-Vought) later became E-Systems

AIRCRAFT LOSSES

Seventy-three C-135 series aircraft have been destroyed as a result of accidents since the KC-135A's first flight on August 31, 1956. The following list is in chronological order by the date of loss.

DATE	SERIAL NUMBER	TYPE	BASE	REMARKS
06/27/58	56-3599	KC-135A	Westover	Heavy weight takeoff, night, light rain, crashed 1 mile off the end of the runway.
11/24/58	56-3598	KC-135A	Loring	Cross wind takeoff, lost No. 4 engine, crashed to right and burned.
03/21/59	58-0002	KC-135A	Bergstrom	Structural limitations exceeded in flight through a thunderstorm near Killeen, Texas.
06/22/59	57-1446	KC-135A	Walker	During fuel cell repair a ground heater air blower caused wing tank explosion. The airplane burned, a total loss.
10/15/59	57-1513	KC-135A	Columbus	Destroyed by in-flight collision with B-52 during air refueling near Litchfield, Kentucky.
02/03/60	56-3628 57-1449 57-1457	KC-135A	Walker	Take-off in gusty crosswind. 56-3628 ran off the runway and into 57-1449 and 57-1457. All three aircraft were destroyed by the crash and resulting fire.
03/08/60	57-1466	KC-135A	Carswell	In fog, aircraft touched down one mile short of runway, became airborne again and hit a power line and small building before crashing on runway overrun.
11/18/60	56-3605	KC-135A	Loring	Extremely hard landing, folded nose gear aft into the body fuel tank.
01/25/62	56-3657	KC-135A	Altus	Fuel-air starter explosion, punctured the wing tank, aircraft destroyed by fire.
05/09/62	56-3618	KC-135A	Loring	Heavy weight night take-off, crashed and burned 2,500 feet from the end of the runway. Angle drive shaft on No. 2 engine had failed.
08/08/62	55-3144	KC-135A	Wright-	Landing accident on approach to Hanscom Field, Patterson, Massachusetts. Crashed 2,700 feet short of the overrun and destroyed by fire.
09/10/62	60-0352	KC-135A	Ellsworth	During letdown for landing at Fairchild AFB the aircraft crashed into Mt. Kit Carson at 4,400 foot level.
10/23/62	62-4136	C-135B	McGuire	Landing approach to Guantanamo NAS, Cuba. Wing contacted the ground 1,000 feet short of runway 09 with the aircraft in a steep right turn.
02/27/63	56-3597	KC-135A	Castle	Night take-off at Eielson AFB in poor visibility, lost power on No. 1 engine after S1 speed.
06/21/63	57-1498	KC-135A	Westover	Aircraft, while making a airborne radar approach in heavy rain, hit a 790 foot hill approximately 5 miles out and 1 mile left of the runway centerline.
08/28/63	61-0319 61-0322	KC-135A KC-135A	Homestead Homestead	The two aircraft were returning in trail formation from Refueling operations over the Atlantic Ocean under VFR conditions. Probably collided.
05/11/64	61-0332	C-135B	Travis	During visual approach at Clark AB in heavy rain the left wing struck the TACAN tower 3,500 feet short of the runway. The aircraft impacted the perimeter road and broke up 1,500 feet short of the runway.
07/08/64	60-0340	KC-135A	Larson	The aircraft was making an air refueling rendezvous with three F-105s under VFR conditions. Confusion put the fighters on a collision course with the tanker. The second F-105 hit the tanker. Both aircraft were lost.
01/04/65	61-0265	KC-135A	Loring	Shortly after VFR take-off the aircraft wallowed and crashed approximately 12,000 feet past the end of the runway. Number 3 and 4 engines were shed prior to impact.
01/16/65	57-1442	KC-135A	Clinton	On take-off from McConnell AFB in support of a Sherman B-52 test, and on its way back to Clinton-Sherman, the aircraft entered a left turn and crashed into a residential section of Wichita approximately 10.5 miles from take-off.
02/26/65	63-8882	KC-135A	Dow	A mid-air collision with a B-47 occurred in clear weather over the North Atlantic. The B-47 was second in a three aircraft cell and struck the KC-135 while attempting to move into refueling position.
06/03/65	63-8042	KC-135A	Walker	On a simulated missed approach at night in blowing dust and sand, the aircraft was flown into the ground beyond the end of the runway.
06/25/65	60-0373	C-135A	McGuire	During a night take-off from El Toro MCAS, the aircraft impacted approximately 200 feet below the peak of a hill 4 miles from the end of the runway.
01/17/66	61-0273	KC-135A	Blytheville	The aircraft was lost following an inflight collision with a B-52 off the coast of Spain during refueling.
05/17/66	57-1424	KC-135A	Amarillo	During landing the aircraft contacted the left wing, then the boom, then the right wing. The aircraft rolled left and right, departed the right side of the runway, exploded and burned.
05/19/66	57-1444	KC-135A	Kadena AB	During take-off in the rain, the aircraft became airborne at 7,000 feet, settled to the runway, became airborne again attaining a maximum altitude of 100 feet. The aircraft contacted the ground approximately 300 feet left of the runway centerline and 450 feet beyond the end of the runway.
01/19/67	56-3613	KC-135A	Fairchild	The aircraft struck Shadow Mountain during penetration for landing at Fairchild AFB.
04/19/67	55-3140	KC-135A	Castle	The aircraft was destroyed during maintenance at Wake Island. The right main landing gear oleo strut was over-inflated during jacking.
07/17/67	59-1465	KC-135R (Reconnaissance)	Offutt	The aircraft stalled out on a high rotation take-off in clear weather.
01/17/68	58-0026	KC-135A	March	The aircraft crashed at Minot AFB during take-off in poor weather.
07/30/68	56-3655	KC-135A	Castle	Fin and stabilizer departed the aircraft during a demonstration flight to a new crew. The aircraft crashed near Mt. Lassen, California.
09/24/68	55-3133	KC-135A	Loring	The aircraft was lost at Wake Island when a go-around was attempted from a three engine landing.
10/02/68	55-3138	KC-135A	Robins	The aircraft ran off the end of the runway during take-off from U-Tapao following a blow-out of the nose gear tires.
10/22/68	61-0301	KC-135A	Westover	Radio and Radar contact was lost when the airplane was approximately 65 miles from Ching Chaun Kang, Taiwan enroute to U-Tapao.
01/13/69	59-1491	RC-135S	Eielson	The aircraft veered off the side of the icy runway during landing roll in light snow at night.
03/25/69	56-3602	KC-135A	Loring	The aircraft aborted after S1 speed due to loss of water injection on the left side. The airplane continued off the end of the runway, proceeded down an embankment with the nose breaking off forward of the wing.

06/05/69	62-4137	RC-135E	Eielson	The aircraft reported inflight vibration 34 minutes after take-off. No further communications were received and no wreckage was ever found.
12/19/69	56-3629	KC-135A	Ellsworth	The aircraft disappeared after take-off from Ching Chaun Kang, Taiwan.
06/03/71	58-0039	KC-135Q	Torrejon	The airplane was lost while making an approach to Torrejon AB, Spain. The crew reported passing 17,000 feet, no further communications received. There was evidence of explosion.
06/31/71	61-0331	C-135B	Wright-Patterson	The aircraft disappeared in the Pacific Ocean between Hickam AFB, Hawaii and Samoa.
03/13/72	58-0048	KC-135A	Carswell	The aircraft hit short on landing and was destroyed.
07/01/72	63-8473	C-135F	French AF	The aircraft was lost on take-off from an island air field in the South Pacific. The aircraft lost power on engine number three, and as the crew turned back to attempt a landing, power was lost on engine number four. The aircraft crashed a short time later.
03/08/73	63-7989	KC-135A	Lockbourne	The aircraft collided with 63-7980 during alert taxi exercise.
03/05/74	57-1500	KC-135A	McConnell	The aircraft crashed on take-off.
12/08/75	60-0354	KC-135A	Eielson	The aircraft had landing gear retraction problems and crashed after takeoff.
02/06/76	60-0368	KC-135A	K I Sawyer	The aircraft crashed during approach to Torrejon AB, Spain.
09/26/76	61-0296	KC-135A	K I Sawyer	The aircraft crashed near Alpena, Michigan while returning to K. I. Sawyer.
03/04/77	62-3522	KC-135A	Griffiss	The aircraft experienced an engine turbine wheel failure during engine trim and was destroyed by fire.
04/29/77	58-0101	KC-135A	Beale	The aircraft, based at Castle, hit cattle on the runway during a touch and go landing.
09/14/77	62-3536	EC-135K	Kirtland	The aircraft crashed into a mountain shortly after take-off.
09/19/79	58-0127	KC-135A	Castle	Veered off the runway during touch and go with a simulated engine out.
01/30/80	58-0007	EC-135P	Langley	The aircraft burned on the ramp during ground water heating.
02/08/80	60-0338	KC-135Q	Plattsburgh	The aircraft was destroyed as a result of an aft body fuel tank explosion occurring during ground refueling.
03/16/81	61-2664	RC-135S	Eielson	The aircraft crashed short of the runway on landing at Shemya AFB, Alaska, sheared off the landing gear and burned.
05/06/81	61-0328	EC-135N	Wright-Patterson	Aircraft entered a rapid descent from cruise altitude and crashed near Frederick Maryland, probably due to runaway elevator trim.
03/13/82	57-1489	KC-135A	Arizona ANG	The aircraft crashed due to a mid air collision with a light aircraft while on approach to Luke AFB.
03/19/82	58-0031	KC-135A	Illinois ANG	The aircraft exploded at 13,500 feet MSL while on approach to Chicago O'Hare airport. It crashed 33 miles north west of the airport.
02/25/85	55-3121	RC-135T	Offutt	The aircraft hit a mountain near Valdez, Alaska while on landing approach.
03/19/85	61-0316	KC-135A	Barksdale	Burned on ramp in Cairo, Egypt during refueling
08/27/85	59-1443	KC-135A	Beale	The aircraft, based at Castle, crashed on go-around after a hard landing.
06/17/86	63-7983	KC-135A	Ellsworth	Crashed after a hard landing at Howard AFB Panama.
02/13/87	60-0330	KC-135A	Altus	The aircraft exploded and burned after landing.
03/13/87	60-0361	KC-135A	Fairchild	The aircraft, while practicing for an air show flew through a B-52s wing tip vortices, lost control and crashed on base at Fairchild.
10/11/88	60-0317	KC-135A	Wurtsmith	The aircraft crashed on landing at Wurtsmith AFB.
01/31/89	63-7990	KC-135A	K.I. Sawyer	The aircraft crashed on takeoff at Dyess AFB.
09/21/89	57-1481	KC-135E	Eielson Alaska ANG	The aircraft exploded and burned on the ramp at Eielson AFB.
10/04/89	59-3592	KC-135A	Loring	The aircraft exploded on landing approach to Loring AFB.
01/11/90	59-1494	KC-135E	Pease, New Hampshire ANG	The aircraft exploded and burned on the ramp at Pease AFB.
05/29/92	62-3584	EC-135J	Offutt	The aircraft ran off the end of the runway on landing at Pope AFB and broke apart.
12/10/93	57-1470	KC-135R	Wisconsin ANG	The aircraft exploded burned on the ramp at Mitchell Field, Milwaukee, Wisconsin.

MUSEUM C-135s (15)

55-3118	EC-135K	McConnell AFB, Kansas
55-3123	NKC-135A	AF Museum, Wright-Patterson AFB, Ohio
55-3130	KC-135A	March AFB, California
55-3139	KC-135A	Castle AFB, California
56-3598	KC-135A	Barksdale AFB, Louisiana
56-3639	KC-135A	Dyess AFB, Texas
60-0377	NC-135A	Edwards AFB, California
61-0262	EC-135A	Ellsworth AFB, South Dakota
61-0269	EC-135L	Grissom AFB, Indiana
61-0287	EC-135A	Offutt AFB, Nebraska
61-2671	C-135C	Tinker AFB, Oklahoma
63-8005	KC-135A	Grand Forks AFB, North Dakota
63-8010	KC-135A	Scott AFB, Illinois
63-8049	EC-135C	Offutt AFB, Nebraska
63-8057	EC-135J	Pima Air and Space Museum, Tucson, Arizona

C-135 GROUND TRAINERS

55-3124	GNKC-135A	Sheppard AFB, Texas
58-0070	GKC-135A	Sheppard AFB, Texas
60-0369	GNC-135A	Chanute AFB (Scrapped October 1991)
61-0282	GEC-135H	Sheppard AFB, Texas
61-0286	GEC-135H	Sheppard AFB, Texas

Destructive Testing Pax River, MD

56-3616	KC-135A	Input	January 1993
56-3617	KC-135A	Input	March 1993
56-3632	KC-135A	Input	February 1993
56-3656	KC-135A	Input	November 1992

AIRCRAFT MODELS BY SERIAL NUMBER

55-3118 – (KC-135A, EC-135K)
55-3119 – (KC-135A, JKC-135A, NKC-135A)
55-3120 – (KC-135A, NKC-135A)
55-3121 – (KC-135A, JKC-135A, KC-135R, KC-135T, RC-135T)
55-3122 – (KC-135A, JKC-135A, NKC-135A)
55-3123 – (KC-135A, JKC-135A, NKC-135A)
55-3124 – (KC-135A, JKC-135A, NKC-135A, GNKC-135A)
55-3125 – (KC-135A, JKC-135A, NKC-135A, EC-135Y)
55-3126 – (KC-135A) First "Speckled Trout"
55-3127 – (KC-135A, JKC-135A, NKC-135A)
55-3128 – (KC-135A, NKC-135A)
55-3129 – (KC-135A, NASA KC-135A WW I, JKC-135A, NKC-135A, NKC-135E, EC-135P)
55-3130 – (KC-135A)
55-3131 – (KC-135A, JKC-135A, NKC-135A)
55-3132 – (KC-135A, NKC-135A, NKC-135E)
55-3133 – (KC-135A)
55-3134 – (KC-135A, JKC-135A, NKC-135A) (ASD and USN)
55-3135 – (KC-135A, JKC-135A, NKC-135A, NKC-135E)
55-3136 – (KC-135A)
55-3137 – (KC-135A)
55-3138 – (KC-135A)
55-3139 – (KC-135A)
55-3140 – (KC-135A)
55-3141 – (KC-135A, KC-135E)
55-3142 – (KC-135A)
55-3143 – (KC-135A, KC-135E)
55-3144 – (KC-135A)
55-3145 – (KC-135A, KC-135E)
55-3146 – (KC-135A, KC-135E)
56-3591 – (KC-135A)
56-3592 – (KC-135A)
56-3593 – (KC-135A, KC-135E)
56-3594 – (KC-135A)
56-3595 – (KC-135A)
56-3596 – (KC-135A, JKC-135A, NKC-135A – USN)
56-3597 – (KC-135A)
56-3598 – (KC-135A)
56-3599 – (KC-135A)
56-3600 – (KC-135A)
56-3601 – (KC-135A)
56-3602 – (KC-135A)
56-3603 – (KC-135A)
56-3604 – (KC-135A, KC-135E)
56-3605 – (KC-135A)
56-3606 – (KC-135A, KC-135E)
56-3607 – (KC-135A, KC-135E)
56-3608 – (KC-135A)
56-3609 – (KC-135A, KC-135E)
56-3610 – (KC-135A)
56-3611 – (KC-135A, KC-135E)
56-3612 – (KC-135A, KC-135E)
56-3613 – (KC-135A)
56-3614 – (KC-135A)
56-3615 – (KC-135A)
56-3616 – (KC-135A)
56-3617 – (KC-135A)
56-3618 – (KC-135A)
56-3619 – (KC-135A)
56-3620 – (KC-135A)
56-3621 – (KC-135A)
56-3622 – (KC-135A, KC-135E)
56-3623 – (KC-135A, KC-135E)
56-3624 – (KC-135A)
56-3625 – (KC-135A)
56-3626 – (KC-135A, KC-135E)
56-3627 – (KC-135A)
56-3628 – (KC-135A)
56-3629 – (KC-135A)
56-3630 – (KC-135A, KC-135E)
56-3631 – (KC-135A, KC-135E)
56-3632 – (KC-135A)
56-3633 – (KC-135A)
56-3634 – (KC-135A)
56-3635 – (KC-135A)
56-3636 – (KC-135A)
56-3637 – (KC-135A)
56-3638 – (KC-135A, KC-135E)
56-3639 – (KC-135A)
56-3640 – (KC-135A, KC-135E)
56-3641 – (KC-135A, KC-135E)
56-3642 – (KC-135A)
56-3643 – (KC-135A, KC-135E)
56-3644 – (KC-135A)
56-3645 – (KC-135A, KC-135E)
56-3646 – (KC-135A)
56-3647 – (KC-135A)
56-3648 – (KC-135A, KC-135E)
56-3649 – (KC-135A)
56-3650 – (KC-135A, KC-135E)
56-3651 – (KC-135A)
56-3652 – (KC-135A)
56-3653 – (KC-135A)
56-3654 – (KC-135A, KC-135E)
56-3655 – (KC-135A)
56-3656 – (KC-135A)
56-3657 – (KC-135A)
56-3658 – (KC-135A, KC-135E)
57-1418 – (KC-135A, KC-135R)
57-1419 – (KC-135A, KC-135R)
57-1420 – (KC-135A)
57-1421 – (KC-135A, KC-135E)
57-1422 – (KC-135A, KC-135E)
57-1423 – (KC-135A, KC-135E)
57-1424 – (KC-135A)
57-1425 – (KC-135A, KC-135E)
57-1426 – (KC-135A, KC-135E)
57-1427 – (KC-135A, KC-135R)
57-1428 – (KC-135A, KC-135E, KC-135R)
57-1429 – (KC-135A, KC-135E)
57-1430 – (KC-135A, KC-135R)
57-1431 – (KC-135A, KC-135E)
57-1432 – (KC-135A, KC-135R)
57-1433 – (KC-135A, KC-135E)
57-1434 – (KC-135A, KC-135E)
57-1435 – (KC-135A, KC-135R)
57-1436 – (KC-135A, KC-135E, KC-135R)
57-1437 – (KC-135A, KC-135R)
57-1438 – (KC-135A, KC-135E)
57-1439 – (KC-135A, KC-135R)
57-1440 – (KC-135A, KC-135R)
57-1441 – (KC-135A, KC-135E)
57-1442 – (KC-135A)
57-1443 – (KC-135A, KC-135E)
57-1444 – (KC-135A)
57-1445 – (KC-135A, KC-135E)
57-1446 – (KC-135A)
57-1447 – (KC-135A, KC-135E)
57-1448 – (KC-135A, KC-135E)
57-1449 – (KC-135A)
57-1450 – (KC-135A, KC-135E)
57-1451 – (KC-135A, KC-135E, KC-135R)
57-1452 – (KC-135A, KC-135E)
57-1453 – (KC-135A, KC-135R)
57-1454 – (KC-135A, KC-135R)
57-1455 – (KC-135A, KC-135E)
57-1456 – (KC-135A, KC-135R)
57-1457 – (KC-135A)
57-1458 – (KC-135A, KC-135E)
57-1459 – (KC-135A, KC-135E, KC-135R)
57-1460 – (KC-135A, KC-135E)
57-1461 – (KC-135A, KC-135R)
57-1462 – (KC-135A, KC-135R)
57-1463 – (KC-135A, KC-135E)
57-1464 – (KC-135A, KC-135E)
57-1465 – (KC-135A, KC-135E)
57-1466 – (KC-135A)
57-1467 – (KC-135A)
57-1468 – (KC-135A, KC-135E, KC-135R)
57-1469 – (KC-135A, KC-135R)
57-1470 – (KC-135A, KC-135R)
57-1471 – (KC-135A, KC-135E)
57-1472 – (KC-135A, KC-135R)
57-1473 – (KC-135A, KC-135R)
57-1474 – (KC-135A, KC-135R)
57-1475 – (KC-135A, KC-135E)
57-1476 – (KC-135A)
57-1477 – (KC-135A)
57-1478 – (KC-135A, KC-135E)
57-1479 – (KC-135A, KC-135E, KC-135R)
57-1480 – (KC-135A, KC-135E)
57-1481 – (KC-135A, KC-135E)
57-1482 – (KC-135A, KC-135E)
57-1483 – (KC-135A, KC-135R)
57-1484 – (KC-135A, KC-135E)
57-1485 – (KC-135A, KC-135E)
57-1486 – (KC-135A, KC-135R)
57-1487 – (KC-135A, KC-135R)
57-1488 – (KC-135A, KC-135R)
57-1489 – (KC-135A)
57-1490 – (KC-135A)
57-1491 – (KC-135A, KC-135E)
57-1492 – (KC-135A, KC-135E)
57-1493 – (KC-135A, KC-135R)
57-1494 – (KC-135A, KC-135E)
57-1495 – (KC-135A, KC-135E)
57-1496 – (KC-135A, KC-135E)
57-1497 – (KC-135A, KC-135E)
57-1498 – (KC-135A)
57-1499 – (KC-135A, KC-135R)
57-1500 – (KC-135A)
57-1501 – (KC-135A, KC-135E)
57-1502 – (KC-135A, KC-135R)
57-1503 – (KC-135A, KC-135E)
57-1504 – (KC-135A, KC-135E)
57-1505 – (KC-135A, KC-135E)
57-1506 – (KC-135A, KC-135R)
57-1507 – (KC-135A, KC-135E)
57-1508 – (KC-135A, KC-135R)
57-1509 – (KC-135A, KC-135E)
57-1510 – (KC-135A, KC-135E)
57-1511 – (KC-135A, KC-135E)
57-1512 – (KC-135A, KC-135E, KC-135R)
57-1513 – (KC-135A)
57-1514 – (KC-135A, KC-135R)
57-2589 – (KC-135A, KC-135E)
57-2590 – (KC-135A)
57-2591 – (KC-135A)
57-2592 – (KC-135A, Turkish KC-135R)
57-2593 – (KC-135A, KC-135R)
57-2594 – (KC-135A, KC-135E)
57-2595 – (KC-135A, KC-135E)
57-2596 – (KC-135A)
57-2597 – (KC-135A, KC-135R)
57-2598 – (KC-135A, KC-135E, KC-135R)
57-2599 – (KC-135A, KC-135R)
57-2600 – (KC-135A, KC-135E)
57-2601 – (KC-135A, KC-135E)
57-2602 – (KC-135A, KC-135E)

57-2603 – (KC-135A, KC-135E, KC-135R)
57-2604 – (KC-135A, KC-135E)
57-2605 – (KC-135A, KC-135R)
57-2606 – (KC-135A, KC-135E)
57-2607 – (KC-135A, KC-135E)
57-2608 – (KC-135A, KC-135E)
57-2609 – (KC-135A)
58-0001 – (KC-135A, KC-135R)
58-0002 – (KC-135A)
58-0003 – (KC-135A, KC-135E)
58-0004 – (KC-135A, KC-135R)
58-0005 – (KC-135A, KC-135E)
58-0006 – (KC-135A, KC-135E)
58-0007 – (KC-135A, EC-135A, EC-135P)
58-0008 – (KC-135A, KC-135E, KC-135R)
58-0009 – (KC-135A, KC-135R)
58-0010 – (KC-135A, KC-135R)
58-0011 – (KC-135A, EC-135A, EC-135P, KC-135A, KC-135R)
58-0012 – (KC-135A, KC-135E)
58-0013 – (KC-135A, KC-135E)
58-0014 – (KC-135A, KC-135E)
58-0015 – (KC-135A, KC-135R)
58-0016 – (KC-135A, KC-135R)
58-0017 – (KC-135A, KC-135E)
58-0018 – (KC-135A, EC-135A, EC-135P, KC-135A, KC-135R)
58-0019 – (KC-135A, EC-135A, EC-135P)
58-0020 – (KC-135A, KC-135E)
58-0021 – (KC-135A, KC-135R)
58-0022 – (KC-135A, EC-135A, EC-135P)
58-0023 – (KC-135A, KC-135R)
58-0024 – (KC-135A, KC-135E)
58-0025 – (KC-135A)
58-0026 – (KC-135A)
58-0027 – (KC-135A, KC-135R)
58-0028 – (KC-135A)
58-0029 – (KC-135A)
58-0030 – (KC-135A, KC-135R)
58-0031 – (KC-135A)
58-0032 – (KC-135A, KC-135E)
58-0033 – (KC-135A)
58-0034 – (KC-135A, KC-135R)
58-0035 – (KC-135A, KC-135R)
58-0036 – (KC-135A, KC-135R)
58-0037 – (KC-135A, KC-135E)
58-0038 – (KC-135A, KC-135R)
58-0039 – (KC-135A, KC-135Q)
58-0040 – (KC-135A, KC-135E)
58-0041 – (KC-135A, KC-135E)
58-0042 – (KC-135A, KC-135Q, KC-135T)
58-0043 – (KC-135A, KC-135E)
58-0044 – (KC-135A, KC-135E)
58-0045 – (KC-135A, KC-135Q, KC-135T)
58-0046 – (KC-135A, KC-135Q, KC-135T)
58-0047 – (KC-135A, KC-135Q, KC-135T)
58-0048 – (KC-135A)
58-0049 – (KC-135A, KC-135Q, KC-135T)
58-0050 – (KC-135A, KC-135Q, KC-135T)
58-0051 – (KC-135A, KC-135R)
58-0052 – (KC-135A, KC-135E, KC-135R)
58-0053 – (KC-135A, KC-135E)
58-0054 – (KC-135A, KC-135Q, KC-135T)
58-0055 – (KC-135A, KC-135Q, KC-135T)
58-0056 – (KC-135A, KC-135R)
58-0057 – (KC-135A, KC-135E)
58-0058 – (KC-135A, KC-135E)
58-0059 – (KC-135A, KC-135R)
58-0060 – (KC-135A, KC-135Q, KC-135T)
58-0061 – (KC-135A, KC-135Q, KC-135T)
58-0062 – (KC-135A, KC-135Q, KC-135T)
58-0063 – (KC-135A, KC-135R)
58-0064 – (KC-135A, KC-135E)
58-0065 – (KC-135A, KC-135Q, KC-135T)
58-0066 – (KC-135A, KC-135R)
58-0067 – (KC-135A, KC-135E)
58-0068 – (KC-135A, KC-135E)
58-0069 – (KC-135A, KC-135Q, KC-135T)
58-0070 – (KC-135A, GKC-135A)
58-0071 – (KC-135A, KC-135Q, KC-135T)
58-0072 – (KC-135A, KC-135Q, KC-135T)
58-0073 – (KC-135A, KC-135R)
58-0074 – (KC-135A, KC-135Q, KC-135T)
58-0075 – (KC-135A, KC-135R)
58-0076 – (KC-135A, KC-135R)
58-0077 – (KC-135A, KC-135Q, KC-135T)
58-0078 – (KC-135A, KC-135E)
58-0079 – (KC-135A, KC-135R)
58-0080 – (KC-135A, KC-135E)
58-0081 – (KC-135A)
58-0082 – (KC-135A, KC-135E)
58-0083 – (KC-135A, KC-135R)
58-0084 – (KC-135A, KC-135Q, KC-135T)
58-0085 – (KC-135A, KC-135E, KC-135R)
58-0086 – (KC-135A, KC-135Q, KC-135T)
58-0087 – (KC-135A, KC-135E)
58-0088 – (KC-135A, KC-135Q, KC-135T)
58-0089 – (KC-135A, KC-135Q, KC-135T)
58-0090 – (KC-135A, KC-135E)
58-0091 – (KC-135A)
58-0092 – (KC-135A, KC-135R)
58-0093 – (KC-135A, KC-135R)
58-0094 – (KC-135A, KC-135Q, KC-135T)
58-0095 – (KC-135A, KC-135Q, KC-135T)
58-0096 – (KC-135A, KC-135E)
58-0097 – (KC-135A)
58-0098 – (KC-135A, KC-135R)
58-0099 – (KC-135A, KC-135Q, KC-135T)
58-0100 – (KC-135A, KC-135R)
58-0101 – (KC-135A)
58-0102 – (KC-135A, KC-135R)
58-0103 – (KC-135A, KC-135Q, KC-135T)
58-0104 – (KC-135A, KC-135R)
58-0105 – (KC-135A)
58-0106 – (KC-135A, KC-135R)
58-0107 – (KC-135A, KC-135E)
58-0108 – (KC-135A, KC-135E)
58-0109 – (KC-135A, KC-135R)
58-0110 – (KC-135A, Turkish KC-135R)
58-0111 – (KC-135A, KC-135E)
58-0112 – (KC-135A, KC-135Q, KC-135T)
58-0113 – (KC-135A, KC-135R)
58-0114 – (KC-135A, KC-135R)
58-0115 – (KC-135A, KC-135E)
58-0116 – (KC-135A, KC-135E)
58-0117 – (KC-135A, KC-135Q, KC-135T)
58-0118 – (KC-135A, KC-135R)
58-0119 – (KC-135A, KC-135R)
58-0120 – (KC-135A, KC-135R)
58-0121 – (KC-135A, KC-135R)
58-0122 – (KC-135A, KC-135R)
58-0123 – (KC-135A, KC-135R)
58-0124 – (KC-135A, KC-135R)
58-0125 – (KC-135A, KC-135Q, KC-135T)
58-0126 – (KC-135A, KC-135R, KC-135A, KC-135R)
58-0127 – (KC-135A)
58-0128 – (KC-135A, KC-135R)
58-0129 – (KC-135A, KC-135Q, KC-135T)
58-0130 – (KC-135A, KC-135R)
59-1443 – (KC-135A)
59-1444 – (KC-135A, KC-135R)
59-1445 – (KC-135A, KC-135E)
59-1446 – (KC-135A, KC-135R)
59-1447 – (KC-135A, KC-135E)
59-1448 – (KC-135A, KC-135E, KC-135R)
59-1449 – (KC-135A)
59-1450 – (KC-135A, KC-135E, KC-135R)
59-1451 – (KC-135A, KC-135E)
59-1452 – (KC-135A, KC-135E)
59-1453 – (KC-135A, KC-135R)
59-1454 – (KC-135A)
59-1455 – (KC-135A, KC-135R)
59-1456 – (KC-135A, KC-135E)
59-1457 – (KC-135A, KC-135E)
59-1458 – (KC-135A, KC-135R)
59-1459 – (KC-135A, KC-135R)
59-1460 – (KC-135A, KC-135Q, KC-135T)
59-1461 – (KC-135A, KC-135R)
59-1462 – (KC-135A, KC-135Q, KC-135T)
59-1463 – (KC-135A, KC-135R)
59-1464 – (KC-135A, KC-135Q, KC-135T)
59-1465 – (KC-135A, KC-135R)
59-1466 – (KC-135A, KC-135R)
59-1467 – (KC-135A, KC-135Q, KC-135T)
59-1468 – (KC-135A, KC-135Q, KC-135T)
59-1469 – (KC-135A, KC-135R)
59-1470 – (KC-135A, KC-135Q, KC-135T)
59-1471 – (KC-135A, KC-135Q, KC-135T)
59-1472 – (KC-135A, KC-135R)
59-1473 – (KC-135A, KC-135E)
59-1474 – (KC-135A, KC-135Q, KC-135T)
59-1475 – (KC-135A, KC-135R)
59-1476 – (KC-135A, KC-135R)
59-1477 – (KC-135A, KC-135E)
59-1478 – (KC-135A, KC-135R)
59-1479 – (KC-135A, KC-135E)
59-1480 – (KC-135A, KC-135Q, KC-135T)
59-1481 – (KC-135A, NASA KC-135A WW IV)
59-1482 – (KC-135A, KC-135R)
59-1483 – (KC-135A, KC-135R)
59-1484 – (KC-135A, KC-135E)
59-1485 – (KC-135A, KC-135E)
59-1486 – (KC-135A, KC-135R)
59-1487 – (KC-135A, KC-135E)
59-1488 – (KC-135A, KC-135R)
59-1489 – (KC-135A, KC-135E)
59-1490 – (KC-135A, KC-135Q, KC-135T)
59-1491 – (KC-135A, RC-135S)
59-1492 – (KC-135A, KC-135R)
59-1493 – (KC-135A, KC-135E)
59-1494 – (KC-135A, KC-135E)
59-1495 – (KC-135A, KC-135R)
59-1496 – (KC-135A, KC-135E)
59-1497 – (KC-135A, KC-135E)
59-1498 – (KC-135A, KC-135R)
59-1499 – (KC-135A, KC-135E, KC-135R)
59-1500 – (KC-135A, KC-135R)
59-1501 – (KC-135A, KC-135R)
59-1502 – (KC-135A, KC-135R)
59-1503 – (KC-135A, KC-135E)
59-1504 – (KC-135A, KC-135Q, KC-135T)
59-1505 – (KC-135A, KC-135E, KC-135R)
59-1506 – (KC-135A, KC-135E)
59-1507 – (KC-135A, KC-135R)
59-1508 – (KC-135A, KC-135R)
59-1509 – (KC-135A, KC-135E, KC-135R)
59-1510 – (KC-135A, KC-135Q, KC-135T)
59-1511 – (KC-135A, KC-135R)
59-1512 – (KC-135A, KC-135Q, KC-135T)
59-1513 – (KC-135A, KC-135Q, KC-135T)
59-1514 – (KC-135A, KC-135R, KC-135A, KC-135E)
59-1515 – (KC-135A, KC-135R)
59-1516 – (KC-135A, KC-135E, KC-135R)
59-1517 – (KC-135A, KC-135R)
59-1518 – (KC-135A, EC-135K)
59-1519 – (KC-135A, KC-135E)
59-1520 – (KC-135A, KC-135Q, KC-135T)
59-1521 – (KC-135A, KC-135R)
59-1522 – (KC-135A, KC-135R)
59-1523 – (KC-135A, KC-135Q, KC-135T)

60-0313 – (KC-135A, KC-135R)
60-0314 – (KC-135A, KC-135R)
60-0315 – (KC-135A, KC-135R)
60-0316 – (KC-135A, KC-135E)
60-0317 – (KC-135A)
60-0318 – (KC-135A, KC-135R)
60-0319 – (KC-135A, KC-135R)
60-0320 – (KC-135A, KC-135R)
60-0321 – (KC-135A, KC-I35R)
60-0322 – (KC-135A, KC-135R)
60-0323 – (KC-135A, KC-135R)
60-0324 – (KC-135A, KC-135R)
60-0325 – (KC-135A, Turkish KC-135R)
60-0326 – (KC-135A, Turkish KC-135R)
60-0327 – (KC-135A, KC-135E)
60-0328 – (KC-135A, KC-135R)
60-0329 – (KC-135A, KC-135R)
60-0330 – (KC-135A)
60-0331 – (KC-135A, KC-135R)
60-0332 – (KC-135A, KC-135R)
60-0333 – (KC-135A, KC-135R)
60-0334 – (KC-135A, KC-135R)
60-0335 – (KC-135A, KC-135Q, KC-135T)
60-0336 – (KC-135A, KC-135Q, KC-135T)
60-0337 – (KC-135A, KC-135Q, KC-135T)
60-0338 – (KC-135A, KC-135Q)
60-0339 – (KC-I35A, KC-135Q, KC-135T)
60-0340 – (KC-135A)
60-0341 – (KC-135A, KC-135R)
60-0342 – (KC-135A, KC-135Q, KC-135T)
60-0343 – (KC-135A, KC-135Q, KC-135T)
60-0344 – (KC-135A, KC-135Q, KC-135T)
60-0345 – (KC-135A, KC-135Q, KC-135T)
60-0346 – (KC-135A, KC-135Q, KC-135T)
60-0347 – (KC-135A, KC-135R)
60-0348 – (KC-135A, KC-135R)
60-0349 – (KC-135A, KC-135R)
60-0350 – (KC-135A, KC-135R)
60-0351 – (KC-135A, KC-135R)
60-0352 – (KC-135A)
60-0353 – (KC-135A, KC-135R)
60-0354 – (KC-135A)
60-0355 – (KC-135A, KC-135R)
60-0356 – (KC-135A, C-135A, RC-135D, KC-135A, KC-135R)
60-0357 – (KC-135A, C-135A, RC-135D, KC-135A, KC-135R)
60-0358 – (KC-135A, KC-135R)
60-0359 – (KC-135A, KC-135R)
60-0360 – (KC-135A, KC-135R)
60-0361 – (KC-135A)
60-0362 – (KC-135A, RC-135D, KC-135A, KC-135R)
60-0363 – (KC-135A, KC-135R)
60-0364 – (KC-135A, KC-135R)
60-0365 – (KC-135A, KC-135R)
60-0366 – (KC-135A, KC-135R)
60-0367 – (KC-135A, KC-135R)
60-0368 – (KC-135A)
60-0369 – (C-135A, NC-135A, GNC-135A)
60-0370 – (C-135A, NC-135A)
60-0371 – (C-135A, NC-135A)
60-0372 – (C-135A, EC-135N, C-135E)
60-0373 – (C-135A)
60-0374 – (C-135A, EC-135N, EC-135E)
60-0375 – (C-135A, EC-135N, C-135E)
60-0376 – (C-135A, C-135E)
60-0377 – (C-135A)
60-0378 – (C-135A, NASA C-135A WW III)
61-0261 – (KC-135A, EC-135L)
61-0262 – (KC-135A, EC-135A)
61-0263 – (KC-135A, EC-135L)
61-0264 – (KC-135A, KC-135R)
61-0265 – (KC-135A)
61-0266 – (KC-135A, KC-135R)
61-0267 – (KC-135A, KC-135R)
61-0268 – (KC-135A, KC-135E)
61-0269 – (KC-135A, EC-135L)
61-0270 – (KC-135A, KC-135E)
61-0271 – (KC-135A, KC-135E)
61-0272 – (KC-135A, KC-135R)
61-0273 – (KC-135A)
61-0274 – (KC-135A, EC-135H, EC-135P)
61-0275 – (KC-135A, KC-135R)
61-0276 – (KC-135A, KC-135R)
61-0277 – (KC-135A, KC-135R)
61-0278 – (KC-135A, EC-135A)
61-0279 – (KC-135A, EC-135L)
61-0280 – (KC-135A, KC-135E, KC-135R)
61-0281 – (KC-135A, EC-135L, KC-135A, EC-135L, KC-135A, KC-135E)
61-0282 – (KC-135A, EC-135H, GEC-135H)
61-0283 – (KC-135A, EC-135L)
61-0284 – (KC-135A, KC-135R)
61-0285 – (KC-135A, EC-135H)
61-0286 – (KC-135A, EC-135H GEC-135H)
61-0287 – (KC-135A, EC-135A)
61-0288 – (KC-135A, EC-135L, KC-135A, EC-135L, KC-135A, KC-135R)
61-0289 – (KC-135A, EC-135A)
61-0290 – (KC-135A, KC-135R)
61-0291 – (KC-135A, EC-135H)
61-0292 – (KC-135A, KC-135R)
61-0293 – (KC-135A, EC-135A, KC-135A, KC-135R)
61-0294 – (KC-135A, KC-135R)
61-0295 – (KC-135A, KC-135R)
61-0296 – (KC-135A)
61-0297 – (KC-135A, EC-135A)
61-0298 – (KC-135A, KC-135R)
61-0299 – (KC-135A, KC-135R)
61-0300 – (KC-135A, KC-135R)
61-0301 – (KC-135A)
61-0302 – (KC-135A, EC-135L, KC-135A, KC-135R)
61-0303 – (KC-135A, KC-135E, KC-135R)
61-0304 – (KC-135A, KC-135R)
61-0305 – (KC-135A, KC-135R)
61-0306 – (KC-135A, KC-135R)
61-0307 – (KC-135A, KC-135R)
61-0308 – (KC-135A, KC-135R)
61-0309 – (KC-135A, KC-135R)
61-0310 – (KC-135A, KC-135R)
61-0311 – (KC-135A, KC-135R)
61-0312 – (KC-135A, KC-135R)
61-0313 – (KC-135A, KC-135R)
61-0314 – (KC-135A, KC-135R)
61-0315 – (KC-135A, KC-135R)
61-0316 – (KC-135A)
61-0317 – (KC-135A, KC-135R)
61-0318 – (KC-135A, KC-135R)
61-0319 – (KC-135A)
61-0320 – (KC-135A, KC-135R)
61-0321 – (KC-135A, KC-135R)
61-0322 – (KC-135A)
61-0323 – (KC-135A, KC-135R)
61-0324 – (KC-135A, KC-135R)
61-0325 – (KC-135A)
61-0326 – (C-135A, EC-135N, EC-135E)
61-0327 – (C-135A, EC-135N)
61-0328 – (C-135A, EC-135N)
61-0329 – (C-135A, EC-135N, EC-135E)
61-0330 – (C-135A, EC-135N, EC-135E)
61-0331 – (C-135B)
61-0332 – (C-135B)
61-2662 – (C-135B, RC-135S)
61-2663 – (C-135B, RC-135S)
61-2664 – (C-135B, RC-135S)
61-2665 – (C-135B, WC-135B)
61-2666 – (C-135B, WC-135B, WC-135W)
61-2667 – (C-135B, WC-135B, TC-135B, WC-135W)
61-2668 – (C-135B, WC-135B, C-135C)
61-2669 – (C-I35B, WC-I35B, C-135B "Speckled Trout")
61-2670 – (C-I35B, WC-135B, OC-135B)
61-2671 – (C-135B, WC-135B, C-135B, C-135C)
61-2672 – (C-135B, WC-135B, OC-135B)
61-2673 – (C-135B, WC-135B)
61-2674 – (C-135B, WC-135B, OC-135B)
62-3497 – (KC-135A, French KC-135R)
62-3498 – (KC-135A, KC-135R)
62-3499 – (KC-135A, KC-135R)
62-3500 – (KC-135A, KC-135R)
62-3501 – (KC-135A)
62-3502 – (KC-135A, KC-135R)
62-3503 – (KC-135A, KC-135R)
62-3504 – (KC-135A, KC-135R)
62-3505 – (KC-135A, KC-135R)
62-3506 – (KC-135A. KC-135R)
62-3507 – (KC-135A, KC-135R)
62-3508 – (KC-135A, KC-135R)
62-3509 – (KC-135A, KC-135R)
62-3510 – (KC-135A, KC-135R)
62-3511 – (KC-135A, KC-135R)
62-3512 – (KC-135A, KC-135R)
62-3513 – (KC-135A, KC-135R)
62-3514 – (KC-135A, KC-135R)
62-3515 – (KC-135A, KC-135R)
62-3516 – (KC-135A, KC-135R)
62-3517 – (KC-135A, KC-135R)
62-3518 – (KC-135A, KC-135R)
62-3519 – (KC-135A, KC-135R)
62-3520 – (KC-135A, KC-135R)
62-3521 – (KC-135A, KC-135R)
62-3522 – (KC-135A)
62-3523 – (KC-135A, KC-135R)
62-3524 – (KC-135A, KC-135R)
62-3525 – (KC-135A, French KC-135R)
62-3526 – (KC-135A, KC-135R)
62-3527 – (KC-135A, KC-135E)
62-3528 – (KC-135A, KC-135R)
62-3529 – (KC-135A, KC-135R)
62-3530 – (KC-135A, KC-135R)
62-3531 – (KC-135A, KC-135R)
62-3532 – (KC-135A)
62-3533 – (KC-135A, KC-135R)
62-3534 – (KC-135A, KC-135R)
62-3535 – (KC-135A)
62-3536 – (KC-135A, NASA KC-135A WW II, EC-135K)
62-3537 – (KC-135A, KC-135R)
62-3538 – (KC-135A, KC-135R)
62-3539 – (KC-135A, Turkish KC-135R)
62-3540 – (KC-135A, KC-135R)
62-3541 – (KC-135A, KC-135R)
62-3542 – (KC-135A, KC-135R)
62-3543 – (KC-135A, KC-135R)
62-3544 – (KC-135A, KC-135R)
62-3545 – (KC-135A, KC-135R)
62-3546 – (KC-135A, KC-135R)
62-3547 – (KC-135A, KC-135R)
62-3548 – (KC-135A, KC-135R)
62-3549 – (KC-135A, KC-135R)
62-3550 – (KC-135A, KC-135R)
62-3551 – (KC-135A, KC-135R)
62-3552 – (KC-135A, KC-135R)
62-3553 – (KC-135A, KC-135R)
62-3554 – (KC-135A, KC-135R)
62-3555 – (KC-135A, French KC-135R)
62-3556 – (KC-135A, KC-135R)
62-3557 – (KC-135A, KC-135R)

62-3558 – (KC-135A, KC-135R)
62-3559 – (KC-135A, KC-135R)
62-3560 – (KC-135A)
62-3561 – (KC-135A, KC-135R)
62-3562 – (KC-135A, KC-135R)
62-3563 – (KC-135A, Turkish KC-135R)
62-3564 – (KC-135A, KC-135R)
62-3565 – (KC-135A, KC-135R)
62-3566 – (KC-135A, KC-135E, KC-135R)
62-3567 – (KC-135A, Turkish KC-135R)
62-3568 – (KC-135A, KC-135R)
62-3569 – (KC-135A, KC-135R)
62-3570 – (KC-135A, EC-135G)
62-3571 – (KC-135A, KC-135R)
62-3572 – (KC-135A, KC-135R)
62-3573 – (KC-135A, KC-135R)
62-3574 – (KC-135A, French KC-135R)
62-3575 – (KC-135A, KC-135R)
62-3576 – (KC-135A, KC-135R)
62-3577 – (KC-135A, KC-135R)
62-3578 – (KC-135A, KC-135R)
62-3579 – (KC-135A, EC-135A, EC-135G)
62-3580 – (KC-135A, KC-135R)
62-3581 – (KC-135B, EC-135C)
62-3582 – (KC-135B, EC-135C)
62-3583 – (KC-135B, EC-135C)
62-3584 – (KC-135B, EC-135C, EC-135J)
62-3585 – (KC-135B, EC-135C)
62-4125 – (C-135B, RC-135W)
62-4126 – (C-135B)
62-4127 – (C-135B, RC-135W)
62-4128 – (C-135B, EC-135B, RC-135X, RC-135S)
62-4129 – (C-135B, TC-135W)
62-4130 – (C-135B, RC-135W)
62-4131 – (C-135B, RC-135M, RC-135W)
62-4132 – (C-135B, RC-135M, RC-135W)
62-4133 – (C-135B, EC-135B, TC-135S)
62-4134 – (C-135B, RC-135M, RC-135W)
62-4135 – (C-135B, RC-135M, RC-135W)
62-4136 – (C-135B)
62-4137 – (C-135B, RC-135E)
62-4138 – (C-135B, RC-135M, RC-135W)
62-4139 – (C-135B, RC-135M, RC-135W)
63-7976 – (KC-135A, KC-135R)
63-7977 – (KC-135A, KC-135R)
63-7978 – (KC-135A, KC-135R)
63-7979 – (KC-135A, KC-135R)
63-7980 – (KC-135A, KC-135R)
63-7981 – (KC-135A, KC-135R)
63-7982 – (KC-135A, KC-135R)
63-7983 – (KC-135A)
63-7984 – (KC-135A, KC-135R)
63-7985 – (KC-135A, KC-135R)
63-7986 – (KC-135A)
63-7987 – (KC-135A, KC-135R)
63-7988 – (KC-135A, KC-135R)
63-7989 – (KC-135A)
63-7990 – (KC-135A)
63-7991 – (KC-135A, KC-135R)
63-7992 – (KC-135A, KC-135R)
63-7993 – (KC-135A, KC-135R)
63-7994 – (KC-135A, EC-135G)
63-7995 – (KC-135A, KC-135R)
63-7996 – (KC-135A, KC-135R)
63-7997 – (KC-135A, KC-135R)
63-7998 – (KC-135A, NASA KC-135A WW V)
63-7999 – (KC-135A, KC-135R)
63-8000 – (KC-135A, KC-135R)
63-8001 – (KC-135A, EC-135G)
63-8002 – (KC-135A, KC-135R)
63-8003 – (KC-135A, KC-135R)
63-8004 – (KC-135A, KC-135R)
63-8005 – (KC-135A)
63-8006 – (KC-135A, KC-135R)
63-8007 – (KC-135A, KC-135R)
63-8008 – (KC-135A, KC-135R)
63-8009 – (KC-135A)
63-8010 – (KC-135A)
63-8011 – (KC-135A, KC-135R)
63-8012 – (KC-135A, KC-135R)
63-8013 – (KC-135A, KC-135R)
63-8014 – (KC-135A, KC-135R)
63-8015 – (KC-135A, KC-135R)
63-8016 – (KC-135A)
63-8017 – (KC-135A, KC-135R)
63-8018 – (KC-135A, KC-135R)
63-8019 – (KC-135A, KC-135R)
63-8020 – (KC-135A, KC-135R)
63-8021 – (KC-135A, KC-135R)
63-8022 – (KC-135A, KC-135R)
63-8023 – (KC-135A, KC-135R)
63-8024 – (KC-135A, KC-135R)
63-8025 – (KC-135A, KC-135R)
63-8026 – (KC-135A, KC-135R)
63-8027 – (KC-135A, KC-135R)
63-8028 – (KC-135A, KC-135R)
63-8029 – (KC-135A, KC-135R)
63-8030 – (KC-135A, KC-135R)
63-8031 – (KC-135A, KC-135R)
63-8032 – (KC-135A, KC-135R)
63-8033 – (KC-135A, KC-135R)
63-8034 – (KC-135A, KC-135R)
63-8035 – (KC-135A, KC-135R)
63-8036 – (KC-135A, KC-135R)
63-8037 – (KC-135A, KC-135R)
63-8038 – (KC-135A, KC-135R)
63-8039 – (KC-135A, KC-135R)
63-8040 – (KC-135A, KC-135R)
63-8041 – (KC-135A, KC-135R)
63-8042 – (KC-135A)
63-8043 – (KC-135A, KC-135R)
63-8044 – (KC-135A, KC-135R)
63-8045 – (KC-135A, KC-135R)
63-8046 – (KC-135B, EC-135C)
63-8047 – (KC-135B, EC-135C)
63-8048 – (KC-135B, EC-135C)
63-8049 – (KC-135B, EC-135C)
63-8050 – (KC-135B, EC-135C, NKC-135B)
63-8051 – (KC-135B, EC-135C)
63-8052 – (KC-135B, EC-135C)
63-8053 – (KC-135B, EC-135C)
63-8054 – (KC-135B, EC-135C)
63-8055 – (KC-135B, EC-135J)
63-8056 – (KC-135B, EC-135J)
63-8057 – (KC-135B, EC-135J)
63-8058 – (RC-135A, KC-135D)
63-8059 – (RC-135A, KC-135D)
63-8060 – (RC-135A, KC-135D)
63-8061 – (RC-135A, KC-135D)
63-8470 – (C-135F, C-135FR)
63-8471 – (C-135F, C-135FR)
63-8472 – (C-135F, C-135FR)
63-8473 – (C-135F)
63-8474 – (C-135F, C-135FR)
63-8475 – (C-135F, C-135FR)
63-8871 – (KC-135A, KC-135R)
63-8872 – (KC-135A, KC-135R)
63-8873 – (KC-135A, KC-135R)
63-8874 – (KC-135A, KC-135R)
63-8875 – (KC-135A, KC-135R)
63-8876 – (KC-135A, KC-135R)
63-8877 – (KC-135A, KC-135R)
63-8878 – (KC-135A, KC-135R)
63-8879 – (KC-135A, KC-135R)
63-8880 – (KC-135A, KC-135R)
63-8881 – (KC-135A, KC-135R)
63-8882 – (KC-135A)
63-8883 – (KC-135A, KC-135R)
63-8884 – (KC-135A, KC-135R)
63-8885 – (KC-135A, KC-135R)
63-8886 – (KC-135A, KC-135R)
63-8887 – (KC-135A, KC-135R)
63-8888 – (KC-135A, KC-135R)
63-9792 – (RC-135B, RC-135C, RC-135U, RC-135V)
63-12735 – (C-135F, C-135FR)
63-12736 – (C-135F, C-135FR)
63-12737 – (C-135F, C-135FR)
63-12738 – (C-135F, C-135FR)
63-12739 – (C-135F, C-135FR)
63-12740 – (C-135F, C-135FR)
64-14828 – (KC-135A, KC-135R)
64-14829 – (KC-135A, KC-135R)
64-14830 – (KC-135A, KC-135R)
64-14831 – (KC-135A, KC-135R)
64-14832 – (KC-135A, KC-135R)
64-14833 – (KC-135A, KC-135R)
64-14834 – (KC-135A, KC-135R)
64-14835 – (KC-135A, KC-135R)
64-14836 – (KC-135A, KC-135R)
64-14837 – (KC-135A, KC-135R)
64-14838 – (KC-135A. KC-135R)
64-14839 – (KC-135A, KC-135R)
64-14840 – (KC-135A, KC-135R)
64-14841 – (RC-135B, RC-135C, RC-135V)
64-14842 – (RC-135B, RC-135C, RC-135V)
64-14843 – (RC-135B, RC-135C, RC-135V)
64-14844 – (RC-135B, RC-135C, RC-135V)
64-14845 – (RC-135B, RC-135C, RC-135V)
64-14846 – (RC-135B, RC-135C, RC-135V)
64-14847 – (RC-135B, RC-135C, RC-135U)
64-14848 – (RC-135B, RC-135C, RC-135V)
64-14849 – (RC-135B, RC-135C, RC-135U)